I'm Only Being Honest

Luton Sixth Form College

JEREMY KYLE

I'm Only
Being Honest

HODDER &
STOUGHTON

First published in Great Britain in 2009 by Hodder & Stoughton
An Hachette UK company

2

A CIP catalogue record for this title is available from the British Library

ISBN Hardback 978 0 340 98079 8
ISBN Trade Paperback 978 0 340 91898 2

Typeset in Plantin Light by Ellipsis Books Limited, Glasgow

Printed and bound in the UK by CPI Mackays, Chatham ME5 8TD

Hodder & Stoughton policy is to use papers that are natural, renewable
and recyclable products and made from wood grown in sustainable forests.
The logging and manufacturing processes are expected to conform to
the environmental regulations of the country of origin.

Hodder & Stoughton Ltd
338 Euston Road
London NW1 3BH

www.hodder.co.uk

To Carla,
for all that you have been and all that you are,
thank you.

I

Look At Me

I know what lots of people think. Just who does Jeremy Kyle think he is? What gives him the right to go around shouting his mouth off at people, telling them how to live their lives? Sitting up there in his ivory tower, with a flash car and a celebrity salary: how could he possibly have any idea what life is really like for those poor people crying out for his help? What possible connection could he have with any of the struggling families that appear on his show? He's never been in their shoes, never had to deal with the problems they face, so how could he have the first idea about what they might need to do to turn their lives around? ... 'I BET THAT JEREMY KYLE DOESN'T EVEN CARE!' I've heard it before and no doubt I'll hear it again.

And here's the truth: I try and give each person I meet on the show the selfsame opportunity to improve their lives. I realise it may not always seem to be the case but at the first time of meeting a guest, I care about them and their problems. And moreover, I care passionately about the help we can offer them. I can't pretend to have liked everyone I have met during filming – plenty have turned my stomach – but that is not to say that I don't feel concern about any of the guests. I do. I have not yet experienced a day of filming on *The Jeremy Kyle Show* during which someone's story, personality, ability to cope or determination to move forward has failed to touch or inspire me in some way. I am not the stone-hearted bully so many cast me as, but neither am I someone prepared to suffer the soft excuses so many offer up for their own personal failings. Honesty is a quality I hold in high regard, and when I know it is being withheld, I tend to react.

The vast majority of my detractors see me as someone who takes great delight in belittling the people I meet each day. As long as my name remains on the wall and the audiences still cheer me on, everything's A-OK with Jeremy, isn't it? It amazes me that people think my sole purpose in life is to publicly prey on vulnerable people, goading them in front of the cameras for my own gratification and in the chase for higher TV ratings. If you believe everything you read, the privileges I enjoy make me uniquely unqualified to comment on the problems of others. Apparently, I have no right to try and help the people who seek it from me because the way I go about it is not entirely to everyone's tastes. To point out someone's flaws is 'hypocritical', and to do so directly makes me 'holier than thou'.

You might believe a lot of what is said about me, but the reality is quite different. I don't trawl the country searching for disadvantaged minorities to pick on. The simple truth is that I am asked to speak honestly to increasing numbers of this country's rank and file who come onto my show looking for the help they say they can't access anywhere else. Whether you believe it or not, Britain is awash with a large number of people who just aren't equipped to cope with the myriad social problems that are sweeping our society. I can't help but fear for the health of this country if what I see played out before me each and every day is a true indicator of what life is like for so many of our compatriots.

I know it might sound dramatic, but I honestly believe that our nation is hurtling towards a defining date with destiny. For some years now, there has been a time bomb ticking beneath the values British society once held dear, and if we continue failing to grasp the fundamentals of a respectful and civilised society, as many of my guests so clearly do, our country faces collapse. But here's the good news: most individuals have it in them to turn their lives around, and equally, this country has all the talent it needs to shape a better future for itself. However, in order for that to happen, all of us, as individuals and as communities, will have to take on the hard work that the rebuilding will require. And we have to start now! The only request I ever make to my guests before they come onto my show is that they be honest with me. Now the time has come for me to be honest with you.

So, look at me: my name is Jeremy Kyle and I am a twice-married recovering gambling addict. I have a brother whose life has been beset by problems with drugs. His wife was anorexic. I am obsessive-compulsive. My name is Jeremy Kyle and some might say I am one of the most hated men in Great Britain.

I am irritating, infuriating, and unlikely to feature on anyone's dinner-party wish list. I have never dragged myself up above the average. Physically, academically or intellectually, my attributes are never likely to score much above six out of ten – and I definitely can't claim that any success I have had to date has been built on good looks! Those who don't like me loathe me. My critics say that I am a pernicious presence on our television screens and that I am the one most to blame for all that has gone wrong since the United Kingdom started selling itself short. But, since starting the show four years ago, the people of this country have come to me in their droves to help them turn their lives around. It is a great honour, and incredibly humbling, that so many have seen fit to put their trust in me.

As to how I dispense that help, I have a great belief in a plain-speaking directness calculated to get the message through to even the most unreceptive of listeners. I readily concede that from time to time I have gone over the top when emotions have got the better of me. I can be brutal, confrontational and pretty unforgiving, and I make no apologies for being curt or to the point – I have never been one to sugar the pill. I no longer see the value in pussyfooting around the issues bringing this country to its knees. Long ago I made a promise to my employers to be as frank as possible and tell any guest on my show – even if they sometimes did not want to hear it – exactly how I saw their situation. If people aren't forced to confront the realities, the seeds are sown for problems to grow and worsen. The more people I meet through my job, the more I become convinced that this country, and far too many of its citizens, need one almighty kick up the backside. I call it as I see it . . . My name is Jeremy Kyle and I AM ONLY BEING HONEST!

The most vociferous complaints against *The Jeremy Kyle Show* typically come from those who have only seen it once. An unscheduled 'duvet day' or time off sick give some people who would not normally catch my show an opportunity to flick around the daytime schedules while curled up on the sofa. Many a teacher or doctor will have stumbled across my offerings on ITV1 without any real knowledge of what the show is about. I don't blame them for being more than a little shocked at some of the more outlandish cases that I'm asked to 'referee'. In the early days of my tenure I too was aghast at just how low some people had sunk. Now, some four years on, the stories are no less shocking, it's just that I am less shocked by them. I guess that the regularity with which I am obliged to confront all that is going wrong in our society has inured me to some of the extremes. I have reluctantly come to accept that the major problems I initially thought might only affect a small percentage of the population are in fact frighteningly commonplace. Every day I tackle tales of family breakdown, delinquency, abuse, addiction, violence, teenage pregnancy and welfare dependency. And the worrying truth is I don't have to look far afield to find too many others adversely affected by these issues; they are queuing round the block to get into our studio to benefit from the help we can offer.

Many critics of the show say that by broadcasting and discussing the problems of our society in an open forum, we are compounding rather than improving them. Well, I can't help thinking that that is absolute bollocks! The current breakdown in society we are witnessing has been brought about by thirty or forty years of successive failures at both a governmental and individual level. The people who argue against my show are seemingly happy to ignore the devastated social environments up and down the country that contribute towards its degradation. My agitators see me as deliberately destroying the fabric of society, profiting from the disadvantaged for cheap thrills. Nothing could be further from the truth – we are actually giving help to some of those whom society has left behind: the evidence is all there. Those critics are wrong and I don't mind telling them why.

If you are one of those who believe that I alone am responsible for every ASBO ever handed out to a hoody, you must be living on a different planet. It is almost as if I'm being accused of mounting a one-man campaign to infect every corner of Britain with ever more deplorable examples of anti-social behaviour, solely in order for me to then have a go at them on the telly! The seeds for the dismantling of British society were sown decades ago. If those fantastical theories were really true, I would have had to embark on a mission to bring delinquency, drugs and despondency to the nation from about the age of three! Well, I am sorry to say (and those who bear with me in this book will soon be able to testify) that, as diminutive and disliked as I may always have been, I am no Bond villain intent on destroying the world.

Nope, forty years ago I was nothing but your average toddler, living with a loving family in Coley Park, Reading.

I went through a fairly unremarkable childhood, playing second fiddle to those around me who had greater talents and far loftier ambitions. My abilities seemed only to lend themselves to crushing mediocrity: I have dawdled through most of my life never really impressing, but not particularly disappointing either. I think I have been a good son, a better father, and sometimes quite the most selfish and reckless of husbands. I readily concede my mistakes; I confess to moments of weakness and temptation. I have been far from perfect for quite a long time, but I don't have it in me to have come up with any blueprint to bring down Great Britain.

When I'm talking and giving advice to the guests on my TV show, I am reliant on my own experiences to help guide the way – the most useful advice, I believe, is founded upon the person giving it knowing what they are talking about. I try to impart an empathy wherever possible, but often brutal honesty is required when I'm figuring out where some people have gone so badly wrong. I know, because that's what I needed when I was at rock bottom with my gambling addiction. Thanks to that pernicious habit, I know the betting game inside out, and so I do realise that the odds are stacked against me really being able to help those who take part in my show. I am not a qualified counsellor and I have no real personal experience of many of the addictions that keep a boot on the throat of so many. However, the evidence of my own eyes is such that I *know* my show has changed the lives of a good many people who might otherwise have been forgotten and abandoned. I may well be an unremarkable host of an unremarkable tele-vision show, but the team I have around me is incredibly good. My colleagues have helped bring positive change to so many who saw no way out from their problems.

My primary role on the show is to identify a person's

problem and frame it in order for them to see that they alone are responsible for sorting it out. I'll call on the help of their friends, family and all the other support networks available to us but, at the end of the day, it is the person with the problem who will have to face up to it. Ultimately, only they have the ability to overcome whatever is holding them back – the most we can hope for on the show is that we supply some guidance and any proper, professional counselling a family or individual may require.

After initially being shocked and then, after a time, becoming accustomed to the stories put before me each day, I started to become deeply frustrated. It wasn't long before I found myself getting more and more livid. The novelty of living my own dream soon gave way to the unwillingness of others to propel themselves out of their own personal nightmares. Each day became defined by the failure of everyone I met to recognise just a few of the most basic tenets that bind families and society together. The anger I express some mornings is not false. Undoubtedly, I am harsher with some than I am with others, but I defy anyone not to lose it at least a little when dealing with teenagers who blithely get pregnant without any thought for the consequences. Or a mother who can't see the wrong in abandoning her kids for a life of drug dependency paid for by prostitution. Sometimes, I honestly feel as though I am bashing my head against a brick wall.

When I was growing up, I always took politeness and common courtesy for granted. Very early on, my parents schooled me on what manners were required around the dinner table or when out in public – they taught me the basics as surely as any good parent could. Whether it was opening the door for a lady or saying 'please' and 'thank you', there was a firm, fair hand guiding me through my early years. They laid down the foundations on which my sense of right and wrong was built, and taught me what was acceptable and what was not. From them I learned respect. In short, they made sure I was prepared for the moment when I would have to make my own way in the world, passing on the lessons that had come down to them through the generations. They set my moral compass, inspired my belief system and provided a set of values that would allow me the chance to contribute, if nothing else, decency and propriety to society.

Beyond the basics of common etiquette, they provided just one of a million possible templates of how people could successfully live alongside one another. From my parents I learned of the nature of sacrifice for the sake of your offspring. I learned the true meaning of unconditional love. I learned the importance of a strong work ethic and the need to provide that still drives me today. Lazing around doing nothing just wasn't an option for me, just as it could never have been an option for them. Consciously and subconsciously, my mind was filled with all of the life lessons they handed out. Through the power of positive parenting, they gave me the principles that I will always abide by and cherish for as long as I live.

Now, mine was not a unique experience. My parents won't seek medals for the sterling job they have both done, any more than I would seek any sort of recognition for basically being a decent member of society. Most of my parents' generation did not see the disciplining and guiding of their children as anything requiring a special effort; it was the minimum expected! OF EVERYONE! Lately, I have been given to thinking that perhaps I am just too old or out of touch to really understand the minds of the younger people I meet. I can never claim to have been cool, but I was young once, and back then I was certainly suspicious about the carping of the older generation. I used to think that people of my grandparents' age had nothing better to do than to moan. I thought retirement had given them too much time on their hands and they eyed young whippersnappers like me with jealousy because they could no longer do the things we were able to do. Now I realise how wrong I was.

Many of the people who write to me now are senior citizens, people who in younger days I would have considered plain old fogies, but I find myself agreeing with most of what they say. Whereas the inter-generational relationship was once characterised by irritation and, at worst, exasperation, it is now sadly ruled by an all-encompassing fear. There is always friction when an emerging youth seeks to create its own identity quite apart from that of its parents', but in modern times, this has been converted into something far worse and more dangerous – an active distrust and even terror from the elder generation of these menacing, directionless kids who espouse no values. Over time, respect has broken down and been replaced by the trend of antisocial behaviour, to the point where you now find fully grown men, let alone frail old pensioners, who no longer feel safe enough to leave their house after dark. I am not scaremongering or concocting a story with no basis in fact. Every single day my production office is besieged by callers looking for an escape from their communities; areas in the grip of problems all brought on by societal or familial breakdown.

To put that in perspective, it is perhaps worth pointing out that *thousands* of Britons are ignoring our cultural legacy of the famous 'stiff upper lip'. No one is keeping quiet about the things that affect them, so bad have they become. Gone is the Dunkirk spirit of stoically and manfully pitching in to help everyone overcome common enemies. Gone is that unity and social cohesion – and what are we left with? A desperation to appear on a national television programme to get the help that has been denied everywhere else. What does that tell you about the state of modern Great Britain?

Now of course I am not slagging off my own show. I am very proud of it and I passionately believe in the good we continue to do for the vast majority of our guests. What really concerns me are the dysfunctions in society that provide shows like mine with an endless wealth of material. Increasingly, I am finding that the people I meet have had none, not one bit, of the guidance that was instilled in me by my parents. More, there seems to have been a wholesale abandonment of those traditional working-class values – honesty, decency, diligence – that kept people proud no matter what hardships they were beset by. There was a steel, a back-bone, a real moral fibre running through even the poorest communities not so long back. People may have lacked money or luxuries, but they were never found wanting when it came to pride. Pride in themselves, their community, their appear-ance, their children and their family.

Please don't get me wrong. I haven't gone all misty-eyed, reaching for the bunting and playing old recordings of the Queen's coronation. I realise certain social problems prevailed back then, just as others do now. However, what seems to be most lacking nowadays is the willingness to stand up for what is right and to insist on others doing the same. When I was growing up, you didn't just look out for your own, the whole estate looked out for each other. I would be just as likely to get a clip round the ear from my neighbour for misbehaving as I would from either of my parents. And that was fine. On my show I'm constantly coming across parents who have no idea what their kids are getting up to and, worse, they don't really care! No examples are being set and no laws laid down. As a result we are seeing the very fabric of our society crumble about our ears.

I am often asked to provide solutions to these problems via *The Jeremy Kyle Show*. Obviously we can only work on a one-to-one basis with any family put before us and will never have the means to effect any great change in the country overall. All we can hope for is that the message filters through from the tiny percentage we do manage to help. There are a great many people out there who can provoke the sort of change this country so drastically needs, though you probably won't find them where you think you would. Writing to an MP is all well and good – government will and should always have a part to play in the improvement of society – and charity groups and the armies of unsung volunteers who help those who have genuinely fallen on hard times can always be counted on to do their bit too. But, and this is the real crux of it, it is each and every person who knowingly brings a child into this world who really bears the most responsibility for the rebuilding of our nation. The best example I can set for my own children is to follow the excellent one that my parents laid out for me. I was lucky enough to have been brought up in a manner that is worthy of passing on to my children – that is surely the first step any new parent should be looking to make, and it's by far the most important step in bringing about real change in this country.

There is no point in hiding from the fact – my show is just the tip of the iceberg where the problems of this country are concerned. We average about ten guests per show, five times per week. We've been making about 250 shows per year, so that is roughly 2,500 guests with serious problems impacting negatively on them and society as a whole. We receive about 300 enquiries per day from members of the public wanting to come on the show to sort out whatever it is that is affecting them. That surely flies in the face of those who think we are deliberately seeking out the worst extremes of an otherwise powerless minority. We are not cooking the books and we don't need to make up the numbers. There are literally thousands of people who have or would like to come onto shows like mine in this country. And they don't want to appear just for a song and a dance and to have me bark at them. The problems we deal with are real and their causes are deep-rooted, sometimes going back years and years. I understand

that not everyone is dealt a fair hand, and that some will go through life with more doors opened for them than others. But, even in the poorest areas and with the roughest of backgrounds, I have to believe that in twenty-first-century Britain there exists some opportunity for all. And I don't blame every individual who failed to grasp an opportunity that came his or her way nearly as much as I blame the parents who helped foster a lack of ambition in their child in the first place.

I am a father of three, and by the time you read this, my wife should have given birth to my fourth child. Whatever my failings, and there have been many as a partner, husband and divorcee, I have always been a constant for my children. The minute I knew my first daughter had been conceived the whole focus of my life changed. My needs became secondary and hers became paramount. I thought that this feeling might be diluted when my second child was born, with my first child in her teens and my middle age fast approaching. It did not. The feeling only intensified. People often mistake my love of my children as a blinkered spoiling of them. That is fine, and I have no doubt there are more severe parents than me out there. That said, I just can't help but keep the promise I have silently made to them a billion times over – that I would always be there for all of them and always do whatever it took to ensure they were safe, secure and happy.

I am the son of a wholly committed father and I myself am currently the wholly committed father of three daughters and, at the time of writing this, the beautiful bump of a first baby boy. There is simply nothing I would not do for my children. I have no doubt that my kids probably get more than their fair share, I have probably spoiled them more than I should, and I still have much to learn about bringing up a family, but I would rather accept the overindulgence of a child over the wilful, heartless dereliction of parental duty that I see played out before me each and every day.

To anyone who does not believe some of the scenes on my show, just look at the evidence. It is irrefutable. It is estimated that the cost to this country from broken families alone is around the £20 billion mark. Apparently the additional costs of crime and antisocial behaviour born of family breakdown and social policy failures is nearer £100 billion! £100 *billion* – and that's without even mentioning the terrible human toll being paid up and down the land by kids with no homes and families with no future. All too often I am standing face to face, trying to reason with parents who see no fault whatsoever in doing nothing at all for their own children. The problems that neglect has caused are pretty plain for all to see, but has anyone yet grasped just how widespread the problems have actually become? The parents I meet on the show are often acting out a twisted game of Keeping Up With the Joneses. Everyone else on the estate is happy to let their kids run riot while they get wasted, so what's the point in acting differently and being the odd one out? You might as well do the same and follow suit. We have got to the point now where being a good parent means taking a stand. And there you have the problem distilled: everyone gets caught up in the general malaise of doing nothing because everyone else is doing nothing!

Not too long after I started at ITV, I decided to do some research to help me better understand the causes and effects of the problems swamping those who came on my show. It wasn't a surprise to find plenty of evidence to suggest that children in homes without fathers:

- are more likely to be truants
- are more likely to face exclusion
- are more likely to become teenage parents
- and more likely to become criminal offenders.

That little list pretty much sums up the make-up of so many of my show's guests. Everyone I try to help via the show is invariably affected by at least one (and usually more) of those issues, and virtually every one of my guests is from a family that is either broken or in the process of breaking up!

In too many parts of our country it seems that responsible parenting is fast disappearing. I may be old-fashioned and I may say this because I am a man, but I think there are just too many young men out there who have shirked their responsibilities. They are strangers to the notion that they should earn their keep before then paying their way. They do not comprehend that creating a life requires a lifelong responsibility to nurture it, financially, emotionally, physically – totally. Those irresponsible young cads who go off gallivanting, spraying their seed as if trying to create an army in their own image (but without ever showing any intent to stick around and lead them), make an absolute mockery of decent dads everywhere fighting to gain access to their children.

Single mothers are not blameless, of course. Getting pregnant definitely takes two, but from what I see on my stage, more often than not it is a distraught woman left holding the baby. Of course there will always be situations where the break-up of a family cannot be avoided. I am the first one to advise any couple to go their separate ways when it is clear they are no good for each other, let alone for the baby stuck in the middle of them. Even so, this is no reason for either of the parents to walk away from their child. How else do these people think their progeny will get ahead in life? If Mum and Dad aren't interested in them, who else is going to be?

I meet parents every day who bemoan their lot. They say they haven't the money or opportunity that so many others have. When I ask them the simple question, 'Well, what have you done to change your own situation?' they seem stumped. Too many are just waiting to be told or given a leg-up. Very rarely do I meet anyone really battling hard to make the best of things, to some day give their children better opportunities than they ever had. Now is the time for each and every parent in this land to stand up and be counted. As I have said on numerous occasions, I don't have the qualifications to be considered any kind of family counsellor. I am no academic authority versed in the minutiae of social justice. That said, under the studio lights, I am exposed to more of society's ills in one week than most will see in a year, and I also know that what kept me from going the way of so many of my guests was the love and support of those around me. My parents stayed together through difficulties that cause too many people nowadays to drift apart. They invested in me and my brother when it might have been easier to just not bother. I know that not everyone will be as lucky as me in having two loving, committed parents, but in this day and age it is possible to succeed with one. As ever, though, it is a case of being prepared to see through the responsibility of raising any child in the proper manner.

My mum and dad often complain to me that everything is so rushed for the younger generation nowadays. They are right. Kids left to fend for themselves seem to bypass the fun that was the most important part of my early teens. They roam the streets, and from too young an age are exposed to drugs, crime, and everything associated with a gang culture that has evolved to usurp the traditional family unit in many areas. There is a rush to get drunk, have sex, get pregnant, get married, get a council flat, all before society deems it legal. There is none of the courtship so prevalent in my parents' day, no time to take stock and learn about oneself, let alone the partner you are pledging the rest of your life to!

I suppose you could say that my mum and dad were the

exception to their own rule. They have stood the test of time, last year celebrating their golden wedding anniversary, but they did rush things a little at the start themselves! My mum was a clerk at Coutts – the royal bank, don't you know! My father swooped in to make her his not long after joining the firm. From the start it was clear he had his eye on more than just the job, though. Within six weeks he had stolen in to secure the affections of the future Mrs Patrick Kyle, when at first it looked as though she might become engaged to another suitor – a dashing charmer, who was also an Olympic fencer with royal connections who would later become the Lord Lieutenant of a remote Scottish island! No joke! Dad was a wily young charmer back then, and he tells me that there was no going back once he'd seen the bird with the immaculate pins, dressed in expensive stockings and seams down the back. They met and were engaged within six weeks, so the Kyle family legend goes. That might seem rather to scupper my (and their) argument about slowing things down. Not a bit of it. They are still very happily married today, as fifty years ago they resolved to work through everything together. They weren't pretending or playing at love, like so many of the seven-times-engaged teenagers I meet. They had found what they thought was true love and they started a journey they were determined to see through together, come what may. They did not have much money but they were both imbued with that spirit and mutual respect so conspicuously absent from many of today's young.

The sad truth today is that many young kids, particularly girls with absent fathers, grow up without ever really having had a male influence to show them what enduring and unconditional love is. As a result, the first sign of affection from the worst kind of spotty-faced teenager can often result in disastrous consequences that both parties are woefully ill-equipped to deal with. Having never known real male love, young girls everywhere are associating their notion of it with sex. This has led to explosions in this country of teenage pregnancies and unwanted babies, not to mention sexually transmitted infections.

I think I have followed in my father's footsteps to a large degree. I have taken forward a lot of the views he espoused and I am slowly getting to the point where we, frighteningly, can no longer be told apart. His marriage to my mother mirrors my own with Carla. My mother is the driving force of my parents' marriage, just as Carla is the rock on which mine is built. Not long into their union, Mum seized control and saw to it that Dad made more strenuous efforts to get ahead. She ripped out an advert she had seen in the London *Evening Standard*, which was advertising a job in the royal household. She bought him a suit, spruced him up and insisted he apply. He got the job and finished there forty-one years later as accountant and personal secretary to Her Majesty the Queen Mother.

Dad's job was not that well paid but he undoubtedly bore the benefit of some unique perks and wonderful, unforget-table experiences that he would never have enjoyed in any other employ.

Dad was there with the Princess of Wales and Fergie when each stayed over the night before their respective weddings, and apparently he was one of the first in the whole wide world to have seen Lady Diana Spencer's wedding dress. When asked later what he thought of that magnificent gown he replied, like a typical bloke: 'It was a bit like my wife's, but longer!'

I remember watching the royal weddings and processions from the gardens at Clarence House, seeing Royal Lodge in Windsor Great Park, and being welcomed into the racing fraternity in the Royal Household Stand at Ascot – all good times. But I also remember Dad being away a lot. Work kept him away, just as my own keeps me away from home from time to time. I don't remember being overly upset by it. I missed him, as we all did, but we always knew he would be back soon and none of us doubted that he loved us all very much or that he was doing everything he could to provide for his own. That work ethic was drummed into me very early on, and his was the perfect example from which to take inspiration. He once told me that he took his own example from the Queen Mother herself. At eighty-five years of age she was still committed to fulfilling three engagements a day, and my father always spoke fondly of the 'Pocket Rocket' who so inspired him to work that bit harder.

I doubt Dad was ever 'establishment' enough to scale the heights his hard work undoubtedly merited within the royal household, but he never let that get in the way of him giving of his best every single day. His commitment to his job was only bettered by the commitment he showed to his family. I was always struck by the reverence with which he was addressed. People showed him a great deal of love and respect, which he had obviously earned through many years of hard graft. He had a pride in himself that can only come with knowing you have done your utmost for all around you. With a man like Dad around, how could I do anything but take on board his fantastic example? He is a man who epitomises the right way to behave in every walk of life. He has mixed with everybody and has always held himself with great dignity. If I go on to command even half the respect, love and affection he did from his peers, I'll know I have done pretty well. One day stands out in memory, when my father was recruiting a second chauffeur for the Queen Mother. He had all the usual applications from the established elite. Oxbridge-educated graduates with first-class honours degrees and the like, but it was the scruffy, long-haired candidate from Liverpool who stood out for the old man.

Sean came to his interview with two earrings and long shaggy hair, more professional hippy than professional driver for Her Majesty the Queen Mother. Dad saw something in him, though. He took him under his wing, got his hair cut and generally smartened him up. Dad has never been one to show too much emotion, but I'm sure I saw him melt a little when I heard Sean's mum on the end of our phone. She must have had him on the line for a full twenty minutes as she recited how proud Sean, with my dad's help, had made her. When Dad came to retire from his post many years later, it was Sean who drove him to collect his medals. It was a proud day for us all to see Dad presented with his CVO but I have every faith he was just as proud of the fact that Sean, his protégé, had taken a day's unpaid leave to drive him around as if *he* was royalty for a day.

As much as possible, I try to live by the principles my father championed. I also try to stress the importance of some of those values to everyone I meet on *The Jeremy Kyle Show*. It never ceases to amaze me that so few of the basic courtesies I take for granted have been passed down through the generations to the young people who appear on the show. I respected both my parents and, though I always knew Mum's word was law, I suppose I followed my Dad's lead more because he was a man. I was more my father's son and we probably generally shared a slightly closer connection. However, whenever I was in trouble with Mum, I knew heaven and earth would shake when the time came for one of her thunderous telling-offs. I always knew I could make Dad laugh, so I wasn't as fearful of getting told off by him as I was of just letting him down.

Much of that bond between my father and I was cemented when we were both coming to terms with my brother's burgeoning drug problem. Throughout that process, I saw his hopes drain away and be replaced by unfathomable fear and confusion. His eldest son was slipping away from him and he could do nothing to stop it. Despite all of the love, investment and guidance he had given, he could not arrest Nick's slide. There were times when I saw him completely break down and his towering strength and iron will to see it through melt away. I can barely imagine what it is like to witness at first hand the demise of your son and first-born despite having only ever loved and provided for him to the best of your ability. But it was what my dad had to face despite having done nothing wrong himself. That was only the second time I had ever seen my dad – my hero – so crushed by an impotence and inability to deal with a problem. The first time was with his own father.

My dad's dad was a huge brute of a man, and I will always remember dreading the frequent visits to that particular set of grandparents. Regularly we would go over to Granny and Grandad Kyle's house. On the way in, we would walk past my grandfather's revolting green Mini, one of those with an extended boot grafted onto it. On the rare occasions I see one on the roads now, a chill still goes down my spine.

We would have to navigate a winding hill of rickety steps to get up to where he lived – Spay Cottage in Berkhamsted – and I remember being increasingly reluctant and timid with each step that brought us closer to the door. Behind it lay nothing but coldness and misery. There was no heating and no fridge and a chilly larder next to the kitchen that housed a paltry assortment of tins. Beside the tins were always some remnants of meals gone by, green and furry; old milk puddings with things growing out of them. These were all the creations of Granny Kyle – a wizened old lady who soldiered on to the age of ninety-six. Quite how the milk puddings didn't finish her off a decade or so earlier I'll never know.

Grandad Kyle hated living in England. He had spent much of his life working in the Indian police force and, from the moment he came back home, it was clear he thought our country couldn't compare. The man was cold, permanently embittered against the world and to me he seemed somehow hollowed out – a husk of humanity. Nevertheless, his unrelenting mean-spiritedness was frequently broken by a visit from his favourite grandson, my brother. Grandad Kyle seemed to have no interest in me; but Nick, his first-born grandson, was the apple of his eye.

I remember the isolation I felt in that cold, lonely house. There were times when Nick would be curled up on Grandad's lap and when I used to come into the room and try talking to him, I would be dismissively waved away. There was a coal bunker built onto the back of Spay Cottage and I remember spending more time there than in the house. I look back and remember shivering outside, looking through the window into the front room and seeing Grandad Kyle reading stories to Nick. The fire would be blazing beside them like some scene from a traditional Christmas card, whilst I would be outside, kicking my heels against the coal bunker, worrying over what I had done that was so wrong.

In fairness to Dad, he had noticed the favouritism and he did confront Grandad about it, but all he ever said when tackled on the subject was: 'We have an heir already; we don't even know Jeremy.' It was no fault of Nick's that he was favoured over me. He sought to include me as much as he could and would often come out and play with me after I had been banished to the garden. Dad stuck to his guns on my behalf and the family had a big fallout for quite a few years. My grandparents remained alien to me and a feud not unlike some of those seen on my stage rumbled on for longer than it should have. I have often said that mine is no perfect life and certainly that mine is no perfect family. We have been through the mill collectively, just as I have personally. We have all emerged the stronger at the other end but it is precisely because we never allowed any hardships we faced to be used as excuses that we managed to prevail. It was never pleasant being shunned by my grandfather and my time around him was practically unbearable. I often thought my parents could have done more to intervene, but never have I used that disappointment as any reason to cause trouble, as an excuse for those moments where I have been squarely to blame for letting people down.

It would be easy to assume that I was born with a silver spoon in my mouth, but that is simply not the case. I was given opportunities that others in life might not have had because my parents scrimped and saved and made sacrifices. I am highlighting the really quite ordinary roots of my family background in order to show those who are happy to reach for the lazy excuse of poverty as reason for never making any effort to better their lot for themselves or their children. We didn't grow up with millions stuffed under the mattress, and we were frequently required to be frugal – there was no such thing as waste in our house – but I can't honestly say I ever went without. My immediate family was close and loving, which was the real reason my brother and I had the opportunities to build a life of our own. Our extended family was not without the odd quirk or infuriating idiosyncrasy, but my parents never allowed such distractions to get in the way of their foremost focus: raising their children properly.

On my show, I have seen people from more appalling backgrounds than I could ever imagine buck the trend and make successes of themselves. I have seen that through effort and sheer force of will people can present a better set of circumstances for their children than they had themselves. On the flip side, however, there are many who allow the cycle of deprivation that caught them up to engulf their own children. My own family has endured some troubled times. I have overcome personal battles that temporarily damaged the fabric of my family. I have on occasion been distracted from my primary purpose, which is to invest in the protection of all of my family's needs. Unfortunately, most people will have periods of difficulty during their lives when their focus wavers, but it is just unacceptable to give up on young children permanently, especially when they are not old enough to know any better. No matter what is thrown at you, what trouble comes your way, your commitment to your children must be lifelong and absolute.

Certain elements of my family shunned me after my divorce from my first wife. There is a strong religious streak running through most of my extended family. The older generation in my family are all particularly God-fearing and none was too impressed at my failure to see my first marriage through. I can't blame them for their disappointment; they all had certain expectations that were way beyond my capacity to live up to. Some of them will have considered me a man more intent on spending time in the bookies than with his family at home. They saw me going through a ruinous phase that I can only now admit was a major reason behind the failure of my first marriage. They did not like me one bit, which is fair enough. I was not the nicest person back then and I was not in the nicest of places either. I remember Uncle Len, once barking at my mother that I had 'brought shame on the whole family.' The way he saw it, divorce was a coward's way out of what should have been a lifelong commitment. His umbrage towards me caused quite a few arguments, but still they were not – nor did they ever become – a reason for throwing in the towel; there I differed from those on my show who make their children the first casualties of the most minor family feud. I'm guessing the 'shame' that little episode brought has been stored away and forgotten about – at least for now that is. It's strange how being on telly has changed so many people's perceptions of me, even those within my own family!

There are too many people looking for reasons to avoid getting on with the basic job of parenting their child. Whether it be a lack of money, a lack of support from their own family, a poor background, or even poverty brought on by their own addiction, most of what is offered up to me by way of defence relies on (normally self-induced) problems that are eminently fixable if someone commits themselves fully to the solution. Some people bury their heads in the sand and claim they did their best when really they know they did anything but. Others, sadly, have never been shown what it takes by anyone around them and so have no idea where to begin to make changes. The chances are that their own children will therefore be condemned to the same dark and directionless upbringing they suffered. That is the situation this country faces; that is the reality of what I confront on my show each day.

None of us can escape the fact that poverty in this country is a very real issue. Poverty must also be THE BIGGEST DISTRACTION to positive parenting, which is adequately displayed by the lives I will go on to talk about in this book. It creates the environment where breakdowns in society flourish. It can't be a coincidence that most of my guests, the people who are emblematic of the social problems facing so many in this country, are living just above, or sometimes below, the poverty line. These people, of course, need help wherever it can be found but, more than that, they need to learn to start helping themselves.

If you ask me, the real poverty affecting this country is a dearth of aspiration, a lack of ambition. You could go into any of the most financially poor communities in the country and find this to be true. Throwing money at this particular problem won't help. The young families I meet who say they are struggling to cope do not find it hard to get by in any financial sense. On the contrary, many have all they need courtesy of a state benefits system that rewards them for creating life they have no clue how to nurture. They have the fifty-inch plasma TV on the wall and plenty of cash to spare for takeaways, alcohol and drugs. What they don't have is the fire inside them to want to make the best of themselves. That fierce pride you hope would be handed down to their children so that they too might make a better life for themselves.

I am dealing on a daily basis with teenagers who come to the show with three children already in tow. It isn't uncommon for me to read in the research notes about women in their mid-twenties who have already had six or seven children taken off them and placed into care for their own safety – I struggle to get my head round that. But when I confront these people, their vacant expressions tell me they couldn't care less that their children have been confiscated by the state. They almost don't see the raising of their own children as their responsibility.

To a large extent I can't blame anyone who has never actually received any guidance. You would hope that there is something inherent inside us all that recognises right and wrong, no matter what our backgrounds, but the truth is that some of the kids I have met have been left to fend for themselves, and never been taught to show or understand human kindness. These 'feral packs' we hear so much about are the second and third generations of families who have become wholly dependent on hand-outs. The youngest have seen their parents paid to sit at home and have more babies without ever having to do anything for the money they receive. Over successive generations, cash has been ladled out without caveat or condition that its recipient contribute to the greater good in some way. The pride that used to beat through the chest of most working men and women has faded away in favour of an indolence that has now come to threaten the basic values most in this country used to hold dear.

There is nothing that angers me more than seeing useless parents sponging off the state whilst giving nothing of themselves, not even to their children, in return. I don't expect too many of the guests on my show are likely to be future captains of British industry, but is it really too much to ask some to just make a bit more effort with their kids? Many young parents come to me and say that they cannot understand why their teen has become so unruly, but when you peel back the layers you see that their 'tearaway teens' have lived their lives unchecked for fifteen years! No punishment when they misbehave; no praise when they have done well. No one telling them they must go to school; no guiding light taking an interest in friends or steering them away from bad crowds. If you believe the bleating of some of these parents, you would get the impression that a once-blissful household was shattered overnight when their loving son suddenly turned into a violent, drug-crazed nuisance! Even now, after all these episodes of *The Jeremy Kyle Show*, I am amazed at how blameless people still see themselves in the development of their children. Many seem to have no concept of cause and effect. They come to me hoping I can instil discipline into children who have run around as they pleased, without boundary or censure, for their entire life! They expect me to cast some sort of spell to make everything all right, unwilling to recognise that they might be the cause of their child's behaviour and that they again have to form the bulk of the solution!

I sometimes can't believe quite how simply I have to explain things. I regularly find myself reaching for ridiculous analogies to make my point more clearly. I've asked some people to consider ancient tribes and to model the parenting of their kids on the templates that see village elders passing down skills and techniques through generations. Their young children, I say, are like sponges, ready to absorb whatever stimulus and experience you put their way. It is not enough to rely on the state or teachers (and certainly not television talk-show hosts) to do the work of proper parents. Every child needs love, affection and attention, but this also has to be offset against discipline, guidance and the setting of proper boundaries. If *you* don't do it for your children, who else will? Unfortunately, we are in the grip of a crisis brought about by generations failing their children in exactly the same way that they were failed themselves. This is the root cause, I believe, of the plethora of social problems I will detail more fully in this book.

What gets me most about this latest generation of failing parents is how easily they give up when tested by the tougher aspects of their children's development. I never tire of saying that no new parent has an innate understanding of what is required, and that there is no divine guide for us to study on how we might become perfect parents. All we have is the advice of our friends, families and betters, all bolstered of course by the experience we pick up along the way. We will all make mistakes, and sometimes life's harsh realities will dictate that we can't have all we hoped for as regards our children. I frequently have to work away from home for three or four days each week. In an ideal world I would work from home and be around to enjoy every wondrous moment of my children's growing up. But life ain't like that, is it?

As much as it kills me to be away from my family, I know I gain more from my absence than I would by staying at home. This doesn't mean that I don't love and want to spend more time with my children – of course I do. But I fulfil a lot of my own needs for self-esteem and pride by working hard and therefore being able to provide for my whole family. The country we live in must be in a really sorry state when

so many of the potential workforce consider it more econom-
ical to stay at home and be funded by the taxpayer. I honestly
believe a lot of the problems we now face could be rooted
out at source if more people took it upon themselves to go
out and earn. I understand the argument and completely
agree that it's ludicrous for the government to make it more
appealing to sponge than work. The only thing I say to those
who view their time purely in pounds and pence is to step
back and take a look at the bigger picture. Even if you are,
say, ten pounds worse off each week by going back to work,
I'd still urge you to do it. The respect you would get from
your family, peers and colleagues would be worth a thousand times more than anything that spare tenner buys you.
The pride you would feel would be worth the effort alone
but, more importantly, the example you would lay down for
your children to follow would be invaluable.

As it currently stands, the benefits system makes no sense
to me. How can it be that you are rewarded for staying out
of work and having more children you are not properly
equipped to raise? We are seeing the effects of benefits dependency percolating through at every level and it is scary as hell.
Many people are living quite comfortably on their plumped-
up portfolio of hand-outs, but so few are using the free time
this generous lifestyle affords for any sort of productive advantage. They don't channel the extra time they have into
improving their own skills or options, and they certainly don't
seem to be using it to steer their children onto better paths.
Where once people used to go out and work all day, now
there are vast swathes of people being paid to stay indoors.
Many seem to have settled for having more kids, perhaps
just to push up the total on the fortnightly benefit cheque.

I see parents every day where one or both of them have
been overcome by problems rooted in excessive drinking or
drug taking. Nobody would suggest that in any but the most

extreme cases the children of these addicts go without the basics of food and clothing. However, even in the less serious cases, what they quickly become starved of is the love, affection and positive role models they need to progress properly in life. All too often I hear tales from teenagers who claim that they are looking after their five brothers and sisters whilst their parents sit around the house getting smashed. And so we end up with whole childhoods lost, opportunities vanished, and future generations destroyed via government-funded addictions. More than ever, I am told tales of kids being forced to pick their way past the cans of lager in the fridge before finally alighting on some mouldy piece of cheese to eat. The 'lucky' ones might get enough of their parents' loot to order themselves yet another pizza before being plonked in front of the plug-in babysitter that is the TV. No doubt these types of problems have much to do with deprivations in other areas, but I think the handing out of money to people with no motivation to do anything other than drink or take drugs all day is only exacerbating an already dangerous problem. Surely we're just feeding their habit?

Every day of my working life, I come across the issues I am covering in this book. I have very real fears for the future of this country if something isn't done quickly, right across the board, to halt what is an alarming implosion of social standards. We have all read about the breakdown of the family unit and the ebbing away of respect on our streets. Well, I have to say I agree with those commentators who say it is taking place. Things seem to be getting more polarised. The problems in the poorer areas seem generally to be getting worse whilst the opportunities being presented to more wealthy communities are seemingly more abundant. I fear a greater sense of divide, a more pronounced 'them and us' battle evolving and one in which the key casualties will be the family unit as well as societal standards of respect, tolerance and aspiration at those traditionally harder hit areas on Britain's financial landscape. I suppose my real fear is that without some joined-up thinking and more people thinking for themselves will we not end up in a situation where the rich get richer and the poor just tear themselves apart?

It would be easy for anyone to argue that my viewpoint might be skewed somewhat. Some may say that I only see the worst elements of today's 'Broken Britain' and therefore have a rather warped view on the magnitude of the problems and how far they have spread into the corners of our society. I take that point, but I have to say that the examples we feature on *The Jeremy Kyle Show* are not the worst extremes of any particular issue we cover; they are the norm of what comes through to our team of researchers. Every day we are obliged – legally, ethically, morally and medically – to turn down requests from people with far more extreme stories than those we currently broadcast. The real horror for those who complain about *The Jeremy Kyle Show* is not actually found in the stories we cover, but rather in those we can't. Therein lies an altogether darker picture of what life is really like for so many in Great Britain.

However, I understand that there are a number of trust issues surrounding television today. If anyone out there chooses not to believe what they see on screen, or if anyone thinks that what they've seen has been engineered purely for entertainment, please consider the evidence. Take London. The capital of this great nation is apparently the sixth richest city on earth. However, inner London is said to house seven of the twenty most deprived local authorities in England. Six hundred and fifty thousand children in London live below the official poverty line. Half of all children are looked after by just one parent. The knock-on effects of this starting point includes there being 171 gangs in London, with a quarter being involved in murder, and nearly half in serious assaults.

London has the lowest working-age employment rate of any area in the UK, and four of its boroughs have unemployment rates above 40 per cent. Beyond this, one million Londoners are harmful abusers of alcohol and it is also home to 23 per cent of the UK's drug-dependent adults. However you cut it, those are some worrying numbers.

Now, not every individual who has contributed to those statistics will be entirely responsible for whatever problem has befallen them in life. There will always be some who slip through the net, no matter what advantages they have been handed (as you will read, I need look no further than my own brother for proof of this). Small percentages of a population will always fall prey to some form of addiction – that is statistically inevitable. However, the vast numbers we are talking about in this country and the massive problems we face cannot simply be dealt with in the classroom. We can no longer wait for governments to wake up and see what part they have to play. We have to recognise sooner rather than later that theirs can only ever be a minority shareholding in the solutions we fast need to find. We have to stop sleepwalking our way to complete and utter meltdown by taking some responsibility. We must get back to a core set of values that sees us do the best for ourselves and give our best to our children. It really isn't that hard. A little more care and effort from all of us at the outset will make a massive difference in the long run.

I am not one for pulling punches. And so it must be that I will not pull any punches now in telling anyone who cares to listen just how bad things in Great Britain are in danger of becoming. By no means do I profess to have all the answers, but I do know who has to shoulder most of the responsibility for turning this country around. It isn't the police, it isn't the teachers and it certainly won't be the politicians. It will be me, you and anyone in this country who ends up bringing a child into this world.

In this book I want to put properly on display all that is served up to me each and every morning I step into work at Granada Television Studios in Manchester. In it I will be able to talk about everything. There is nothing that has to be lost to the cutting-room floor here: it will be exactly what I see each day, exactly as I see it. I'll warn you now: some of it will not be pretty, but everything I'll tell you is true. You may not like what you read – and on one level it is to be hoped that you don't.

I want to speak truthfully about everything that lies at the heart of this country's problems. I have looked into the various facts and figures and they merely confirm what I long ago knew to be true: this country is slipping away from us. It is being stolen away by a growing band of people who simply don't know how to be better. I try my best each morning, but it seems that my television show will never make the difference to many of the 1.5 million who watch it every day; we can only help the few who take part.

I have vowed to speak honestly to them as I have vowed to speak honestly to you. I am not without blame here and I would certainly never tout myself as the perfect example of how a member of our society should be. No, I am pretty damned far from perfect. As such, it is only fair that I also tell you about some of my own faults and failings, my own mistakes, the personal battles and a few of the vices which so nearly destroyed me. I have hurt some people along the way and I have been down on my knees on more than one occasion. I'll tell of the tears I've shed and the sometimes selfish misjudgements that carried me to rock bottom. Believe me, I won't do it for my own gratification – I am not the sort of person who takes any delight whatsoever in reliving past mistakes, but here they are necessary to highlight that we are all capable of making serious errors and indeed of recovering from them.

I'd bet (though only a modest sum, of course!) that I am not half as talented as most of the people who are reading this book. I know I owe a lot of any success I have to luck, but I will never accept that it was serendipity or coincidence that led me to make the most of the opportunities that came my way. I have always worked bloody hard to make the best of whatever abilities I had, just as my parents did. I only have to look around my family to see how those with boundless natural talents can end up if they waste them. I'm sure it must still rankle with my brother when he sees the runt of the Kyle litter doing so well, particularly given that he had all the tools to have everything that's mine – and more. When he comes to look back at his own failings, once he strips away the smart answers and complex excuses, he'll know at once that he alone screwed up. He had the best of starts like me but he messed it up. It has never been my parents' fault and it will never be my fault. It was his decision to experiment with drugs that very first time and it is he alone who bears the responsibility for taking drugs at any time since. He still has more talent in his little finger than I have in my entire body, and now it is down to him to make the best of it.

One common trait – which shines malevolently through all those who never see that they might escape troubles through resolve and hard work – is apathy. This is *the* most insurmountable thing I come up against, each and every day. I can provide tools, introduce people to Graham Stanier, the show's psychotherapist, and encourage them to do well. I can give pep talks and gee-ups, but I can't provide people's motivation for them. Not in the long term, anyway. People need to be able to look themselves in the mirror at the end of each day and honestly assess if they have done all they can. Only they will know. Whether you have ambitions to be the local plumber, or even the prime minister, you need to know in yourself and for yourself that you have done all you can to achieve your goals. And the conviction and belief that you can achieve, that you will achieve, and that you should achieve, should be passed down through to your children. I fought hard to get where I am by making the most of my abilities. If enough people could honestly say the same, there wouldn't be nearly so much for me to write about in this book.

As I have said, I have made some huge mistakes and I have taken some unconventional paths getting to this point in my life. I met my wife in the most bizarre circumstances imaginable, but you have to see beyond the headlines to understand why our marriage works so well. It is not the where-you-meet or how-you-met that matters, it is what you are prepared to invest to make it work that ultimately counts. We are a team and we both abide by the rules and tenets laid down for us by our parents, guidelines that have stood the test of time for both of us. We are now trying our best to pass those things on to our children in the hope that they will go on to greater heights – and with any luck make fewer mistakes along the way, too.

My great fear for the UK right now is that we are not preparing our future generations for the ups and downs that lie ahead of them. The failures of some parents in recent generations are now coming home to roost, and we have to act quickly, and as one, to ensure that fixable issues don't become permanent problems.

Every instinct I have tells me that nothing is impossible. For me to get where I am today is proof positive that anything is possible if you work hard enough to earn the breaks, and then make the most of them when they arrive. The society we need to rebuild in this country is one that need only be founded on responsible and decent people to whom good deeds come naturally, without undue coercion or correction at any Boot Camp. Nobody needs to be perfect, though perfection should never be discouraged if aimed for. All anyone needs to adhere to are the basics of good parenting. If everyone does just that, placing greater emphasis on the ethical and moral development of their children, this country will soon shake off the parasites draining it of all its former glory. I am not picking on anyone undeserving and I am not trying to sensationalise. The problems this country faces are real and plentiful, but also very fixable. I have looked at this country, as I have looked at myself, and called things as I see them. Hopefully, you will appreciate that I am only being honest.

2

Kids Having Kids

If there's one subject that is guaranteed to drive me to distraction, it is that of youngsters having babies when they are patently ill equipped to care for them. Unfortunately, this seems to be one of the issues I come across most frequently. Even if the story of a broken home might come under a different headline, you can bet your bottom dollar that somewhere woven into its fabric is an incident that saw another unwanted life conceived on a thoughtless whim. These stories are typically rooted in the all-too-familiar theme of poverty: not only in the obvious financial sense, but also a dearth of ambition and aspiration, and a lack of education. The lamentable liaisons that culminate in an appearance with me (usually to get DNA results on children that no one can ever quite seem to remember creating) tend to be blurred by the cocktail of drink and drugs that one, other or both parents consumed on the night 'love's young dream' met 'high romance' in some mate's spare room. Then, nine months later, everyone gathers round in shock, horror and surprise to learn that they have perpetuated a cycle which will see another baby born to parents that did not foresee or care about the consequences of their actions.

I am forever preaching contraception and always demanding that people, young girls in particular, aim higher and demand more of and for themselves. Despite government statistics showing that things are getting better, I have to say that my experience says different. It is well known that Britain has the highest teenage birth rates in Western Europe. I'll repeat again for the hard of hearing: the UK's statistics are *twice* as high as Germany. We are *three times* more likely to have a teenager give birth in this country than our cousins in France, and our teenage birth rates are a whopping *six times higher* than those of the Dutch. Some people in this country sneer and scoff about the supposedly open and easy approach to sex in the Netherlands, but it seems to pay dividends for their society. They appear have an altogether more adult attitude towards sex, underpinned by a maturity that shows up our 'kiss-me-quick' sensibilities as childish and embarrassing.

Now, some may argue that there is a generational issue at play here. British 'reserve' abounds in a lot of people of mine or my parents' age. Sex has never been known as a topic for open, honest debate. No, a few double-entendres and a bit of *Carry On Camping* banter have always sufficed, when what was perhaps required was a proper dialogue about the implications of having sex as a teenager – or at any other time, for that matter. Now, I haven't suddenly turned into some stereotypical hippy uncle who is about to preach about free love, peace and harmony. As kids we all knew *that* chat was coming and it still looms large on the horizon for any parent. It can be embarrassing, but it has to be done, if only for parental peace of mind.

I can still remember the fishing trip my father took me on. He paced about nervously all day as we cast line after luncheon-meat-baited line in search of chub. My father, bless him, stumbled, muttered and couldn't pick the right words as the subject was nervously broached. I could feel his pain, and I was none too comfortable myself, but the speech was given, the message understood and something that was almost a rite of passage for kids of my age was concluded for another generation. Many years later I was to repeat the feat, though typically even more clumsily, with my daughter, Hattie. I actually remember driving in the car with her and nervously trying to steer the conversation away from the radio and onto this chat that all parents must have with a seventeen-year-old daughter who was attracting the sort of looks mine was from the horny young lads of Cirencester! Luckily, I needn't have worried: she is pretty clued up about these things. She stopped me dead in my tracks, both rescuing and cutting me down at once with the killer line: 'Dad, nothing's happened yet. I haven't gone beyond first base, but when I do, I'll let you know. Now, carry on driving and stop making yourself look like a twat!' I guess with that we were done!

Still, if the nation's teenage pregnancy problems stemmed exclusively from parents getting tongue-tied at the thought of saying 'penis' and 'vagina' in the same sentence, I think I'd be all right. Unfortunately, the fixes needed for the issues go way beyond overcoming the embarrassment of that brand of people who still snigger when Bill Oddie talks of blue tits!

What is perhaps even more worrying than those teenage girls who carelessly get pregnant on a drunken night, thanks to their equally thoughtless young Don Juans, is the number of girls who get pregnant knowingly and willingly whilst still being unable to cope with having a baby. Symptomatic of the broken homes and families that feed this booming British teenage pregnancy trend is the stock line I've heard from kids as young as TWELVE and THIRTEEN who tell me they want a baby because 'they want something to love and to love them back.' At first, I naively thought that such girls were just trying it on with their parents, throwing a few toys out of the pram for extra pocket money or to get some more attention. Not so. I was genuinely shocked to meet Shannon, a girl of thirteen, who was so intent on having a baby 'that will love me like I want to be loved' that she had already lured *eight* different men – UP TO THE AGE OF TWENTY!

– into bed for sex, which she had deliberately planned should be unprotected. This taught me there and then that we were dealing with commonplace scenarios that could not just be straightened out by Mummy and Daddy getting to grips with a competent telling of 'The Birds and the Bees'.

Let me lay out the bare facts:

In 2003, the last time such figures were properly updated, in England and Wales there were 59.8 conceptions per 1,000 15–19-year-olds. There were 42.3 conceptions per 1,000 15–17-year-olds, and an average of 8 conceptions per 1,000 13–15-year-olds! This isn't a problem confined to southern Britain. I've met hundreds of kids, from every corner of the country, and they all seem to be falling into the same trap. I have no reason to disbelieve the figures that tell me young women under the age of 20 in Northern Ireland (in 2003) produced 1,484 live births whilst in Scotland in 2003/04 there were 68.2 conceptions per 1,000 16–19-year-olds and 7.5 conceptions per 1,000 13–15-year-olds.

People tell me these overall figures are dropping, and thankfully it is true that the rate of teen pregnancies is slowing. We still lag behind our obviously more cultured and considered European neighbours in even the most optimistic statistics but, for me, the issues that lead to these still deplorable numbers remain there for all to see. If you turn your telly to ITV1 at 9.25 on any weekday morning, you will see the manifestation of these issues for yourself.

The majority of the 'kids having kids' I meet tend to come, I am sorry to say, from the same sort of stock. An unfortunate start in life, one in which they were denied the quality and amount of opportunities that many of the rest of us enjoyed, has been compounded by poor personal choices that see them locked into the same cycle that led to their own creation. I sympathise wholeheartedly with anyone out there whose start in life is handicapped in this way. I wish there really was equal opportunity and upward social mobility for all. However, the simple facts show us that the playing field is uneven. I have to remain positive that there is no such thing as a class gulf or any sort of sociocultural chasm dividing 'haves' and 'have-nots'. I instead accept that there always has been and always will be a discernible difference between the 'have-mores' and 'have-lesses'. That last distinction is very important to me, and I believe it is a key concept to grasp for any young person not wanting to add to the teenage pregnancy stats that shame our country and ruin lives. There will always be people out there who have more money, more opportunities, or more supportive family, friends or loved ones. It is not hard for anyone in life, even the most blessed, to pick out a peer who has seemingly been dealt a better hand. The key to unlocking anyone's potential, to increasing their options in life, is surely not to concentrate on how little they start with compared to any contemporary. The focus for any individual – from any background and any part of the country – should always be to play *their own* hand as best they can.

I have regularly spoken to people from the poorest backgrounds and the most hard-pressed of families. Their stories can all be heartbreaking, and I am lost for the words to articulate properly the very real suffering some have endured through no fault of their own. These people can be born into situations that obviously put them at a disadvantage to the vast majority. But one thing is clear: at some point along the way they, and they alone, have made a personal choice to take a particular path. They might not have had the best of starts; they might not have had a network of people ready, able and willing to point out the potential repercussions of any bad choice they might make. They may have come from communities where prioritising right and wrong or the personal risk attached to any decision does not really rate as important. I understand that, in these cases, the actions that lead to unwanted or unplanned teenage pregnancies can be bound up as much in youthful exuberance, misadventure or thoughtlessness as the need to escape a depressing set of circumstances. But no matter what the background, if you drill down far enough into anyone's personal story, there will always be that one moment, a personal crossroads of sorts, where we either *choose* to do something or we don't. We take the drink or we don't. We say 'yes' to the drugs on offer or we pass. We think 'contraception!', or we have sex and hope for the best.

I wouldn't be motivated to write this now, nor would I front the show, if everyone always did their utmost to play the cards they're dealt to the best of their ability. But I'd be lying to myself if I concluded, as so many do, that there is no way out for anyone from certain social or economic back-grounds. No matter if you're from *the* hardest of backgrounds, doesn't everyone at least have access to schooling and basic education in this country? If that is the only card you're dealt, then I'd say play that and milk your school for all it's worth. At school, if you choose, you can escape whatever troubles you have at home for six hours a day. You can throw your-self into the learning and study that will ensure your options increase as you progress. You take fate back into your own hands. Do well enough – which anyone can with the right application – and you will ensure that you are no longer waiting for the next hand to be dealt. To continue the metaphor, you can deal from your own deck!

On the show, it is sometimes too late for me to intervene. Thankfully, a lot of those who have got themselves into a mess and given birth do recognise how their personal choices affected the outcome. Many resolve to **learn** a lesson and then make the best of their new set of circumstances. I always hope that anyone watching might heed the mistakes of people on my show. Certainly I've always found it preferable to learn from others' mistakes than suffer the ignominy of learning through my own. However, the regularity with which I am confronted by young kids having yet more children shows that the message clearly isn't getting through as it must. I shall therefore point to some more sobering statistics that might prompt any teenager considering pregnancy as an option – and certainly the parents who are either fully complicit or not sufficiently invested in such a decision – to think a-bloody-gain!

Government statistics show that by the age of thirty, teenage mothers are *more likely* to be living in poverty than any mother giving birth aged twenty-four or over. Those same teenage mothers are also much *less likely* to be employed *or* living with a partner. Teenage mothers are 20 per cent more likely to have *no qualifications* at age thirty than mothers giving birth aged twenty-four or over.

This evidence frustrates me more than any other in the issue of teenage pregnancy. So many of the young mothers I've met have got pregnant purely to engineer a move out of the family home and into council accommodation. Worse, certain young mums with two or three kids in tow already, and often to different dads, are embarked on a deliberate policy of selfish and inconsiderate 'postcode procreation' to then move themselves from one free house to another one that is bigger, better, but always still paid for by me and every other taxpayer. Family units have broken down to such an extent that some kids think that risking unprotected sex with any old stranger is worth it to secure alternative accommodation for themselves.

And surely that is key to what is wrong in Gordon Brown's Britain. We can warn against dangers and endlessly give guidance, but no word we preach will ever ring true so long as

the government's welfare system seems so heavily incen-
tivised in favour of single parents, the key constituents of any
broken family. My understanding of the welfare system was
that it was meant to catch and help those who were unlucky
enough to fall through society's cracks. Nowadays the whole
system is being wilfully and strategically abused, in some
cases by those who would rather scrounge than earn a living,
and in others by those who are almost encouraged by government to abandon traditional notions of family values in favour
of a system that so many tell me actually rewards households
where there are no fathers, single mothers with no job and
whole flocks of children.

Certain viewers tire of hearing me spout the same mantra
to certain guests in similar situations. I sometimes get bored
myself at constantly having to repeat the same stuff to kids
for whom sound advice or common sense seems complete
anathema. I am forever telling young teenage couples who
are convinced they are in love after only seven days together
– days in which one of them has often transgressed sufficiently in the other's eyes to warrant demanding that I put
them on a lie detector! – that they are in no position to know
if they really want to have a baby together. Moreover, as I
am also always telling them, what's the bloody hurry? Having
a baby does not make a relationship easier. It does not cement
and fortify love in the way that so many of our teenagers
naively expect it will.

In my experience, and as most parents will confirm, adding
a child to a relationship only ever makes things more complicated, more stressful and more difficult. What stresses and
tensions existed in any relationship before are tested to previously unimaginable limits. Furthermore, adding your own
little critter, no matter how much you love them and each
other, is almost guaranteed to expose fault lines in your relationship you did not even realise were there. Don't take my

word for it, look again at the stats: teenage mothers have three times the rate of postnatal depression of older mothers *and* a higher risk of poor mental health for three years after the birth.

Let me spell it out for anyone who still can't see the potential problems on the horizon. Any money that was previously yours to spend will now be going towards nappies and milk and all that other essential stuff that kids need to survive. Sleep goes out of the window, as does any semblance of the social life you once knew. Staying up late and going round mates' houses on a whim (should) all get sacrificed at the altar of good parenting. You will become more tetchy and irritable as the sleep deprivation kicks in; you may well contract postnatal depression – but still that baby will be there, needing feeding, deserving attention, and wanting to cry whenever anything isn't just so in its big new world . . . And yet people still come to me and think all of this will be easy, or somehow make an already rocky relationship more harmonious?!?!?

If your, or your relationship's, health is still not enough of a consideration to halt the inexorable march towards teenage motherhood, you might like to consider the health and future welfare of your child. Even those who feel well equipped to have a baby at a young age; even those who have considered the personal pitfalls but are still sure this is the best way forward for themselves should just consider the following: the stated infant mortality rate for babies born to teenage mothers is 60 per cent higher than for babies born to older mothers. SIXTY PER CENT HIGHER! Now, I'm not saying that there aren't teenage mothers out there who have done a fantastic job in raising fantastic children. I am merely asking that, before having a baby, even the most mature and adult of teenagers should consider the possible outcomes and probable impact on all elements of not just their own psychology, health and welfare but also their baby's too.

Continuing the theme, I note that teenage mothers are statistically more likely to smoke throughout their pregnancy. You don't need me to point out the blindingly obvious; surely anyone with even half a brain can by now deduce the negative impacts of smoking on one's health – be they child, adult or unborn child. To be fair, I run the risk of hypocrisy in criticising smokers, because both my wife and I smoke ourselves. That said, Carla has always given up smoking the minute she has known she could be pregnant, never once having a puff until well after our children were born. Clearly I have never been pregnant, but any cigarette I had while Carla was expecting was always lit well away from the house (and from a hormonal wife who may well have slain me for giving into a craving she knew she could not indulge). Contrast that with people I see outside the studio and in the streets, drawing on countless fags whilst their bellies are massively swollen with their unborn child. Again, no thought for their babies, just a slavish devotion to their own fixes, typifying in microcosm the selfishness of the decision to have a kid in the first place.

The best hope any of us has for fixing this and all the other issues in our society is for each individual to take responsibility for their own part in the massive repair job we face. Sir Winston Churchill once said that 'attitude is a small thing that makes a big difference.' Whereas he was engaged in the Battle of Britain, today we should be much more concerned by this Battle for Britain. I appeal to everyone just to think of the consequences. Do you really want to be part of a trend that gets worse with each deteriorating downward spiral? It is one thing to be dealt a bad hand and poor start in life, but it is quite another to knowingly deal out that same disadvantaged start to your own children. Rather than repeating the same mistakes as your parents or those all around you, isn't it better to buck the trend? I am fed up of talking to kids and parents in this country who seem content to be sheep, unable or unwilling to stop perpetuating this cycle. Children of teenage mothers apparently have a 63 per cent higher risk of being born into poverty compared to babies born to mothers in their twenties. The former are also more likely to have accidents and the very behavioural problems I am called upon to sort each day. How many times do I have to say to each (f)ailing mother that I don't want to see them back on the show in twenty years' time to fix the same problem between them and their offspring that currently exists between them and their parent(s)? I don't say these things glibly. I bloody well mean them because I know only too well how easy it will be for these scenarios to repeat themselves. Please people: seize life, build on it and experience all it has to offer. Improve yourself, broaden your horizons, and in doing so improve the well of opportunities that your future children will have to tap into. Sir Winston Churchill also once said, 'a man does what he must – in spite of obstacles and dangers and pressures – and that is the basis of all human morality.' Not for the first time, the citizens of this country could do a lot worse than to listen to his words and heed their advice.

I honestly believe that part of the problem stems from there being too much pressure on kids to succeed, or at least subscribe to the media definitions of success. I didn't truly know what I wanted to do until I was forty years old. My eldest daughter, Hattie, is eighteen and she hasn't yet settled on a career path. One lady recently approached me and asked me about her own daughter, a sixteen-year-old she was aghast to report did not yet know what she wanted from life. She was expecting me to advise her to 'get a job', 'knuckle down', and all the rest of it, but to me it was a perfectly understandable predicament for any sixteen-year-old to be in. Harder to fathom was the pressure being projected onto this girl by her mother. I calmly explained that I was happy that my own daughter, in the absence of any concrete career plans, had instead decided to broaden her horizons by travelling the world. And, more than that, she has my full backing!

If you can't yet find the right professional path for yourself, why not get out and see the world and discover a bit more about yourself along the way. I'm sure most people would get a lot more from travelling foreign lands and dealing with the challenges of speaking new languages, embracing new cultures, and meeting new people than they would from labouring at a dead-end job in the same town they've spent their whole lives in!

I know worldwide travel isn't readily accessible to all, but there is nothing to stop that same sense of ambition and curiosity that leads so many to seek pastures new replacing the apathy present in so many of our youth. My production office is full of people, some of whom come from very tough backgrounds, who have rounded themselves out with experiences that took them far beyond the confines of the estate they were brought up on. Many have travelled internationally and, those that have, all tell me that they did so by working first to save enough for the plane ticket, and then again to sustain themselves in Spain, France, Greece, the USA, or wherever they ended up. All tell me they would not swap those experiences for any career opportunity that might come up in future. Their travels gave them a grounding, a confidence, and a sense of themselves that helped set and drive them on the paths to the successful careers I am proud to be a part of.

I can already see half of the readership of the *Guardian* piping up to deride or dismiss the above, but they will have missed the point. I know it is unrealistic to push for everyone on a tough estate to suddenly broaden their horizons in this way. That would be ridiculous. But if they harnessed that same spirit of adventure, of trying things and believing things can be done, they might well breach new frontiers a lot closer to home. Rather than doing whatever everyone else around them has always done, they might actually be the ones to break out. No more 'sheep' locked into a cycle of crime, poverty and teenage pregnancy. Perhaps we'd see new waves of kids applying their 'street smarts' to altogether more inspiring and entrepreneurial pursuits. Imagine how that might change the landscape of this country on every level.

That is still the dream, of course, but for now we've all got to tackle the realities of everyday life that see so many of our young caught in the teenage pregnancy trap. If the trend for British kids having kids is to be abated, then we really do have to take a good look at ourselves, understand who we are and what we've become. On the broadest and most basic level, we need to raise the expectations of our nation's young. Unfortunately, horribly low rates of expectation exist in our young in terms of everything from education to employment opportunities. Our kids don't demand more of themselves because they can't see any way off a path that has failed so many of their own predecessors. They feel destined to follow failed footsteps, and that leads to a grim expectation that they too will fail. They can't see that with a little effort or some extra guidance there are still options that are loftier than having Martini sex – any time, any place, anywhere (and usually with anyone), claiming state hand-outs and queuing up for the next available council house.

If the kids from the poorest backgrounds have fewer options than others, then they really have to be shown that the one option all of them have – a school education – really is their ticket to a better life. Young girls need to think and aim for something bigger, and I don't mean a chest as large as Jordan's. Though actually if they could channel her sense of drive, purpose and ambition into more productive pursuits for themselves, then that would be something positive.

It was recently pointed out to me that the only thing that these kids can do that is both free and fun is to have sex! This is particularly the case on the neglected estates from which many of my show's callers come. Well, if that is the case, the consequences of thoughtless procreation need to be properly spelt out too. As I've pointed out above, rates of teenage pregnancy are far higher among deprived communities. In these areas, the likelihood of becoming a teenage mother is nearly one in three but, worse, the effects of deprivation and social exclusion are passed from one generation to the next, and so the sorry cycle continues. We need to get back to that two-pronged attack that did the job so well in my formative years. Parents need to step up and take responsibility for keeping their kids on the right path and, where that is not possible, teachers have to take up the reins and guide their young charges away from the teenage pregnancy trap. Of course, you'll never stop kids experimenting. Teenagers all over the world will always be invited to parties where illicit drinking takes place, and for boys the compulsion to try out that newly awakened 'toy', which before had only ever dangled, becomes overwhelming. If we can drum it into these kids' minds before the hormones kick in and their behaviour becomes directed by booze and appendages, we might just begin to turn the tide. If that means the return of awkward father–son moments such as the one I faced whilst failing to catch any fish on the Holy Brook in Reading, so be it. If that means our classrooms are once more populated with kids embarrassed by teachers clumsily sheathing bananas with condoms whilst preaching safe sex, I say: bring it on! At least we can say we are attempting to get the message through.

In schools, sex education needs to be compulsory and accessible. As well as the obligatory biological tour of the Fallopian tubes and whatever else, there also has to be a concerted effort to talk to today's teenagers on their level about what having sex means and where it will lead. I'm not saying teachers should come armed with a copy of the Kama Sutra or the thoughts of Dr Ruth to every lesson, but an impassioned plea for them not to join some of the statistics I have outlined in this chapter might well make some of the inroads required. Properly given sexual education before sexual activity takes place can only help, surely? I don't believe, as some do, that this will lead to more teenage sex. I feel that it will lead to more *safe sex* for teenagers who were always going to have sex anyway. And I defy anyone not to be at least a little discouraged from wanting a baby by having one of those baby simulators we have occasionally featured on the show. They scream and gurgle and burble and whine all day and all night – just like a real baby constantly demanding a feed or a change. They most certainly do not make anyone charged with looking after one want to jump into bed and create the real thing, do they?!?!

Culturally, we could learn a lot from some of our European neighbours. A lot of cultural commentators put that down to the fact that they just aren't as fixated as us on the sex lives of others. Their papers aren't full of celebrity 'sexposés' because there just isn't the appetite to know or care about them. They seem to focus on the realities of their own sex lives, not on fantasies or gossiping about someone else's.

Social policy needs to be robust and designed to help UK citizens meet the targets that the government has set. In 1998, New Labour insisted that our teenage conception rate should be halved by 2010. It is true and fair to say that between 1998 and 2005 the conception rate fell by just over 11 per cent among under-eighteens and just over 12 per cent among under-sixteens. The year 2008 gave us the lowest figures since 1998, but just imagine how much faster they would fall if the government did not so demonstrably incentivise life as a single mother. If young kids knew that in future they might have to stay in their family home and raise their baby with the parent(s) they so want to be rid of, that might change attitudes – or at least provide a teenage pregnancy deterrent.

Two-parent families in work are being remorselessly milked to support the misguided lifestyle choices of others, and that is just not fair. The reward for making the right choices in this country is to get clobbered with ever-higher taxes while reading about how the money taken from your pocket is being siphoned off for any miscreant who can't be bothered and would rather exploit a system (s)he knows is there to be used. If these kids having kids were actually made to face up to the consequences of their own actions without sponsorship from the state, we just might see a change. If teenagers were denied the council home they saw as their divine right by virtue of being pregnant, the current ignorant attitude towards contraception that pervades might necessarily become more enlightened. Moreover, if these teenagers were forced to remain in their family home, new baby *et al*, their parents might *have* to become more invested in the lifestyle choices of their offspring. If parents knew they would be held accountable on some level for their child getting pregnant, just as they are at present with regards to truancy, I bet they'd be a whole lot more interested in where their children were disappearing at night, what they were up to, and with whom!

As I have said, the overall rate for teenage conception, the particularly British trend of kids having kids, has been falling. However, at the time of writing this, I am just starting to read a slew of articles suggesting that teenage pregnancy rates are recently on the rise again. Whatever the truth of whatever stats we read, there is no escaping that fact that we could all do more to quicken the pace of change. The trickle of overall national trends bears no resemblance to the stories I see on society's front line each morning. The message is getting through to some, but clearly not everyone, so it follows that we have to get more coordinated and consistent in our approach. Government policy needs to be backed up in the classroom and followed through in the family home. We all need to be singing from the same hymn sheet on this one: that is the only way a consistently clear message will get through to this and the next generation of Britain's young.

It can be done because I have seen the message get through to a great many of the individuals I speak to on *The Jeremy Kyle Show*, and I have seen previously carefree, careless and wayward teens turn their life around and opt for choices that can only improve them and society as a whole. But I can only speak to one individual at a time. Imagine what we could do if we ALL took the time and opportunity to turn around the life of just one teenager, be they our son, daughter, niece, nephew, pupil, family friend or neighbour. Imagine the difference that might make, not just to the statistics, but to our society as a whole. I'll keep trying to do what I can. Will you?

3

Discover Some Backbone

I never cease to be amazed by the amount of people that call my show to seek help or guidance with the basic fundamentals of parenting. *The Jeremy Kyle Show* receives literally thousands of enquiries per week and my producers tell me that a significant proportion of that number is made up of despairing parents, at a loss to explain or contain the spiralling misbehaviour of their miscreant offspring. 'Tearaway teens' have been something of a staple for us, and the sheer number queuing at our doors searching for help is, for me, every bit as frightening as the issues they repeatedly seem unable to resolve without our intervention. That there are so many is further proof of my contention that our society, the way we contribute to it, the way we function in it and the way the authorities seek to govern or manage it, needs drastic over-hauling at every level.

Recently, on the show, I was invited to try and make a nineteen-year-old ne'er-do-well see that terrorising his frail, partially disabled and petrified mother (she was a penniless sixty-one-year-old pensioner with osteoporosis), wilfully vandalising her property and possessions, then looting her purse for the incapacity benefits he felt *he* was entitled to, in order to feed his pathetic cannabis habit, was not actually on! Like so many of my guests nowadays, he thought his decision to call the show had somehow made his actions less deplorable, that picking up the phone to ask someone else to take responsibility for his problems had somehow absolved him of any guilt in the disgusting behaviour he daily doled out to his mother. She, bless her, came to the show under threat of eviction, bankruptcy, and even being given an ASBO, all because her son would not move out, make a life for himself – or at the very least not involve her in the funding of a drug habit he wouldn't have had the time to maintain if he'd just applied himself to something as simple as looking for work! That he had hitherto failed to acknowledge or under-stand that his actions were unacceptable left me somewhere between incredulous and incandescent, but it is only writing this now that I am left to reflect on an altogether more tragic footnote underscoring this family's plight.

His small-minded thuggery, claims of an addiction that patently did not exist (the show accepts the research in respect of cannabis abuse that asserts it is not physically addictive to even the heaviest of users), and the wanton destruction of every possession or ideal his mother held dear was bad enough, but it was failure to see, or even conceive of the possibility, that he might be the one to provide support – financial, emotional and in every other sense of the word – that now cuts through my rage and moves me to genuine sadness. This woman lived in shel-tered accommodation and was genuinely unable to work but, despite all her afflictions, the only problem truly preventing her from making the best of her autumn years was the son she refused to turn her back on, no matter what he so regularly and shamelessly subjected her to.

If anyone was in need of a caring, loving son to help out, take some of the strain and make life a little easier, it was her, but this idea had not flickered for even one moment in her son's mind. And that, I am sorry to say, is all too common an occurrence these days among the increasing numbers of families and communities that seem to be disintegrating before our very eyes. He did make the call and I applauded him for it, but he really had no idea why he'd done so. He didn't really see any problem; certainly he couldn't bring himself to acknowledge its heartbreaking effects on one mother I could have easily forgiven for showing him the door. He wanted me to fix a problem without being able to see what it was and how he was responsible for it. In short, he had no bloody backbone!

That story sticks in my mind principally because I heard it so recently. It's true that such abhorrent and unwarranted violence against an innocent victim should be difficult to forget, but the shocking probability is that the minutiae of this story, which so enraged me, will soon fade in my memory. Why? Well, the even more sickening truth is that I confront this type of story and meet these types of people pretty much every time I film a show. That particular story will soon be superseded in my mind by something even more shocking and more unbelievable. These sorts of people and these sorts of stories come to us in their droves and I have seen no sign of that trend abating. Moreover, I have to say, the type of violence being perpetrated by those who seek the show's help is only getting worse.

In our first block of filming, four years ago, we made a show called 'Terror on the Estate', which featured a host of parents who feared their own teenage children were out of control as they regularly ran amok about their homes and local community. Virtually every show I have filmed since has featured a story where a parent has 'lost', or failed to control, guide, or understand a child, whom they then come to view as beyond help or hope. Increasingly I am called upon to act as some sort of emergency parent to a child I have never before met. In twenty minutes, I am beseeched to instil a short, sharp shock of discipline, and somehow railroad errant youths into treating others with tolerance and respect. The more horror stories I read in the press about the worsening misdemeanours of this country's youth, the more I am convinced that there are whole swathes of the population looking to teachers, community leaders, the police – even government or fed-up talk-show hosts – to provide the basic care, attention, instruction and guidance that all kids should be able to count on by right from their parents.

This country is in the grip of a frightening and escalating wave of knife and gun crime among youths now being written off as 'feral' by the authorities struggling to contain them. What I demand daily from those who seek *my* help with *their* children is to know just what part *they* expect to play in their child's development and future progression. Where is their backbone when the going gets tough and the hard yards of parenting a child have to begin? As with that teen I described earlier, who brutalised his mother, so many of today's parents seem not to have factored in their own failings to the equation. If little Tommy or Johnny gets bad grades or plays truant, then that is somehow the teacher's fault. If they get caught defacing public property, hurling abuse at members of the local community or generally being a foul-mouthed, law-breaking menace, then that must be because 'they fell in with the wrong crowd'. If they are caught smoking or taking drugs, then it must be because the police have failed in their duty to keep the streets clean, right? WRONG! These pitiful excuses might be offered up unthinkingly or by way of distraction, but the bottom line is that in most cases it is the parents who have palpably failed. These people, in the vast majority of cases, are *the* key reason their kids have 'strangely' gone so far off the rails.

It can't be coincidence that a good proportion of the world's David Beckhams, captains of industry, or any other high achievers credit their success in part to the solid grounding afforded them by a family who loved, supported, nurtured and guided as necessary. I benefited enormously from the backing of parents I know have been openly supportive of every positive step I took to better myself – even when they didn't agree with my reasoning. They gave me the space and security I needed to make some almighty cockups and very questionable career choices. They found it in themselves to support me when I told them I was ditching the well-paid job I'd had in London for two shows a week on a local radio station in Kent. They could not quite believe I was swapping a job I loved and was very good at for a break in radio that paid an annual salary of just £5,000, but they put that to one side to support the dream I was chasing.

As you will read later, there were some pretty catastrophic flights of fancy in the life of Kyle the Younger, but I was dusted down after each failure, was assured I was loved and supported, and encouraged to start chasing my dreams all over again. I contrast my own experience with the worst examples of parenting found by my show's researchers and have to conclude once more that I have very real fears for this country's future. The true extent of the problem goes way beyond any parent's failure to acknowledge a responsibility for their part in either the problem or potential solution to their child's behaviour. More often than not, now, I hear of mindless parents defending their guilty children at all costs, thereby exacerbating both the individual problem and the wider social curse that infects our communities like a cancer.

I heard recently of an incident that is apparently becoming all too common. One of my producers told me of a friend of his who works tirelessly as a proud and dedicated schoolteacher. He actually described him as a rather staid, almost boring character – redoubtable, reliable but not very rock 'n' roll, a friend who regularly eschews group parties or friendly reunions until every last schoolbook is marked and lesson plans are prepared for the coming weeks. I've never met him, but apparently he, like me, is no big drinker, not the greatest fun on a night out and would never dream of a catch-up over a pint on a 'school night' . . . sounds all right to me and just the sort of committed professional this country can be proud of having in its schools. Anyway, I digress.

This dedicated teacher was dreading a forthcoming parents' evening with all the fear and anxiety that I used to reserve for those same nights when my teachers passed judgement on me countless years ago. 'What could he be scared about?' I asked, bemused. I tactlessly joked that 'he was probably just scared of working to a proper hour in the evening like the rest of us have to.' I was shocked to learn that this man's fear was genuinely held because of a particularly unsettling encounter at a previous parents' evening. Apparently, being the bastion of standards and good teaching that he is, he felt compelled to tell a parent that one of his class was struggling academically as a direct result of this parent's son being unruly, rude and disruptive in most lessons. The parent took umbrage, failed to believe that his blue-eyed boy was anything but a reflection of his own 'perfection' and promptly thumped the teacher for daring to be in any way critical of his son. Furthermore, he maintained that the teacher must be wrong about the child's abilities and that any of his son's limitations or academic failings must lie squarely at his teacher's feet.

Now, I could rant ad infinitum about how and why that is so gallingly wrong, but I hope and trust you can all see that for yourselves. What is really worrying is how common-place these kinds of stories are: we live in a world where our teachers, nurses, doctors and even police are ever more fearful of coming to unprovoked harm from members of the public, simply for doing their jobs properly and to the best of their abilities. I hear of depressingly similar tales coming from the streets where we once expected everyone to look out for each other and uphold the rule of law.

I have genuine sympathy with those people of my parents' generation who mourn the loss of the local bobby on the beat who could keep any wayward scamps in order with a stern talking-to or even a clip round the ear. Seemingly gone are the days when we could all expect to keep an eye out for one another's kids, justifiably chiding or disciplining anyone who stepped out of line. I remember being dragged in front of my headmaster once after stupidly throwing conkers into the road whilst waiting for a bus at the local stop. One hit a car and the driver, a complete stranger, thought nothing of demanding his pound of flesh from the headmaster, to whom he spilled (and exaggerated!) every last detail – with the full support of my parents, as it later turned out. I fully expected them to stick up for their offspring in the face of this stranger's tale but they backed him every step of the way over my idiotic actions that day. I was gutted, but thinking back on it now, they were right!

Nowadays, if you were to go around to number 32 and tell Mr X that his son had been behaving abominably, you would be more likely to be assaulted or humiliated than listened to. The disciplining of the child would also get lost in the ensuing fracas, with the only lesson learnt being that smacking neighbours is good, hard and gets results. The kid gets away with his original misdemeanour and is encouraged to re-offend against the neighbour, safe in the knowledge that 'good ole dad' will give him another kicking if he ever dares complain again.

Just as more traditional notions of family have given way to the dysfunction so eroding modern society, so our trad-itional sense of community, in which everyone played their part in the all-round upholding of standards, has given way to a more tribal, feudal and territorial division of this country's residential estates. Gang mentalities have been fostered and the universal need for 'respect' now dictates that no one can be criticised or approached about bad conduct without fear of violent reprisal.

I am often ribbed by my colleagues, and sometimes chastised by certain viewers, for the frequency with which I use certain phrases. Chief among them is 'where I come from'. I don't speak geographically but, as I have attempted to outline at the start of this book, I try to refer to a time and set of circumstances that laid the foundations of the values I live by today. I have described certain elements of my own upbringing that helped shape the code and creed by which I live today, the backbone that dictates the way I live, work, interact with the world and indeed bring up my own family.

As important and enduring as my own family's influence over me was, it is also important to note and remember the era and society of the time that allowed, nay encouraged, my family and lots more like us to function as successfully as we did. I would be just as scared of getting in trouble with one particular neighbour, a lady who regularly informed my mother whenever I stepped out of line, as I would be of crossing either of my parents. In fact, the most chastening experience of my formative years came when I managed to crushingly disappoint my father and myself all in one go!

My dad had always been a tireless worker and provider for our family, but I was now fourteen and he put the usual self-sacrifices aside for once to perk up his own life with a brand-new car. The new Fiat Regatta was duly deposited upon the drive, its gleam mirroring my father's delighted gaze whenever he stole another glance at it. Of course, I knew that I wasn't allowed to go anywhere near it, far less drive it, but, ever eager to impress and show off, I decided an impromptu spin might be in order. A hundred yards to the Post Office and back should do the trick, I thought, and leave that terrifying neighbour's son, my best friend at the time, suitably impressed with my intrepid spirit of adventure. Not for the first time, showing off landed me in hot water and the car into a lamppost. My crash wrecked the car, my dad's pride and joy could function no more and his irksome little son also managed to break his middle finger (with it bandaged up into erect attention, the first sight my returning father would have of his car's destroyer would be a frightened son, strangely, inadvertently flicking him 'the bird'!).

Needless to say, my mother gave it 'the full bananas' and turned into some sort of whirling dervish during one of the most almighty rollickings I had ever had from her. Her apoplexy ceased as she thundered the final words of her tirade: 'AND JUST YOU WAIT UNTIL YOUR FATHER GETS HOME!' Now, there can't be many fourteen-year-olds who just ignore a broken finger; however, that was instantly forgotten as I sat frozen with nerves on the end of my bed and waited for my father's return. I was expecting something apocalyptic from him as I heard him pace up the stairs to confront me. But the man who walked through the door showed not even a flicker of rage. He was loving, warm, kind and gentle. All he asked, looking at my bandaged finger, was: 'Are you all right?' That was the best bit of parenting I ever received from him. I was expecting *The Guns of Navarone* but I actually got undeserved kindness. I was left crushed by my own failings, mortified that I'd let such a loving and giving man down – not least depriving him of the one thing he had got for himself in the last fourteen years. I resolved there and then to make my dad proud.

That fear of letting down one's parents seems to have been lost; in the vast majority of cases I think that is the fault of parents who have – over successive generations – failed to properly plan for or invest in their children's development. I believe that the failed parents I meet on my show, and those like them whose messes I am forever required to help clear up, are chiefly responsible for the lawlessness, undermining of authority and the erosion of respect on the streets. I mean, where is that little bit of fear of their parents that kids used to have? I'm not advocating a return to Victorian extremes of corporal punishment, but I think it healthy that all children know when they have crossed the line between right and wrong. Moreover, I think it healthy that children should be more than a little apprehensive about what punishment will be meted out by Mummy or Daddy if they do stray beyond acceptable moral boundaries, boundaries that should have been set out and explained to them. That way, surely more of the behaviour that ultimately leads to crime and to our fear of crime could be prevented at source, right?

As 'nice' as my dad was over the car incident – although he knew what he was doing all right – he could also lay down the law when needed. He mixed his approach to disciplining us and got great results by virtue of having previously invested time to truly get to know us, to understand what made us tick. If a shock to the system was required, either of my parents was more than up to the task of dispensing it.

I didn't want even to disappoint my parents, far less incur their wrath by breaking the law. I invested in my own family and was encouraged to value its reputation. I was proud to be a Kyle and wanted to strive to make Mum and Dad proud of what I did. Of course I strayed from time to time. I experimented and chanced my arm with various bits of naughtiness of which I knew my parents would not approve. That said, when I got caught, my own sense of disappointment would be just as crushing as the fair and proportionate punishment I knew would follow the similarly firm but fair telling-off. Sometimes just a 'look' was enough, but when that was insufficient for Mum's needs, she also had a fine line in public humiliation. Upon finding that a four-year-old Jeremy had helped himself to a sherbert lemon from a Woolworths pick'n'mix counter, my mother took it upon herself to frog-march me back to the shop to atone for my theft. Shouting all the way, she left no stone unturned to achieve her desired effect: toe-curling embarrassment, I think it was. I was forced to apologise to the rather bemused shop assistant, Mum's hand still vice-like on my ear. With that apology ended my one and only foray into the world of shoplifting. It was a lesson I have never forgotten and one that helped set the boundaries that ensured I never got caught up in anything like theft again.

These experiences helped shape my sense of right and wrong and set my moral compass. Mum and Dad truly loved and invested in me, dedicated time to me; they helped me create my own set of standards, values and aspirations by which I still live today. All of these experiences helped instil a strong work ethic in me: the need – and desire – to provide for my family and contribute to society. In short, they helped provide me with the backbone missing in so many I meet on stage.

When I first started my new life in television I mistakenly thought that the stories and people I dealt with represented societal extremes. I was wrong. The people I meet daily, I am increasingly convinced, represent the norm, and that strikes me as downright scary. So, as I have often maintained, I believe *The Jeremy Kyle Show* is a reflection of the society we live in, not a skewed or exaggerated sideshow featuring one section of an unfairly targeted minority. Many maintain that all I do is set out to exploit some of the most vulnerable on society's fringes, but that is just rubbish: I don't invent these problems! If we are honest, none of us has to look too far from our own front doorsteps to find evidence of underage sex, drinking, drug taking, crime or violence. The statistics show that these things are getting worse; certainly our news-papers are full to bursting with terrifying and tragic tales of lives being lost to increasingly violent crime amongst the nation's young people.

I have been gripped and appalled in equal measure by the reprehensible spate of killings that culminated in mid-2008 in the untimely death of Ben Kinsella. I read at the time that he was the thirty-second UK teenager to have been murdered on our streets in 2008, one of a total of eighteen in London in the first six months of the year. The 2007 death toll of teenagers in London was at the time the worst on record. 2008's statistic got worse again. What hopes do we have for 2009? Or 2010 or beyond? Just seeing the figures is almost as distressing as reading the tragic stories of loss that now fill our papers each week: 27 MURDERED in London in 2007, 18 STABBED, 8 SHOT, 1 BEATEN – YES, BEATEN – to death. Now, those in power will tell you they are winning the war against violent crime. Well, let me tell any political leader who might care to listen: there is a very real fear among young and old alike that things are getting worse, a lot worse. Don't quote us figures on how things are getting better when the reality for so many people is that they are afraid to go out on the streets.

The Metropolitan Police say they saw a 3.5 per cent rise in firearms offences in 2007, up to 3,607 reported incidents. The Centre for Criminal Justice claimed there could have been anywhere between 22,000 and 57,900 victims of knife crime in 2004. The Youth Justice Board claim there has been a 40 per cent rise in violent crimes committed by under-eighteens in this country whilst other research suggests that one-fifth of all crimes committed by under-eighteens are violent. No matter which way you look at it, or whom you choose to believe, you can't escape the *threat* of this sort of violence and the fear most of the people my age feel towards so many of our young. I am scared – I don't mind admitting it. Every time I meet a new gang member on my show, or read of another needless killing, I fear for my family and the country my eighteen-, four- and two-year-old daughters might inherit. I am scared of this culture, I am scared by the climate that has allowed it to grow and I am scared for the people so blindly caught up in it.

I have met people at all stages of a gang member's evolutionary cycle. From people on the verge of initiation to those who feel too entrenched and drawn in by this culture to retreat or withdraw. Whatever these people's differing perceptions on why it is imperative that they either immerse themselves further or try to make good an escape, one thing remains the same, no matter who you speak to. All agree that violence is a regular occurrence and that the violence being witnessed each day is getting more brutal, more bloody, more severe. At the same time 'respect' – ironically the one currency on which all street gangs feel the need to be judged – is receding to a level where nobody seems to care about the value of a life or the potential consequences of getting embroiled in altercations that seem only to have three likely outcomes: hospital, jail or death.

It does not take a great imaginative leap to see where a lot of these problems begin. Deprivation, poverty and a lack of social mobility are all problems in those areas of the country where gangs now appear out of control. But if you're not living in these areas, and don't see the problems every day, it would take an extraordinary determination to really examine and attempt to tackle these problems. However, even those of you living in the most leafy and Utopian suburbs might want to sit up and take note because, trust me, this violence and these gangs are closer to you than you might think. After all, Islington, which is in parts one of the most affluent and wealthy postal districts in the UK (certainly if the council tax bills are anything to go by), has also regularly been home to some of the more heinous and needless of these killings.

No matter where you are in the country, you are not far from a group of people who, if what they tell me is true, feel the need to carry weapons as a matter of course. Most will carry and conceal kitchen knives but, ever ingenious, they will be prepared to use fence posts, broken glass, whatever they can get their hands on to *shank* (stab) you.

Their motivation for any attack can be as simple as theft. If you're carrying a mobile, wearing a pair of trainers, or carrying money that they want, you'd better watch out; you are a justifiable target in their eyes. Some are even less ambitious; they are prepared to attack and maim you just because you may unknowingly have strayed into the wrong part of town. Various gang members I have talked to and read about have explained the importance of territorial division and sticking to safe streets or postcodes where you are either known or can be vouched for. If you stray, things can get nasty; if you're new to an area you are a target.

I am reliably informed that all people in these gangs carry some form of weapon, whilst anyone in the area not affiliated to a gang would probably also feel obliged to carry something, if only for protection when becoming embroiled in the seemingly inevitable confrontations you can see for yourself on every news bulletin, newspaper or YouTube download.

This attitude is one of the things we surely must root out. More knives on the streets means more chance of them being used and, ironically enough, it would appear that those carrying a knife for protection have as much chance of being killed or injured with that SAME knife as they ever do of protecting themselves with it. I recognise that there must be a coordinated response at every level of society to really, properly respond to this problem. Prevention is every bit as important as punishment, but the punitive measures available to the authorities must surely act as a deterrent.

A lot of the youngsters I meet on the show have already been to prison two or three times by the end of their teens. Like an ASBO, for some a prison sentence can almost seem like a badge of honour, so I'd back anyone who proposed allying prosecution and a fair sentence with the unbreakable promise of hard time for the offender. I'm not talking about a few weeks on remand in a cushy home-from-home, with Xbox, satellite TV and all manner of creature comforts. I am talking about hard time, with a minimum of privileges and where the maximum possible time is spent with every offender trying to improve their education and understanding of their responsibilities to the wider world. If the reaction I get from certain guests is anything to go by, prison as an institution is little feared by the young, and most go to court expecting to get treated leniently by a judge before being almost pampered inside.

That has got to be wrong. We can't be like lazy babysitters to our lags, just shoving them in front of the telly and counting down the hours until we clock off and the next shift takes over. We have to make every effort to make these people understand their crimes, give them the tools to follow other, more productive paths whilst making those hours in between hard. Bloody hard, in fact – if ever my own child was sent to prison, I would at least want to hear on their release that they 'never wanted to go back to that awful place again'. Sadly, that is not the case right now; too many people are content to do another stretch, safe in the knowledge that their last time inside was not too taxing.

The huge proliferation of gangs has, it seems, been born of a pack mentality that understandably dictates that people are safer in numbers. All such gangs have to use their foot soldiers to mark out the boundaries of their own safe zones;

anyone straying beyond these boundaries is vulnerable to attack. The street law by which these gangs live can't leave any slight or attack unanswered, and so revenge attacks comprise a significant proportion of the whole. Of course this creates a never-ending circle of conflict in which the ante keeps getting raised ahead of yet more bloody reprisals taking place but, although they get it, they just don't care – most consider it better to lose life than face!

Certain guests on my show have really enlightened me as to how and why this growing subculture exists. I don't accept the violence, I deplore it on every level; but I can at least understand the reasons behind the genesis of gangs in places where people feel it just makes sense to stick together. What I have never been able to understand is how or from where someone can summon up the hatred – or whatever emotion might be required – to go out and murder someone they don't know. Thankfully the teens I have interviewed and tried to help have come to me before things have got to this stage, but all of them have seen this sort of thing going on all around them. I even watched a programme recently where one street enforcer, a nineteen-year-old from London who had coined the moniker 'The General', spoke of his own rise through the ranks. He explained his current preference for using guns over knives. Terrifyingly, he candidly explained not only how easy it was to get a gun and bullets, but also how it provided him with the means to an easier kill. He described the 'effort' it took to stab one of his first victims, how hard it was to summon the 'determination' to keep going beyond that initial plunging of the knife and to keep twisting and working the blade as it scraped against his victim's ribs. That image, that description – one that made me feel physically sick – will likely remain with me forever, while that programme, although shocking for certain reve-lations that were new to me, did seem to chime with what

I read in the national press and hear from my show's own guests. The problem areas were not isolated little pockets; they were big, sprawling estates in major cities the length and breadth of the country.

To my mind, the real problem underpinning all of the wastefulness and wickedness I have only really touched upon stems from a real poverty of ambition and aspiration amongst our young. More parents need to be investing a whole lot more to provide their offspring with the sort of collective moral backbone that might just have seen off this sort of problem before it began. The kids in these gangs are seduced and enlisted at a very young age. Children as young as seven or eight are recruited and in some cases tutored by older gang members, schooled in the art of knife-wielding and petty crimes. I am told that these kids then graduate from using knives to guns by about the age of fourteen. Apparently it is possible to rent a gun by the hour if you need to (how many fourteen-year-olds actually 'need' a gun?), though most are slightly wary of getting caught in possession lest they get charged for other murders carried out by other people using that gun.

In the same show that featured 'The General', other youngsters told of the ease with which they could access all types of weapons. In Bradford, machetes could apparently be purchased for 'under a tenner' and without the need for ID. One youth boasted of being able to get a hand grenade for £450! A HAND GRENADE! UN-BE-LIEV-A-BLE!!! Whatever happened to saving a pound a week's pocket money for football stickers?!

As I have mentioned, some gang members have come to *The Jeremy Kyle Show* looking for a way out, but others are resolutely determined to stay where they are and do as they please, despite any pleadings from loved ones. Why? South Wales's chief constable, Barbara Wilding, once hinted at part of the problem when she described how the loyalty and unity felt by gang members had replaced loyalty to the family. The breakdown of the family unit, so prevalent in her region and so many others, had contributed, she said, to the increase in gangs and gang-related, often violent crime. What people couldn't get at home from Mum, Dad and a loving family, they were manufacturing for themselves, with loyalty to their gang superseding everything else.

I agree with her, but there are wider social considerations also playing their part. Many of the people I have seen, even the brightest sparks and ones with most promise, don't want to give up a lifestyle that appears to feed self-esteem and provides material wealth. So used to just taking what they want, many young criminals say they can steal or drug-deal in a day what they might otherwise have to work hard for, nine-to-five, five days a week for a month. They distance themselves from what they perceive as a 'boring' treadmill of work and focus instead on the kind of lifestyle that every glossy magazine and hip-hop record tells them is glamorous. Through their ill-gotten gains come the cars, clothes and material trappings of success. From these follow the girls and kudos, and from the whole ensemble comes the 'respect' they demand of their peers. How do we tackle that? How do you tell a kid from a poor and broken background that he should give up the keys to what he sees as his dream and try and make a go of something that is harder to achieve and pays less when you achieve it?

I have thought long and hard on this and I have some ideas of my own. Unfortunately, we can't turn back the clock and give back to these youths the positive parenting they never experienced. We can, though, attack the culture that has sprung up from these failings with ideas and policies that have their roots in ambition and positive aspirations. As I have intimated throughout, positive parenting is as much about listening to as it is about instructing your child. And with this lesson in mind, let us all listen to the words of Ben Kinsella himself, who weeks before losing his life to a needless stabbing in June 2008, aged just sixteen, wrote a letter to our current prime minister as part of his English GCSE coursework.

Dear Gordon Brown,

In society today violence is part of our culture. In a recent survey of the borough of Islington, 85 per cent of teens from fourteen to eighteen admit they've assaulted someone with a group of people . . .

The problems are caused by a lack of respect between parents and their children. Parents feel like they have no control what their son/daughter does on the streets and feel like they can't tell their own kids what to do. Mums and dads have to wait at the door until three a.m. hoping their child returns alive and well. Parents need to consider bringing their children to parenting classes or else lose them for good . . .

Lack of trust between parents and their young also leads to violent behaviour . . . youths stay out until the early hours . . . become bored, frustrated and aggressive . . . There have been cases where fifteen-year-old boys have brutally attacked for no apparent reason and when questioned by the police as to why they state 'I had nothing else to do' . . .

Ben went on to suggest changes and demand they be implemented before it was too late. I would love to have met him and have him try and talk sense into some of the guests on my show.

Ben suggested curfews for all under-eighteens, which apparently dramatically reduced gang-related crime when implemented in New York in 2003. Conservative leader David

Cameron advocates, through his party's Knife Action Plan, and among other things, a National Citizens Service scheme, which is meant to be a little like National Service for sixteen-year-olds. I'd agree with that. I have seen the benefits to be gained over a very short period of time with teens on some of my own show's Boot Camps and feel sure a disciplined environment akin to those in some of our armed forces would serve some sixteen-year-olds well.

I have stressed before that positive parenting must play a large part, but besides this must come a greater understanding of why things have degenerated to the level they have. Successive governments have presided over policies that allowed the selling-off of school playing fields. Competitive sport was almost done away with by the political correctness cabal in the Nineties. Listen to Ben Kinsella: our youth need somewhere to play and something to do to alleviate the boredom that can apparently all too easily become murderous rage if left unchecked. They need to be allowed to be both aggressive and competitive, but in disciplines or sports where those instincts can be trained, honed or channelled. We need more community centres and more funding for the sorts of inspirational leaders I have met on the show, leaders who do so much to engage and invigorate the young in their communities.

Where consistent, committed action to prevent this societal deterioration fails, harsher punishments must follow. It is impossible to stop anyone getting hold of a knife, of course (you only need to go to the kitchen drawer), but you can take steps to deter these kids from leaving the house with one. It is often argued that of the thousands who still see fit to daily carry a knife, too few are ever effectively dealt with when apprehended for doing just that. Too many get let off with meaningless cautions and not enough go to prison for the danger they pose to everyone around them merely by choosing to leave the house armed in this way. People should automatically be sent to jail for carrying a knife. Prosecutions and cautions are no longer enough. I would also enhance the deterrent by making the sentences longer and of definite length. If you knew for certain you were going to jail for, say, seven years for carrying a knife – no exceptions – would you really take it out of the house? I wouldn't, and I bet that message would soon get round once the authorities really started to deliver on the promised and much-needed clamp-downs. Don't misunderstand me, though, I want stronger punishments only where packages of prevention have failed. It is estimated that eleven times more is spent each year on locking up people after a crime than goes into spending on the initiatives that might prevent it. Unfortunately my show does not have the exposure or resources to make a real difference on a national level. That said, I remain proud of the help we have been able to give some individuals and families alike.

I believe we need to do more to hone the obvious intelligence, 'street smarts' and spirit of entrepreneurialism that exists on our streets. There are some very smart cookies out there who feel failed by education, family, or society in general, and they turn their intellects to making money in a way that only causes fear and further damage. Why not have in place a system whereby their talents are spotted early and harnessed for their own and the greater good, turning them into future Richard Bransons and captains of industry, not drug dealers? Football clubs make it their business to identify young talent at an early age; communities and schools, prompted by national initiatives with government backing, need to do the same. These kids need to re-learn the true meaning of respect, not their fantasy version of it, which is built entirely on fear. They need to have a work ethic instilled in them; they need to learn the value of 'a pound note', as my mate Martin and most of my dad's generation used to say, and that might help lay foundations that will truly help them to understand the value of the life they seem so ready to squander.

   People need to see the virtue in being a good parent; how much 'richer' that makes you than acquiring the garish accoutrements of today's bling-bling plastic gangsters. They need to see the value of a community and take pride in it, not just defend their patch of it. In the community centres and classrooms of this country, people should be making every attempt to refocus their efforts away from easy options and into the talents that, hard-won and worked at, *really* give someone their sense of pride and worth. All I hear is that these gangster kids want 'power, money, respect and glory' – well, if you can be the best at any one of a billion things in the world, you can have that and more besides. If you earn it through your own talent, intelligence and practice, you will discover your own worth, as well as the value of what it is you are striving for. Stabbing someone for drugs won't buy you a whole lot of anything that will last.

There are those bucking the trend and making an effort. I applaud the interactive task forces set up by police and community groups across the land. They have long since learned the need to address these problems from the inside out. They toil each day on dangerous streets and strain every sinew to become a presence that is liked, truly respected, and accepted by local youths. They don't preach or issue diktats. They talk, they learn, they understand and persuade people via the power of better ideas. These good people show the way for young people who might otherwise have been led astray. They show that respect is earned through the quality of one person's deeds. Anyone in any doubt about that only needed to see the dignity, reverence and true respect shown to the families of Ben Kinsella and Jimmy Mizen. People spoke of those two tragically murdered victims in only the most glowing terms. Hundreds turned out to mourn and pay their respects. They were not obliged to go out of loyalty to a gang; they were not instructed to be there. No, hundreds of their family and friends brought traffic to a standstill because they felt compelled to pay their respects. They recognised the worth of the lives so scandalously cut short. They felt moved to act. The kids who turned out in their droves showed their backbone in standing up for something they believed in, making a stand against yet more pointless murder – now is the time for the rest of us to do the same.

I truly believe that when people know better, they do better. Not enough of today's young have been helped along at key stages in their life, and we are all seeing the consequences of that now. Knife and gun amnesties won't ever work. Weapons will always be easily sourced or improvised. We have to battle the belief in so many young that they necd a knife. Work harder with them to give them back their confidence, their belief that all things are possible and their desire to make these good things happen for themselves. We all need to stop spreading the fear that distances us from our young succes-sors and put the energy reserved for sound bites into the hard work that will facilitate all young people in reclaiming their pride, hearts and minds. Just as we ask kids to take responsibility, so we must all take responsibility for the awful way in which we have failed some of them. If we can show we have found our backbone in understanding where we went so badly wrong, surely they will then acknowledge the need to find a backbone of their own to make the best of the hand they have been dealt . . .

4

Am I Just Old and Boring? (Part I)

Of all the things I say that so regularly enrage the nation, there is one phrase above all that I'm told provokes the ire of a good number of my television programme's loyal and dedicated following: 'Am I just old and boring?' It's not the most contentious thing to fall from my lips, nor do I think it particularly confrontational or even that offensive. No matter, it is that phrase which generates more written complaints than anything else on *The Jeremy Kyle Show*.

I often don't realise I am saying it. I certainly don't repeat it deliberately and I honestly do not intend to mock or offend any of this country's more senior citizens, a great many of whom provide the viewing figures that keep me in work and continue to put a roof over my family's head. More studious viewers of the show will recognise that I actually espouse a great many of the views, values and beliefs of my parents' generation. In fact, I often find myself wishing we could turn back the clock and have our country's young re-learn the true worth of so many things that now seem lost to them. I see so many people, day-in, day-out, who just have no will or desire to work.

We all read about the breakdown of the family unit, the continuing need for a new 'respect' agenda and the steady erosion of law and order. However, it is the rising rates of drink and drug abuse, which must by now be nearing epidemic proportions if the 'extracurricular' intake of some of my guests is anything to go by, which cause me most concern. Too often

I am confronted by people who have slipped into shameless and wantonly self-destructive patterns of behaviour that could so easily be rectified if only people were prepared to call on the slightest percentage of the personal willpower at their disposal. Many times I find myself trying to spell out the patently obvious to people half my age, unbelievably having to explain that a life dominated by repeated boozing is in no way good for that person's health, relationships or indeed offspring. It is at times like these that I find myself extolling virtues and borrowing well-worn phrases that might well have come from my father's own 'Manual on Modern Life', had he ever written one. More often than not it feels as if I am turning into him.

Even on stage, in front of an audience of millions, I regularly find myself having that dawning moment of realisation that almost all blokes will go through at some stage in their life; that moment when they can no longer escape the mounting evidence that they are in fact becoming their father. In the last three years I have found this happening increasingly to me. I catch myself saying things, thinking things and doing things that feel more him than me. At home I find myself decrying the 'angry noise' that passes for modern music and at work I reach for adjectives or champion views that unmistakably echo those of a man who has begun to despair of this nation, just as I and so many others have.

My rhetorical questioning of age and the relative tedium of my existence compared to every jobless, witless, directionless kid seemingly hell-bent on living life as one long, endless party is not meant as a slight on anyone older than me. Far from it. That phrase is trotted out as much in fear as it is in acceptance of the fact that I am outgrowing and failing to grasp certain choices being made by young people in this country. I don't think I am entering any midlife crisis, but I do get a little panicked when it becomes obvious that

I am not getting through to someone who can't see a correlation between the misery they say they are experiencing and
the alcohol they are pouring so prolifically down their necks
every day.

I do a lot of soul-searching after those shows where I just
know that I did not make the real connection with a guest
that I know I can. It frustrates me to see someone wasting
so much of their own potential whilst bringing nothing but
hurt and heartache to all those around them, and all the while
being unable to see how easily fixed the whole mess could
be. I don't expect to be best mates with everyone I meet, but
I have always backed myself to be able to build some sort of
rapport with pretty much anyone, and it is from that foundation that I have historically been able to dish out honest
advice that is heard, understood and responded to.
Undoubtedly, those with the hardest shells to penetrate are
those angry young kids who have been sucked into a routine
of getting plastered every day. Most other guests come to the
show with a problem they want me to help fix, but these
hardened young drinkers don't seem to realise they have a
problem in the first place.

I sometimes feel I've tried every tack in pointing out the
severity of the situation, but still acknowledgement does
not register in the glazed eyes staring back at me. It is at
these moments that I am given to wondering out loud
whether it is the message or the messenger that they are
so reluctant to respond to? Is what I am saying complete
anathema to them, or is it just that they can't buy into me?
When I question my own ability to do the job I'm paid to
do, I'm sure I'm just like every parent who has ever failed
to get through to a stroppy teenager. I, like them, wonder
if it is my accent that they don't like, or my background?
Maybe it's the fact I'm on TV; maybe I'm not 'street' enough,
hip enough, cool enough, or whatever. Or maybe, in their

eyes, I am just too 'old and boring' for them to pay me any heed.

I want to help everyone I meet on the show, but there seem to be ever greater numbers of people who don't want to help themselves and therefore just look at me as if I am talking to them in a foreign language. Some of them view me with contempt and disdain, but others treat me in a manner I recognise from my own past. They look at me the same way I once looked at my dad, or anyone I thought too old or too far removed from the realities of my life to ever properly invest in the lecture they were giving me. I was often being given sound advice, but a petulant streak that was born of a perceived invincibility that many young lads have in their early twenties won out, good guidance went ignored, and I ended up making a mess of quite a few things that could easily have been avoided if I'd just stopped to consider the older, wiser heads around me. They weren't always right, but then neither was I. I look back now and sometimes wish I'd been a bit more respectful of some of the lessons various people tried to teach me. Maybe my penance for earlier arrogance, impetuosity and contempt is to now be treated similarly by all those who eye my attempts at positive intervention with all the suspicion I used to reserve for my dad's. Just as he questioned me disapprovingly when I gave up my 'proper job' for a stab at a life in radio, so I can't help but comment with equal censure on those who are giving up their futures for little more than another look at the bottom of a bottle.

Turning gradually into your dad in front of two million strangers each day is, for me, a fairly daunting prospect. For most people, any similar experience takes place in far more private surroundings. Most will have heard themselves ticking off a young relative, or complaining about 'telly not being the same any more' in exactly the way their parents used to.

To hear yourself say things that you've only ever heard before from parents or teachers can be quite sobering. I have no real desire to get or seem old, but I can't help but feel the advancing years when speaking to people of a generation whose values seem so out of kilter with my own.

When I entered the world of work, I always thought of myself as something of an independent young firebrand, grateful for the solid grounding given me by my parents, but at the same time believing I was an altogether more modern man, from a different generation and living for a different time. It is only now I have had children and resettled into a second marriage and family life that I realise the importance of everything that my own parents advocated all those years ago. Far from being as 'old and boring' as their occasional (but always very sensible) lectures could make them sound, they were in fact just pointing out right and wrong, whilst imploring me to make the best of myself.

I see the look many of my show's younger guests shoot me as I try to get through to them, just as my parents tried to get through to me, and know that they see me as little more than some ancient irrelevance with no grasp of what it was like to be their age. They think I don't know, won't understand or can never have been burdened by any of the issues that they seem to feel are exclusively theirs. Well, of course I wasn't always a middle-aged man. I have actually lived a little, and have been fortunate enough to pick up a few nuggets of wisdom along the way.

It gives me no great pleasure to remind myself that my youth is now well behind me. I don't much like the frequent prompts that I am becoming a clone of my father, either; but sometimes there just ain't no escaping the fact that some people need to be told where they are going wrong. I don't mean to condescend or come over all schoolmasterly with anyone, but if you're sending your life down the toilet and you come to me for advice, I won't stop short of telling you exactly where I think you are going wrong. And why. In a great many instances, my guests could be said to be literally flushing their life down the toilet, literally pissing away all hopes of happiness in a blur of endless boozing. Their personal crises are all too commonplace in this country and born of a problem that also lies at the heart of British culture: alcohol dependence.

In many ways the alcohol-related problems I deal with are typically, if not quite uniquely, British. Such problems are everywhere in this country and they cut mercilessly through any preconceived barriers of class, wealth, background or breeding. More worryingly, research shows that these problems are no longer any respecter of age. Alcohol Concern recently calculated that 22,000 Britons die each year of causes directly related to this country's burgeoning alcohol consumption. Around one person in thirteen in this country is considered alcohol dependent, and admissions into hospital of those with alcohol-related liver disease has risen by 21,000 in ten years!

When I first began presenting *The Jeremy Kyle Show* I naively thought that an alcoholic was someone swigging meths on a park bench morning, noon and night. I had no idea of the scale of the genuine physical and/or psychological addiction which now has nearly 10 per cent of this country in its grip. Indeed, it was only after meeting some of the show's first-ever guests, and therefore having to research more fully the issues raised, that I started to grasp just how widespread this problem of alcohol is. I also began to see just how hard it will be for Britain, more than most other countries, to get on top of it.

On the one hand, drinking is something of a sport in this country. People are chided by their peers for missing a round, drinking too slowly or opting for beers that are anything less than the super-strength required to knock out a horse. Getting 'bladdered' is celebrated without any thought of the consequences, and anyone who preaches moderation is again, apparently, too old, too boring or too out of touch. I have seen people ostracised from social groups principally on the basis of their not 'joining in' or, more accurately, not wanting to get as smashed as everyone else.

In some quarters people are revered for little more than their seemingly infinite capacity to consume alcohol. He who drinks most and fastest seems to be king in the Great British pub, guaranteed special status by a small coterie who, unbelievably, seem to be held in thrall by the sight of a pint being downed. Contrast this adulation with the contempt held by most for those 'diagnosed' as alcoholics, and you'll begin to understand the hypocrisy and unfairness that rightly rankles with those charged with remedying one of our society's most widespread ills. On the one hand we promote and celebrate a laddish/ladette culture of copious consumption, but on the other we cast out as hopeless 'alcies' anyone who can't last the pace without succumbing to problems that are a statistical inevitability. I mean, how can we laud those able to drink everyone else under the table and then lambast the ones who can't stop once started along a path to society-endorsed addiction? This is when the peer pressure imparted on all to drink, and drink a lot, in this country is shown to be at its most vulgar.

That said, I also believe that we can't impinge upon people's freedoms and overly police the pleasures enjoyed quite properly by the vast majority. Personal choice must prevail, and the failures of the few cannot be allowed to ruin what still remains a fun and relatively harmless release for so many. Surely, where alcohol is concerned, we have to educate people sufficiently well to make the right choices and know their own limits. Give people sufficient confidence in themselves so that they no longer blindly follow peer pressure. Have them begin to understand their own tolerances – just as they do in France, right?

This would be a step in the right direction, of course, but the attempts to usher in a new more 'continental' culture of drinking in this country do not seem to have made much difference at all. The patterns of drinking I am told about each day remain dangerously harmful, and the problems associated with them are getting worse. I look around my studio sometimes and wonder if enough of our countrymen actually have the capacity to responsibly embrace anything so 'sophisticated' as twenty-four-hour licensing. From what I have seen, people were drinking round the clock long before that law was passed, and those same people still are. Twenty-four hours, twenty-four cans – and all from the comfort of their own living rooms. People tell me that the price of a pint is too expensive now, so they stay in and get as pissed as they can on beers that are twice the strength but not even half the price. And so the problems continue.

I said earlier that alcohol problems are no respecter of age. The trends in harmful drinking are rising across all age groups in this country, but it is probably no great surprise that British kids (along with the Irish and Danish, actually) are the heaviest underage drinkers in Europe. Deaths from drink-related causes are now occurring at younger ages than ever. People in their twenties and thirties are dying from liver failure! I met a couple of people on the show who had reached rock bottom and came for one final attempt at beating their alcohol addiction. I could not believe that sitting before me were young men in their mid-twenties. Yellow-skinned, bloodshot eyes, faces dazed and bloated by sustained alcohol abuse from ages as young as ten or eleven. I have met people on the verge of having their lives ended before they had even really begun.

In the corridors of our studio, and on into the detox/rehab centres where we have been able to send certain guests, I have been truly sickened at just how low full-blown alcohol addiction can leave you. The shaking, the sweating, and the frenzied convulsions are all well-known symptoms that, although expected, were still pretty shocking to see up close when face to face with an alcoholic suffering withdrawals. What I could never have prepared myself for was the constant retching, vomiting and spitting of blood from two men I am told had pretty much sacrificed their stomach lining at the altar of excessive drinking. The incessant intake of alcohol had literally caused corrosion of the throat at the top of the oesophagus, which had then gradually spread down into a stomach that had become one big weeping sore.

Their physical toll only told part of the story, though, for these were two guys who, by their own admission, had lost everyone close to them, despite being given countless chances to change. I am glad to say that we were able to help bring about change in one of these men. The other's story, I am sorry to say, did not end nearly so well. After successful completion of a detox programme, he slipped back into old habits and died from heart failure brought on by liver damage and other ailments associated with decades of alcohol abuse.

In the same way that I was once ignorant in my assessment of what an alcoholic was, so I was also once guilty of laziness in my assumption that alcohol-related problems tended to affect middle-aged and older generations. I had read, like everyone else, about how teenagers could run amok and occasionally get out of hand after an illicit boozing adventure. If I am being honest, though, I also just thought that these were stories that might have been blown out of proportion. After all, me and most of my mates – in fact most teenagers I knew growing up – were all guilty of looting our parents' spirits cabinet from time to time. I'm surely not the first to have siphoned off half a pint of whisky to sneak into the punch at a friend's sixteenth or seventeenth birthday party, am I? I merely assumed when reading stories of 'wild teenagers' that it was probably a party that had got out of control and the teenagers at the centre of it would likely be reprimanded and punished by incandescent parents as soon as the dust had settled and neighbourly relations were restored. It was not until filming this show that I got a much truer glimpse of the blight our binge-drinking young are on society.

Now, before I press on, I feel another confession coming on. It would be unfair to bash the binge-drinking habits of others without at least owning up to some failures of my own. I admit I have had my fair share of excessive drinking experiences. I take no pride in retelling them here, but do feel it is important for people to know that I am not just sitting in judgement, blithely bashing all and sundry without ever having had any experience of what they are going through. I try to bring as much empathy and past personal experience as I can to bear on any situation or issue I am confronted with.

As far as alcohol goes, I have had my flirtations with it. During one particularly fevered onslaught by the press, I retreated to my hotel room after the filming of my shows had finished each week and greedily sank a minimum of two bottles of wine per night. I'll talk more on this later, but there is no getting away from the fact that I began to drink heavily, like a fish in fact, in a bid to escape the realities of the troubled times enveloping me. I guess some could call me hypocrital for preaching moderation – or indeed ordering someone on my stage to give up boozing altogether – before going back to a lonely hotel room and getting drunk myself, but I think there are distinctions to be drawn. Yes, I hoovered up two bottles of red per night and sometimes carried on a little longer with glass after glass of Baileys too. I was frequently drunk, and got that way quite deliberately, to quieten my mind and fall asleep at the end of never-ending days that I was truly hating. However, I was not putting my family's future on the line. I was not failing them as either father or husband; I was providing for them, working as hard as I could. Nor was I waiting for a hand-out from anyone – I certainly wasn't expecting society to buy the booze that accompanied me through a troubled six weeks or so in 2007. Even so, I was drinking to excess, and I did not stop until I myself realised that it was not helping me achieve anything much more than a hangover and a postponement in dealing with problems that never went away, no matter how much I drank. I knew it and I stopped it, thankfully whilst I was still in control of it.

Of course, many cases of alcoholism start in this way. A means of unwinding or coping becomes a habit that does not seem to particularly hamper or hinder until it is pointed out many years later that the drink has been the only constant in a person's life. Different problems may have been and gone, different partners may also have flitted in and out, but drink, invariably, has been the one permanent fixture. In too many cases, the recognition of a need to cut back or give up comes too late to save the really important things that have been lost – marriages, jobs, children.

I spoke earlier of the culture of drinking in Britain and I too was caught up in that. In my early twenties I had just started at Newman Personnel in the City of London and was getting a good deal of success in my life as a professional recruiter. The deals were being made, I was placing people in jobs, the bonus commissions were flowing in and life was good as never before. There was a close and competitive camaraderie amongst my colleagues. We all wanted to beat each other on the work leader-board; each of us strove to be top dog in that office every week; but we were also a team that lived by that City mantra of working hard and playing hard. As anyone who has seen my knees go wobbly after two piña coladas will testify, I am not the world's most hardened drinker. It doesn't take a lot to have quite an effect on me. That said, in the testosterone-fuelled, ego-driven, money-motivated and distinctly male-dominated world I found myself in back then, going out after work was the only option available to me. Don't get me wrong, I had some pretty good times, toasting the good days or drowning sorrows after the bad with equal commitment. My colleagues and I felt a bit like the legendary Spice Boys who made up the Liverpool FC football team throughout the Nineties. Apparently their motto was 'win or lose, we're on the booze', and I guess we adhered as closely to that as anyone else I knew.

After work each day, regardless of whatever successes or failures we had endured or enjoyed, there was an almost ritual marching of 'the boys' over to The Punch & Judy in Covent Garden. One pint would soon be followed by seven more, as late afternoon dissolved into the next morning's early hours. I guess I was getting drunk every night, though I just told myself I was 'going out'. The fact that I was always getting up the next day to go and do a hard day's work, allied to the fact I had started to do my job really quite well, masked the true nature of what I was getting sucked into. Thankfully I know my own limits, I know my own tolerances and I have no great love of being out of control. I therefore instinctively knew, mostly, even if quite tipsy, how much more I could take before I would have real problems getting home or, worse, getting up for work the next morning.

Often I was that one in the group, so derided everywhere, who pretended he was going to the toilet before actually sneaking off home. Even when being obliged to carry on with 'just one more drink', I would plot my self-preservation. I would volunteer to get the next round, duly buy it, but always make sure that my 'vodka tonic' was straight lemonade. These measures and many more like them ensured that I stayed straight enough for long enough. I could keep face and maintain a place in the group, but without giving myself completely over to the demon drink. So I too have been exposed to sustained peer pressure to drink in an environment where it was considered, in some cases, career suicide to shun your colleagues in favour of a quiet night in.

Obviously I was young at the time, but passing years and a bit more maturity soon saw me grow out of this phase. Not completely, for there were always moments when one 'quick drink after work' unexpectedly turned into one almighty session, which was instantly regretted the minute the horns from the brass section of the next morning's hangover sounded. So yes, there was a time in my life where it was easiest to go with the group and get leathered, despite me sometimes not wanting to be there. Thankfully, I was eventually sufficiently strong-willed and self-aware not to let things slide too much. And I was always driven by a desire to succeed at work. That motivation to succeed professionally also ensured I did not follow a path that can start with just a few drinks after work and end in a long-term addiction to alcohol.

For lots of young people, the choice between having a few illicit drinks and giggling drunkenly in the park with friends, or spending a long night working or studying with no tangible reward at the end of it, seems to throw up an obvious winner. Many of you see your parents and other adults take drinks when they like and recognise the hypocrisy that allows them to foolishly misbehave whilst you are expected to study and keep quiet. Many of you feel safer and more loved by your group of friends than you do at home, so why wouldn't you want to spend more time with them and do the things *they* want to do rather than the things you are told you *should* do by a family that sometimes seemingly could not care less. It's one rule for them and another for you, right?

I'm probably going to sound just like the people who said you should knuckle down and do more before they settled down to drink and smoke in exactly the same way you had planned to with your friends before getting caught by the front door. Well, hypocrites they may be, but at least they are saying the right things. There are a great many people out there who don't benefit from any sort of guidance at all; those making your rules should literally have earned the right to do so by virtue of the hours invested each week in raising and providing for you. They care for you, and they care about what your future holds.

They are right: you should make something of yourself. And when you do, the beer you long to have with your friends will taste all the sweeter because of it. Enjoy it when you are old enough to drink it. Don't break the law now; bust your balls instead to get ahead and forge the career that will see you able to afford any beer, or even champagne, you want in later life.

There will be some out there who won't thank me for saying so, but I really don't see too much of a problem when someone who's worked hard all week to put food on the table goes out on a Friday night with some friends to let off steam. I've done it, we've all done it and – do you know what? – after a hard week of work, there's sometimes nothing like getting a bit tiddly with your mates and forgetting about the pressures of work.

The odd blowout is fine. I recently returned from Magaluf and the filming of a show that opened my eyes to the good and bad of what the papers call 'Binge-Drinking Britain'. In the main I didn't have any problem with boisterous Brits saving up all year to go away for some fun in the sun. Yes, there were people who took it too far, and yes, there will always be those who can't be trusted to say 'enough is enough' once too many beers have taken hold. There were some sickening sights of everything from vomiting to violence, but in the main people were having the good time they were probably entitled to after toiling away in their jobs throughout the cold winter months in anticipation of this, their summer holiday.

The problem only comes when all you do is drink. What are you building up to at the end of the week? Where's the fun to be had next summer on holiday if all you've done is drink round the clock and bummed around all year anyway?

Don't be a statistic and don't fall into a destructive pattern of behaviour, drinking every day out of little more than boredom. You might not realise it because it is so readily available, but alcohol is a drug and addiction can creep up on you. If all you do is drink all day, no matter how tough or resilient you think you are, it will take over. You will go from being cheered on by your mates to being ignored by them. Very few stick around when true alcoholism grips you. Your family and friends may scatter and your very own body, the one thing you've always been able to count on above anything else, will start to fail you. Coughing blood, liver failure, constant sweating, shaking and an all-consuming need to pour another bottle down your neck is all that will await you. And that doesn't seem like fun to me.

Now, I have spoken about the very real problems we as a nation face with alcohol. But, as I said earlier, we can't ban alcohol or enforce prohibition. Why should we? That would be like going back to the classroom and having teacher, in this case the prime minister, saying: 'There's always one, and this one took it too far and spoiled it for the rest of you.' There are a lot of people who can no longer adequately control or moderate their alcoholic intake. These people should be supported, helped through recovery and reintegrated into society, confident that they won't relapse and once more become guided by past demons. We do our bit on the show to help people beat the booze, whilst also supporting the families affected by one person's drinking. To a large extent, I think that's all we can do as a society. Educate the masses effectively and help those individuals who, for whatever reason, slip through the net.

There will always be those for whom a family breakdown, bereavement, unemployment, or some other personal crisis proves too much to cope with. They may well find temporary comfort at the bottom of a bottle, and it is our duty as a society to help such people through their difficult times before their lives are made all the more complicated by a full dependence on alcohol. Equally though, there are those who do not deserve to be propped up by society or encouraged to continue their flirting with a lifestyle that in so many cases becomes their ultimate undoing. I am sick of seeing teenagers on my show who complain that their compulsion to drink is born of boredom or because someone at home 'doesn't understand' them. They insult with their selfishness those whose genuine problems with addiction have in no small measure been brought on by past abuse and/or abandonment by people they should have had a right to expect would be there to love and protect them. We should not be doling out endless benefit cheques to people who do not want to do much more than sit around and pickle themselves. Surely that is just asking for trouble later down the line? NHS budgets are already overstretched, so why store up vast hordes of liver-damaged dependants to throw at our hospitals in twenty or thirty years' time? Surely it is better to get a grip on this problem now?

Of course there is no accounting for personal choice, and some will always just choose to drink instead of doing anything else. I can't understand that prioritising of beer over family,

but I have seen enough of it to know that it exists, and sometimes with no valid reason that I can fathom. Such people I
tend to hold in contempt for an attitude that is as destructive to the hopes and dreams of their loved ones as it is to
their own physiology. Nevertheless, these people still have it
in them to change. Again I have seen and played my part in
helping make that change. To that end I am always grateful
for the support of the great many agencies and charities out
there that guide, advise and take referrals from Graham and
his remarkable backstage team.

I believe the reasons for alcohol abuse in this country are
too varied to be tackled in one head-on policy. That said,
there are things we can do to redress some of the balance
and get the statistics back to a more palatable level. I am a
great supporter of our armed forces, but I have been shocked
to see the number of ex-members of the forces who are seemingly returned to 'Civvy Street' with no real advice on how
to readjust. Not a day goes by when my show is not called
by someone seeking help for an ex-forces person with an
almighty drink problem. Many of those personnel I have met
tell me that they have not been able to adjust back to life
without an infrastructure in place to guide them. Some have
re-acclimatised after institutionalisation, but are still trauma-
tised by the horrors of war, memories they try to block out
with booze. In other cases, booze has been supplemented or
even usurped by hard drugs.

One such guy told me that he was haunted by the site of
a bomb blast in the Balkans. He was serving out near Sarajevo
and was caught in a roadside explosion. Above him a sniper
was picking off his friends with deadly accurate fire, and
opposite him, as he crouched in a wheel arch for safety, was
the image that he now took with him wherever he went: that
of a pregnant woman who had been partially blown apart. I
say partially because he said he could still see the unborn

baby coiled inside the mother who'd had half of her front ripped away from her torso in the explosion. He delivered that baby but now was battling all sorts of personal problems as a result of the horrors he witnessed. Chief among them was a burgeoning crack addiction.

I can't imagine seeing, far less surviving, such things, and perhaps it is no surprise that there are so many who can't cope once they return to a life shorn of all the friends and camaraderie they enjoyed in the services. Too many, it seems, have been left to struggle on alone with images and memories that no one who wasn't there will ever truly understand. Having met more than a few brave soldiers who fought for us but can no longer cope with the physical or mental legacy of their time in service, I am more sure than ever before of the worthiness of charities such as Help for Heroes, the Army Benevolent Fund and The British Forces Foundation. I wish there was more we could all do to help them too; it seems to me that there are people keen enough to pack them off to war on our behalf, but not nearly as anxious to provide support for those who return broken from what they experienced so we didn't have to.

I have met and tried to help people at every stage of an alcoholic's cycle of drinking and recovery, and there is one measure I think we could all take note of to ensure things do not deteriorate in successive generations. There are myriad reasons for a person to drink, and many do without causing any harm to anyone at all. Sustained alcohol abuse might be more difficult to deal with politically, but we could, at a stroke, reduce the harmful effects of binge-drinking in this country if we just resolved to tackle the pricing and availability of certain drinks.

Those young people I'd watched going too far in Magaluf had been wooed into bars with ludicrous promises of twenty shots for a fiver. It is these places that need to be kept in line, as what they are offering is just plain irresponsible. I can scarcely blame a youngster, looking for a good time on a budget, trustingly putting themselves in the hands of what he or she has every right to expect is a responsible businessman running responsible licensed premises. What they actually buy into however is a cowardly situation where dangerous, even life-threatening consumption of alcohol is encouraged. I saw young people having endless bottles of spirits tipped down their necks by bar workers before then being urged to cavort as drunkenly as possible by them. It is from this starting point that we will all read about lewd acts, date rapes, violence and bad behaviour. And of course these reckless promotions are not confined to holiday hot spots. If we know we are living in a culture that prizes irresponsible drinking, then surely it is incumbent on the government not to compound the risk by endorsing crazy drinks promotions. That is not to say that I am against any credit-crunch-busting promotions out there, designed to fill pubs with punters looking for fun on a budget. All I'm saying is that such promotions have to be managed responsibly, by the long arm of the law if necessary. At present it seems certain licensees are all too happy to scream 'Two-for-one!' when they should perhaps focus more on saying 'Too-many-time-to-go-home!'

Town centres are no-go areas for many people on Friday and Saturday nights, purely because of the drink-fuelled aggression that pervades. It goes without saying that binge-drinkers are more likely to have accidents from slips, trips or falls, but beyond this fairly innocuous possibility, there is the very real likelihood of becoming involved in crime – as villain or victim. It is estimated that 76,000 facial injuries each year are the result of drunken violence, and alcohol is thought to be a major factor in as much as 50 per cent of all street crime.

In 2007 there was a 40 per cent rise in underage drinkers being referred for treatment. This shows everyone that the problem is getting worse, not better. Too many youngsters are obviously thinking it is cool to drink, or are otherwise just so bored or disenfranchised that they consider getting wasted as a fun if not entirely productive way to spend time. The traditional tenets I will be banging on about increasingly in this book – those of parental guidance and investment in community projects and spaces – need to win through but, even with all that in place, it becomes a matter for the individual to take responsibility for their own actions. Good friends will tell you you've had enough, but it is far better if you know your own limits beforehand.

I may well sound old and boring to them, but so many of the people I meet today need only to get back to a time and lifestyle where common sense prevails and temporary pleasures are earned, and where transitory pleasures are NOT prioritised above permanent responsibilities – which are in any case, in my experience, even more pleasurable. For example, offer me a night out and ten pints or a quality day out with the wife and kids, and I'll take the latter every time. It's not that a boozy night out with the lads won't appeal; there will always be times when it definitely does. It's just that it is no longer the be-all and end-all for me. And if that kind of night out means more than anything to anyone reading this, I would urge serious caution and a chat with your GP, because the path you are on leads to a dangerous place.

I can't help feeling old and boring when I forever plead with kids to stop drinking, start thinking and put themselves first before recklessly fighting, breeding or wasting their lives at daily parties. Just imagine a situation where a show like mine is no longer called by pissed-up teens getting pregnant at the drop of a hat, or by whole generations of people more content to take benefit cheques to the nearest off-licence rather than go out and build a life for themselves. As well as finding myself out of work, I'd also suffer the ignominy of becoming an irrelevance, with pearls of wisdom and words of advice that were no longer needed by young folk who were now in complete control of their destiny. By then I really would be old and boring. And I'd be loving every minute of it!

5

A Massive Own Goal!

'The pale-looking punter anxiously watching the horses line up on the bookies' TV does not look much like a confident, smooth-talking TV presenter.

'And as Jeremy Kyle sighs and throws away his betting slip as another nag fails to deliver, the controversial agony uncle is for once lost for words.'

EX-GAMBLER KYLE BACK AT THE BOOKIES was the headline I woke up to on 24 March 2008. Cue all manner of phone calls from concerned colleagues and loved ones who feared I'd frittered it all away at the local bookies in Ascot.

Nobody need have worried. I was fine, the mortgage was safe, we all still had a roof over our heads and I hadn't pawned off any of my children to pay for a bet on a horse race! I can only presume it was a slow day at the *Daily Mirror*'s news desk, because I was doing nothing more than meeting a friend for lunch and indulging a passion for the occasional flutter. This was no clandestine, cloak-and-dagger operation. I was on a two-week holiday from filming and doing what I sometimes like to do most to unwind.

I am not really the sort who can sit still long enough to while away hours lost in literature and, as you will soon read, I am not perhaps the easiest person to have around the house. I had some hours to kill before the kids needed picking up from school and I thought I'd take advantage of what was quite a rare opportunity for me to enjoy some downtime that did not involve work, wife or children. 'Sod it,' I thought, 'I'll go to the bookies.' There was no premeditation, no sweaty-palmed need for me to get any fix. I was doing what I'm sure a great many blokes do, whenever work allows, in getting out from under my wife's feet and spending a few hours with a friend before returning home to once more play happy families. Carla knew where I was (typically she had already made me promise to hand over half of any winnings to her!), and she stopped by to pick me up with a car full of kids on the home leg of the school run. I am not a big drinker, I have never taken drugs, and this is what I sometimes like to do when I am not at work and my wife has made it patently clear I should make myself scarce for a few hours. I really don't feel the need to stand up and say, 'My name's Jeremy Kyle and I'm addicted to gambling' because, today, that is just not true. But that is not to say I have never been under its spell . . .

I think it's fair to say that gambling is the only vice that has ever really 'got' me. I didn't realise it at the time but, looking back, I can see that there was a time in my life when gambling was more in control of me than I was of it. In my early twenties I got to a stage where I was betting every single day. My reasons for visiting the bookies had long since stopped being about having some fun: I was there as a creature of dangerous habit. My first marriage was crumbling around me and I sought solace in the only place I now felt truly accepted. Of course I was accepted – I and all the other sad bastards wasting away our lives, bet by bet, were always welcomed with open arms by shop managers gratefully relieving us of all our cash. And none of the 'friends' I gambled with each day were likely to speak up about any fears about our habits. The collective silence was essential for us all to cover the true extent of the damage we were doing to every part of our lives.

The sad truth was that I had deluded myself. I convinced myself that the betting shop was the hub of a loyal coterie of friends my life could not be without. This was just one of a million lies I kept telling myself and others as a means to excuse a burgeoning addiction that had placed me unwittingly in over £10,000 of debt. I had become the very cliché of an addicted gambler. I was borrowing money to fund increasingly fantastical punts. I became incredibly secretive about where I was and what I was doing. I jealously guarded the nature of my losses whilst aggressively concealing the place I was accumulating them. A range of pressures in my life seemed to converge at once and, instead of confronting them as I should have, I buried my head in the sand and escaped each day to a place that had gradually become my second home.

I often wonder how simple pleasures and pastimes graduate to the state of full-blown addiction. At what point does a hobby become a habit? I daily meet people struggling to accept that their 'normal' everyday behaviour is actually something wildly out of kilter with the rest of society. Often people cannot see how something they once chose to do to relax is now something they could not be without. I have lost count of the families I have tried to help where a loved one's 'quick drink after work' each night has steadily deteriorated over the years into alcoholism. One drink per night can soon become one bottle of wine each night. Sooner or later drink can become the dangerous centrepiece to every single evening when it was only ever intended as an occasional relaxant. People who have fallen into bad habits – or, worse, addictions – have a tendency to normalise what is very abnormal behaviour, and I guess I fell into that category, though I didn't see it at the time.

I have looked back a lot. I have thought long and hard about the moment things started to go wrong for me. There were times when I trawled my soul for the smoking gun that would signpost the start of my own destructive love affair with gambling. I can't find it. And I am not alone. I've spoken to more than a few people who similarly can't recall that single event or moment that started their own relationship with whatever stimulant has come to control them.

I don't really get to go out on a Friday night. Weekend drinks aren't really my thing and the days of me venturing out to nightclubs have long since passed. Work takes up the bulk of my time; family commitments take up most of the rest. On those occasions when I am afforded time off, I will occasionally play a round of golf. Each weekend I will take the kids swimming. Those apart, there isn't really a lot I look forward to, to get away from it all.

It goes without saying that I love the time I get to spend with my children. They remind me each time I come home just why I was missing them all so much in the first place. Days apart from them can be tough, but thankfully that is all forgotten when they bound into my bedroom at some ungodly hour each Saturday morning. They don't care that I have been away working fourteen-hour days all week, and they couldn't care less about the career stresses of 'TV's Jeremy Kyle'. All they want to know is that Daddy is getting up because today is Saturday and Saturday's the day he always takes us swimming! That is exactly how it should be, and I wouldn't swap my Saturday mornings, no matter how knackering they can be, for all the tea in China. I cherish those moments above all others in my week. Those moments with the dynamic duo – my two young daughters, Alice and Ava – remind me what I am working so hard for and what sort of future I am striving to secure. That said, a trip to the local swimming pool with toddlers intent on drowning either themselves or each other is anything but relaxing!

Time at home with my wife and the family is all I look

forward to as I toil away in Manchester, but again, I would hardly advertise the Kyle household as the ideal place to unwind. Put it this way, we're not top of our friends' lists of places they want to go to when they need to chill out. Pregnant wife plus two toddlers and the occasional presence of a nomadic teenager in love rarely equals peace and unbridled tranquillity.

My wife occasionally escapes the madhouse to ride horses. Every now and then I get to hack my way around a golf course. This is another of those things I love to do. Golf is the one sport I can honestly claim to be anywhere near good at. However, even a round of golf is still not, for me, relaxing. A few sliced drives and the odd lost ball does nothing for my Zen-like state of calm (!!) and I frequently return from playing eighteen holes feeling far more stressed than when I left. My inner competitiveness won't let me relax into a round of golf. I'll berate myself for any missed opportunity and beat myself up over every shot I know I could have executed better. And if I've lost to the friend I'm playing with, God help anyone who wants to sit down for polite chitchat afterwards. As I have said, I am no guzzler of wine, and so I certainly don't take anything else to de-stress. No, for the best part of twenty-five years I have found I can quiet my mind best and restore some inner peace whilst betting on the odd horse race.

From a very early age I always loved a day out at the races. I defy anyone not to be blown away by their first visit to Ascot, Cheltenham or Newmarket. I was lucky enough to have been introduced to this other world by my father. His job with HM the Queen Mother meant we were often welcomed into the Members' Stand at some of the country's most prestigious race meetings. I always remember enjoying such events and forever pestering Dad for news of the next. Back then, though, gambling was never really a feature of my days at the races. The pageantry, pomp and ceremony, the smells and sights and sounds, all held me in thrall. I particularly loved the fact that so few of my classmates ever went to the races with their parents – it gave me a story that no one else could beat when we swapped news as we all filed out from lunch. It somehow granted me temporary status as someone interesting. For a few fleeting minutes each day I was considered just about cool enough to be allowed into conversation with people who never normally gave me a second glance.

Try as I might, I can't remember my first bet as such. But I do still get a tingle when I think of my first big win. That came so early in my betting career it was probably part of my undoing in later years. I guess I was like so many who first dabble with drugs and love what they are experiencing. I kept going back and doing it again and again. It wasn't long before I got caught up in something that I thought was only providing positives in my life. At first, anyway . . .

I remember the local Coral's betting shop in Caversham. My route back from school at the age of sixteen took me past it, and curiosity compelled me to venture in. This smoky, dimly lit hive of activity seemed so adult to me. Growing up, every kid knew that this was where men went to enjoy themselves, but no one ever knew what actually went on behind those doors that were so resolutely shut to us. Being barred so conspicuously for so many years only added to the allure, I suppose. Many of my classmates used to talk excitedly about how they one day looked forward to joining their dads for a drink in the local pub – that other place where 'real men' went to enjoy themselves, and which also disapproved of kids. Drinking never really held any appeal for me, but I was increasingly transfixed by what all these men were concentrating on when hunched over their copies of the *Racing Post*. They lingered longer on a page of times and numbers than any of my mates ever did on Page 3 – and we were testosterone-fuelled teenagers! What was it that could keep some of the loudest, most rowdy men in town quiet for so long? I soon discovered they were studying form.

It was as though they were trying to break some sort of code from the assorted facts and figures printed before them. All were convinced that they could unlock the secrets contained within them and find for themselves a passport to untold riches. I'd never seen a rich man among this odd collective, but I was definitely taken in by the promise of potential winnings. I started to study form too, and was quickly schooled in the mechanics of gambling. I wanted to be one of them and they were only too happy to teach me what they knew. Men I began looking up to as wise old sages were passing on tips that I took to be ancient secrets that no one else knew.

I was told always to back a horse that had finished fourth in its last two races or, failing that, to go for the second favourite. I was taught that you should back the second of any trainer's two horses – not the favourite – if he/she had two in the same race. No one explained why, it was just passed on as gambling gospel to be adhered to at all times. (By the way, 'knowing' all of this stuff only makes it all the more infuriating when Carla occasionally bases her picking of a winner on nothing more than the aesthetic majesty of any one steed! I'll never understand how good looks triumph good form on the racecourse but my wife has the knack of knowing just when the odds will be upset in this way!) The odd visit after school soon became the daily must-go trip to Coral's as I continued my gambling apprenticeship. It was fun to learn and exciting to be a part of something that none of my peers were ever really into. This was my little project, for me and no one else. I flung myself into it fully.

By the time I was seventeen or eighteen I had become such a regular feature at the Caversham Coral's that I was actually given my own stool in the shop. I knew everyone by name, they knew me, and I rather revelled in the fact that I was 'friends' with such an eclectic assortment of people. By the time the 1983 Grand National came around, I was fully conversant with all the tips and tricks of the betting trade. I was confident. Emboldened by my rise through the ranks at Coral's, I sought to make my most daring bet yet: a faintly daring tri-cast for the National in which I should pick the first three home in any order. Corbiere romped home, Greasepaint finished second and Yer Man trailed in third. Jenny Pitman had just become the first female trainer of a National winner but, more importantly to a young Mr Kyle, I had picked the first three finishers correctly and had just won about £5,000!

If my early days as a gambler had been defined by the losses that are the norm and not the exception for most punters, life over the next few years might for me have been markedly different. As it was, I felt invincible. Five thousand pounds to a kid in 1983 was a hell of a lot of money and winning it only fuelled my enthusiasm for gambling. Apart from really, *truly* enjoying myself whenever I met up with my new friends at Coral's, I now had a taste of the money that I thought might always easily be made from betting. I should have got out while the going was good for me. I should have listened to 'Johnny Johnson'.

'Johnny Johnson' was my mentor when I worked at BT-Yellow Pages. I was earning what felt like about 4p an hour as the young, dumb thing there to stack files. It didn't take long for me to notice that he too was another of that select band of people who studied racing form on the back pages each lunchtime. What made 'Johnny' different, though, was that he never used the information he had deciphered to make a bet. I asked him why, and he explained a lesson in his broad Jamaican accent that I have never forgotten. I might as well have been sitting on a grandfather's knee as he regaled me with his tale of a trip to the dogs at Walthamstow in 1973.

There are six greyhounds in each dog race, and bookmakers pay out on the winner and runner-up. 'Johnny' was at Walthamstow with friends and it was his first time at any racetrack of any sort. Almost as a joke he placed the £2.58 he had in his pocket on a bet in which he speculated on the winner AND runner-up of all TEN RACES he watched that night. He was too busy taking in the experience and his new surroundings to concentrate on what was happening on the track that night. He knew he'd had a couple of winners but was probably too tipsy to know what was really going on with his ridiculous bet. It wasn't until he checked his paper at work the next day that he realised the extent of his unprecedented good fortune. 'Johnny Johnson', on his first-ever bet, at his first-ever race meeting, had won £17,800! In 1973! I saw some similarities between our victories and was hopeful of him passing on some more tips that I might use to propel myself to even greater triumphs. But the only advice he offered me was to stop gambling!

He told me that with his winnings he had bought a house without ever needing a mortgage. He bought a brand-new car, which was still going strong by the time I rocked up to work with him, but he also said that since that day he had never once bet again! He reasoned that he could never repeat that kind of good fortune and reckoned that anything that could make you feel that good on the one hand might only lead to misery and despair on the other. He'd had his good times in one big hit and he never wanted to put himself in temptation's way again. Only bad times could follow, he argued. Since that day, whilst never betting again, he had always sought to study the form at the back of any newspaper, I guess to see for himself if there was any science behind the magic of his good fortune.

Of course I am no 'Johnny Johnson', and I was more than just bitten by the gambling bug, I was consumed by it. It had ceased to be a simple pastime. It was no longer an extracurricular curiosity; it had become something I needed to do each and every day. I convinced myself I was seeing old friends without ever realising that the people I hung out with were just sad old gambling junkies with no interest whatsoever in me. They couldn't tell you one thing about me but my name. They wouldn't bat an eyelid if I showed up or not the next day. They would be there – guaranteed. And they would do exactly as they did yesterday, exactly as they would do tomorrow, with nothing but fags and televised horse racing to sustain them. Many had frittered away fortunes and lost whole families in the process, but none had been sufficiently moved to deviate from their daily diet of gambling.

So caught up was I in the ritual and routine of my daily visit to the bookies that I could not see how much more of my life it was taking up than ever it used to. A quick half-hour after school had moved on in later life to intense three-hour sessions during or after work. I would ensure that I got to the betting shop in good time to make the start of four full race meetings. I didn't mind what meetings or other commitments were cut short to get there. Four meetings meant twenty-four races. If I was lucky I could squeeze in two dog races too, and if I had any spare change in my pocket I might also bet on whether it was going to snow in Trafalgar Square on Christmas Day! I avoided going home to a wife I could no longer bring myself to confide in about the extent of my problem. I spent less and less time at home whilst wasting more and more money in the betting shop. I became the very epitome of the 'mug punter', who chases his losses while concealing them from the very person he should be being most honest with about them.

With my life disintegrating and my gambling losses

mounting, I turned to, of all people, a bank manager for help. He had called me in but, in truth, I'd probably gone into Lloyds of Caversham fully intending to lie my way to a loan that might help me continue chasing the untouchable dream of a big bookies' payday, one that might solve all of my problems. Thankfully my bank manager saw through my pitch and jolted me back to reality. I will never forget Mr Roger Bishop, nor anything he said to me that day.

He explained, quite plainly, that he was retiring the following year and could not really care less about my plight! He said he understood it, though, and presented me with two options to clear the £12,000 I now owed. Option 1 was to declare myself bankrupt and face the prospect of never having any credit-card company or mortgage lender ever looking seriously at me again. Option 2, he said, was to pay £487 each and every month for the next three to four years until my debt was paid in full. I was warned that if I missed just one payment under the terms of Option 2, I would default and be declared bankrupt anyway. He could sense the panic in my voice but he knew something had hit home. He had said from the outset that he wanted to teach me a lesson, and to be fair his lesson got through far more clearly than any of the teachings my former pals in the bookies had ever passed on.

I had no choice but to get my house in order. The delusion gave way to shame, but soon after that I found the determination to turn things around. I redoubled my efforts at work and built a life no longer bent about the need to gamble. What problems I had I worked at, and the loan I took out to clear my debts I paid back, bit by bit, pound by pound. All in all I made forty-two payments back to Lloyds and was stunned to learn that in total I had paid back £16,850. The bastards had made 30 per cent on me! To add insult to injury, I received a letter from my branch not ten days after I had made my final payment to them. In it they offered me a £5,000 overdraft. Unbelievable!

To be fair, I learned Mr Bishop's lesson and have never since been so reckless with the personal finances that are my family's future. I reached the age of twenty-nine and was finally debt-free. The upshot was that I became almost overly ordered in the management of my money. I have become obsessive about every penny that comes and goes from every account I have ever held since that day. And, I'm sure out of guilt, I have always done my utmost to provide all of my family with absolutely everything they need. Nowadays there is no hiding place. If I have a problem I talk to Carla. If there is a crisis on the horizon we face it together, as a team.

Before, I probably took on too much. I selfishly indulged what I thought of as a passion without realising that it had become a dangerous addiction. I buried my head in the sand and neither talked about nor dealt with any of the problems I myself was to blame for causing. I can only say sorry to those who worried, and anyone who was neglected or left out as I came to terms with my own issues. It can be of little comfort to any who had to suffer as they did that I am now OK, but there is little more I can do but get on with my life whilst trying to be the best husband and father I possibly can be. I made mistakes. I scored a massive own goal, but I have tried to make amends. I faced my demons, paid back all I owed, and I strive to provide my family with all they need each and every day.

Of all the guests I meet on *The Jeremy Kyle Show*, it is those with gambling problems I have the most direct affinity with. I can only bring the benefit of personal experience to my job, and when I am told about someone's struggles with gambling I feel a truly empathic connection born of shared experience. I can take an imaginative leap into most situations, am well informed on most others and believe that I will always be able to give guidance on the rights and wrongs of a situation. However, gambling is the mistress that truly seduced me. She convinced me all was well when really it was anything but. The gambling buzz that so gripped me I can actually see in others as they talk about it. I can see the cogs spinning in a gambler's brain as he works out the next set of crazy odds that he'll need to claw himself back to the black. I fccl the nervousness and excited anticipation all hardened gamblers get when having a punt they know they shouldn't. I'll never understand what a hit of heroin feels like, but gambling I get. Big time.

There are about 284,000 problem gamblers in the UK by most recent estimates, about 0.6 per cent of the population. I am not convinced we need to do anything too draconian to combat what has only become a serious issue for quite a minor percentage of the population. I know some might view this as a softly-softly, out-of-character approach that is perhaps irresponsible. However, as with most things in life, I believe it has to come down to personal responsibility. The 0.6 per cent of the population who have a problem should not be allowed to spoil what is a perfectly pleasant form of entertainment for everyone else. Sixty-eight per cent of the country, 32 MILLION PEOPLE, will have taken part in some form of gambling in the last year, and the overwhelming majority will have come to absolutely no harm at all. Some might even have won!

There are a great many more alcoholics than there are gambling addicts in this country but, no matter how bad the associated problems can be for some, I can't ever see a case for banning either. In reality people would always find a way to gamble and drink anyway. Banning pursuits enjoyed by so many would only force them underground. I have been a problem gambler, and if that Coral's in Caversham had never stood I might never have been tempted down the paths I was. Still, the fact I did succumb was down to no one other than me. I alone was to blame for allowing something that started as a means of passing time to consume and control me as it did.

I am all for investing more money into the treatment of problem gamblers. There are some fantastic organisations out there, like Gamblers Anonymous and Gordon House, which could all do with increased funding to support the great work they do. Maybe they should be entitled to money raised directly from the pockets or profits of bookmakers? If there was a small windfall tax placed on bookmakers, which could be siphoned off directly to fund treatment for problem gamblers, that might be a start. I feel also that tobacco companies should be obliged to pay a percentage of their profits to those underfunded, over-worked NHS departments struggling to stem the tide of people being admitted with smoking-related diseases. They drain resources that could be spent elsewhere on diseases that are not self-inflicted or built on the back of Fifties ad campaigns to get everyone puffing. Using that rationale, it seems only fair that bookies should make their contribution to help those who can't help themselves where gambling is concerned. It will hardly break the bank for these people to help out 0.6 per cent of the population. And, let's be honest, I've never seen a broke bookie!

I must be fair, though. This does all come back to personal responsibility. As with all things in life, gambling is some-thing that should be approached responsibly and in moder-ation. If anyone wanting to gamble remembers a few basic principles – AND STICKS TO THEM – they won't go far wrong. Essentially, if you are starting out in gambling to make money, DON'T! In the long run you won't win. The odds are always going to be stacked in favour of the person you keep handing over your hard-earned cash to. It is far better to set yourself a budget of money *you can afford to lose* at a bookmaker's, casino or wherever, and stick to that. Enjoy the experience, but once you've spent your budget, be it £10, £100 or £1,000, just say thanks very much and leave. Never borrow to fund your gambling and never hide it or in any way otherwise let it affect your relationships with loved ones. Always start from a position of a) knowing whether to gamble and b) knowing how much you will spend. Never chase losses: I've been sucked into that mug's game and, let me tell you, it is not good for your health! Beyond that, it is probably just as important that you leave any betting establishment the minute you have been fortunate enough to win. There is a powerful temptation to keep betting so you'll keep winning, but sooner or later you'll have handed back every penny of your winnings. And more besides.

It is easy to feel invincible after one big win and even easier to get carried away to the point where you end up handing back more than you won in the first place. I mean, how many times have you seen someone playing on the fruit machine in a pub for countless hours? Ask them why they are playing so intently and they will say they are playing for the jackpot. Three hours later they'll return to the table having finally won the £30 top prize on offer, seemingly oblivious to the fact that they have just spent £80 to get it!

Trust me, as far as gambling is concerned, if you break even you are having a good day. I probably got caught up in the fallacy of there apparently being loads of easy money to be made, all in a setting that seemed so fun to me. The appeal of gambling will never go away, of course. The whole point of making a bet is based on the promise that you *could* stand to get more money back than you first put down. Everyone loves a bargain, and what could be more of a bargain than getting given free money just for predicting the winner in a race? Where things have perhaps changed and become more dangerous to those susceptible to problem gambling is in the actual betting environments themselves. Casinos, which were once the exclusive preserve of high rollers in five-star hotels or Las Vegas tourists with money to burn, can now be found in most large towns and cities. When I was growing up I remember casinos having their own mystique. They seemed incredibly hard places to get into, and I never remember them being so commonplace. Nowadays they are everywhere, and you don't have to jump through many hoops to get in. Fill in the form, pick up your card and in you go.

Similarly, I have seen betting shops change immeasurably over the last twenty years. The thrill-filled oases on offer now bear no resemblance to the smoky back rooms that I used to inhabit. The whole feel of betting establishments is much more welcoming than in days gone by. That sense of it being a place where only a certain sort of man could congregate has given way to much more of an open-door policy. They no longer look like the school caretaker's nicotine-stained broom cupboard. Now they cater for anyone who wants to spend whole days there. Grab your coffee, play fruit machines (surely just computers programmed to make money, no?), bet on virtual horse or dog races as well as the real thing – and then there're whole banks of video roulette and computer poker machines.

I was just curious when I first stepped through the doors of Coral's, Caversham. I only found a few old boys who were happy to explain how betting on live horse racing worked. That was it. Now there is much more to tempt us, so there has to be greater awareness from us to keep ourselves in check. Similarly there should perhaps be some onus of responsibility on the managers of these outlets that now offer such a dazzling array of ways in which we can part with our cash. Just as landlords now rightly bear responsibility for allowing certain people to get far too drunk on their premises, so betting-shop managers or owners should reasonably be expected to turn away punters who are dangerously chasing losses with no fear of the consequences. If you know someone is up to their eyeballs in debt, don't you have a moral obligation not to keep taking their money?

Most people will say that anyone who was as consumed as I was by gambling should probably never gamble again. That is the only advice I can reasonably be expected to offer an alcoholic who has proved they can't control their booze consumption or a drug addict who has become controlled by whatever they are putting into their system. I'm guessing the experts wouldn't approve, but there's no point in lying: I STILL GAMBLE. The point is I now gamble responsibly. Undoubtedly one of the privileges my position as a well-paid television presenter offers me is the chance to spend a bit more money on the things I enjoy than ever I could before. To a large extent I can now bet without the fear that used to grip me when I was racking up debts with bookies. Back then I would bet £20 when I couldn't afford to lose £10. Now I set myself a modest budget I know I can afford to lose and once it's gone it's gone. If I win before it's gone, I get out of Dodge, count my lucky stars and hand over half to my wife's latest shoe fund!

That, in a nutshell, is about as much as I can say to anyone who comes to me seeking help for a gambling problem. If you have consistently shown that your gambling controls you and not the other way round, if it is destroying the relationships around you as you haemorrhage more money than you will ever be able to afford to pay back, then get out and get out for good. However, I believe my 'addiction' was more about me not confronting the real problems I had going on in my life at the time. I wasted hours each day in betting shops precisely because I was avoiding going home until the very last minute. At home I knew I would have to come clean about certain aspects of myself of which I had become deeply ashamed, and I bottled it. As a result of spending the time I did in those betting shops, the problems at home got worse. As they got worse, I chose to stay out more. The more I stayed out, the more money I spent on bets. The more I spent, the more I lost, and the more I lost, the more I chased in order to avoid going home to face even worse conse- quences that were all the result of my own failings.

In Carla, I have a wife in whom I can confide about anything. The minute I have a problem, I go to her. The minute I have made a mistake, I know *I can* go to her. She may well call me all the names under the sun behind closed doors. Indeed, there have been more than a few occasions when a dinner plate has whistled by my head as she bawled at me over some cockup or other. She'll defend me to the hilt in public over whatever allegation is doing the rounds, though.

When I lost my job at Virgin radio, the old me would have been more than tempted to avoid going home. Before Carla, I would probably have kept the bad news to myself, worried constantly about it and made every possible attempt to avoid confessing my failures to loved ones. However, Carla has seen to it that there is nothing that I don't feel comfortable enough to talk about in my marriage. No subject is off limits. Carla is more bold than I ever am about tackling problems head- on, and she gives me the strength to do just that where other- wise I might wait and stew and avoid and . . . bet?

People who only know me from TV may be surprised to learn that I am the pussycat in our relationship. She is much more inclined to tackle our problems aggressively. She'll grab our problems by the balls long before I've coughed and begun looking for mine! When I got back from my sacking at Virgin (having definitely not stopped at any betting shops en route), I told her straight away. Her infinite capacity to surprise was again in evidence as she cracked open a bottle of bubbly and set about preparing a lovely barbecue for both of us! We 'celebrated' long into the night and at the end of it all she told me not to worry about losing a job in radio. She assured me we'd always be OK, come what may, and then she told me to knuckle down and try and get my dream job in TV. Amazing. Her mantra at any time of personal crisis, especially one I have brought on by my own idiotic behaviour, has always been: 'You may be a stupid bastard but you're my stupid bastard and if anyone so much as looks at you funny in the next three months, I'll blow their head off!'

Carla knows me better than I know myself. She knows that gambling is no longer a problem for me. Nowadays, making a bet is as much about meeting up with friends and enjoying a social occasion as it is bound up in my passion for horse and dog racing. Carla often orders me out of the house or, if I'm bored, asks if I fancy going to the bookies or not. When it is put to me in those terms, I'd really rather stay at home and risk the wrath of my wife as I continually get in her way. I rarely, if ever, go to betting shops any more. I will have bets from time to time, but in the main I make them when out with friends who share the same interests. I still love racing (I once even owned a racing greyhound which seemed to specialise in going backwards! I remember Gary Newbon commentating on the TV and pointing out that *Crafty Disco*, the dog which had just stopped most of the others halfway round so all could take turns to sniff its bum, was actually owned by 'chat show host Jeremy LYLE'. No mention was made of my sidekick, The Prince of Darkness, Brett Capaldi, who must have worked wonders to find the only racing dog in England who had no interest in running and got repeatedly lost going round an oval track!) so I will occasionally be found at some track or other with a few friends. But the emphasis on such occasions is always on the social side of meeting up and having fun. Betting is something of an incidental transaction that can take place as and when we do meet up. It is no longer the reason to go and meet up. Whereas before I used to escape to gamble and gamble to escape, now I go out to meet friends and sometimes choose to bet with them if I do.

I don't blame the *Daily Mirror* for following me as they did. They are more than welcome to follow me again if they are concerned my holiday habits might one day get the better of me. However, I can assure them that the propensity for the odd punt no longer dominates my life. The massive own goal I scored came in not following the advice I now give to so many I meet. I was not honest about my problems. I did not identify them, nor did I attempt to resolve them by talking them through with the people I should have. I buried my head in the sand and let things spiral out of control, but in the end I turned things round. I took my medicine, heeded the advice and learned my lesson. I did all that was asked of me and I believe I paid every penny of my dues ... Not many thought I would, or could, in particular a certain bank manager called Bishop. I wonder what odds he would have given on things turning out the way they have ...?

6

Am I Just Old and Boring? (Part II)

I work in an industry that most people agree is absolutely rife with drug taking. I front a show on which drug taking is or has been part and parcel of everyday life for most of those invited to contribute. I have seen at first hand how drug abuse has affected my own family and still, at forty-three years of age, I haven't taken anything more exotic than chemist's cough mixture!

Anyone rooting through my bins for evidence of any rock-'n'-roll excesses will be sorely disappointed. In amongst the usual domestic detritus might be found the odd finished packet of Marlboro Lights, maybe even an occasional betting slip, but beyond that my household waste will reveal little more than a love of chocolate and perhaps a propensity to prepare more spaghetti bolognese than my family can ever eat in one sitting. The only needles my family have ever discarded have been those once used for knitting, the only powder to come near my nose is Carla's make-up as I kiss her and the only green herb I've ever seen in the house is locked in a jar marked 'oregano'.

Having not once taken an illegal drug might make me uniquely *unqualified* to dispense advice to anyone suffering from drug-related problems. That said, I have plenty of experience of seeing the terrible toll taking too many drugs can exact on individuals and families alike. I know that a majority of my guests on *The Jeremy Kyle Show* are or have

been regular users of illegal drugs. And let me be plain: NO
ONE comes to *The Jeremy Kyle Show* just to tell me how
fantastically things are going for them. No, they come with
a vast array of problems endemic in our society but particularly prevalent in certain pockets of Britain. Many of those
complaining of problems don't see the compounding effect
that even recreational drug intake has on those problems,
whilst there are others who won't see rampant drug addiction as any problem at all! I cannot identify with any of the
rituals or paraphernalia of drug taking – put a crack pipe
in front of me and I'm sure I wouldn't know which end to
use! I certainly have no empathic connection with the highs
that drug abusers chase, but I do know the price that is
regularly paid by people who flirted with a substance that
later came to control them.

To be frank, I do not personally understand the need to
take drugs. I just can't handle not being in full control of my
faculties. The very idea of deliberately doing something that
would take me so far out of myself, so far beyond the boundaries of what I understand to be real and right and normal,
is something that fills me with terror. Of course I understand
that there are a huge number of people who love to escape
the confines of their lives with a helping pharmacological
hand. There are those who feel hemmed in by humdrum
routine, and those who see chemical expansion of the mind
as more fun and adventurous than any literal broadening of
intellectual or geographical horizons.

Let's be honest about it, most people in this country do
drugs because they have done them before and liked them.
The millions of Brits who will this weekend fuel themselves
with ecstasy, cocaine or cannabis are not likely to be doing
so for the first time. They will be repeating or attempting to
re-create a past substance-induced experience that they found
to be positive rather than negative. I hear, know and indeed

have worked with such people, who argue that their weekly sorties into a world of criminal excess are justified under the banner of 'recreational drug taking'. 'Smoking weed chills me out'; 'If more people took "E" than got pissed on a Saturday night, there'd be a lot less fighting on our streets.' 'I work for a living. It's up to me how I spend my money' and, 'I'm not doing any harm' seem to round off most of the arguments put to me by those who claim their use of drugs should be better understood by people like me who are 'just out of touch'.

I have been tut-tutted and looked at disdainfully by whole hosts of talented, successful, bright young things who almost feel sorry for my fusty insistence on doing without what they so regularly take and claim to be relatively harmless. They roll their eyes at me at the start of an evening, unaware of the irony inherent in their mocking of me. They will be unaware of the prophetic precursor they have provided of things to come. They wouldn't appreciate how misplaced this gesture seems when – not three hours later – they will be struggling to keep them from *not* rolling, once whatever they've consumed has taken a proper hold.

I find myself feeling particularly 'old and boring' when continually forced to state the obvious about drugs. Of course I have to bang on about the illegality of drug taking or the dangers it poses to any individual's health, but I'm not saying anything new when I do, and surely these dangers can't come as any surprise to anyone. Warnings in this area have been stark and particularly plentiful in recent years, and most people are fairly familiar with some of the more catastrophic consequences of drug taking. Most know that depression, paranoia and psychosis can follow sustained abuse of anything from cannabis to cocaine. Most things in life have to be paid for at some point, and the undoubted highs experienced by a great many on drugs are also followed by crushing 'comedowns' that not every human mind is able to take. Just as some are susceptible to the ravages of alcoholism where most of us can take or leave drinks as we choose, so there are many I have met who just could not handle or enjoy drugs in the same way that most of their mates could.

I understand and have an element of sympathy for those who wish to see certain drugs reclassified to be commensurate with those publicly taxed commodities of alcohol and tobacco. I understand the few who tell me that they 'really can handle' whatever they have taken without posing a risk to work, family or friends. As I say, I have worked with people who perform brilliantly day to day, despite having written off the odd weekend to chemically constructed excesses that they have funded and made time for. I have *more* sympathy for the arguments put forward by these sorts of people than those who come to me having done nothing but sponge off the system in order to take drugs. I agree that there seems to be little in the way of personal consequence or repercussion for some in their situation, but no amount of reasoning along those lines can ever persuade me that taking drugs is anything but a deadly lottery. As Leah Betts found out, it only takes one dodgy pill. It only takes one bad wrap or one questionable line and a life might be lost.

So while taking drugs might seem safe to the vast majority of those who regularly choose to do so, no one will ever convince me that anything bought from a shady bloke in some backstreet pub before being snorted off the lid of a public toilet is anything other than disgustingly dirty and unsafe. I mean, let's be honest, the only people selling drugs are criminals. The alternative economy that arises from the booming drugs trade in this country is not regulated; there is no quality control, health and safety or any other of the checks we insist upon for even those areas of least concern to us in the rest of our lives. I've no doubt that chicken feed, birdseed or the sawdust bedding for some kid's pet hamster has to conform to a whole host of EU regulations designed to protect Little Hammy and his human family, but no recreational drug user (and certainly no addict) I ever met has ever thought anything of greedily hoovering up substances they know might well have been cut with anything ranging from Ajax to rat poison! Are drugs really that much fun to warrant taking that much risk? Well, sorry if I sound old and boring, but I'm quite happy to never find that one out. Put it this way, I've done my share of gambling in my time and I don't much like the odds on me and drugs.

Are drugs really that fantastic? What is it about them that gets so many under their spell? The reasons not to do them are clear. The potentially fatal consequences of negative narcotic experiences are widely reported. Maybe people are buying into a sense of glamour when taking drugs; either that or there really is nothing going for them in this country.

The drugs themselves would have to make you feel bloody fantastic to be any sort of compensation for how they make you look. I have seen people, even during my sheltered life, that have been rendered little more than sweaty, gurning wrecks by whatever they have taken, their faces like some sort of contorted human compass with eyes pointing east and west simultaneously whilst tongue goes north and the chin zigzags frenziedly south. I remember Frankie Boyle once describing Amy Winehouse as looking like a campaign poster for distressed horses as she stumbled incoherently from one party to the next, and that image perfectly encapsulates some of the sights and sounds I have been confronted with when watching people 'just having a good time' on drugs. I mean, I know I suffer from seemingly incurable verbal diarrhoea, but the cacophonous, cocaine-laden squawking of some usually quite erudite professionals never fails to leave me as shocked as it does irritated. People on cocaine, I have learned, just do not shut up, and they rarely make much sense. How can anyone think *I'd* need any of that?

I have been accosted by a few people on drugs and the experience always reminds me never to be tempted myself – but more compelling than anyone making an unintentional show of themselves is the evidence provided by the thousands (literally) I have met who have had their lives destroyed in some part by drug taking. Those who have lost careers, families, relationships – and sometimes all three – as a result of 'just having a good time' on substances that have come to conquer and control their abuser; all these tell of the misery brought on by spiralling addictions. When not getting through to their loved ones, people on my stage sometimes look at me and implore me to understand the message. I tell them as I tell you now that I already know. I understand the toll drug abuse can take. Drugs are a tax on the soul that can hollow out whole families. I know this for I have seen what abusing drugs did to a member of my own family.

Before starting this book, I vowed to be as open and honest about *my* life as I could. That remains the case now; I am prepared to put my life, my experiences, my thoughts, my feelings and my opinions under the microscope, offer them up for public consumption and subject them to public scrutiny. However, what I am not prepared to do – not yet at least – is go into detail about certain members of my family.

It will be no secret to anyone who has watched my show regularly that I have a close family member who has had his battles with drugs. I can't go into detail about them or him here and now because it would upset the people who have given and mean so much to me: my family. If I was to speak about those experiences and the terrible times endured by my family, I would expect to be able to do so with the same unbarred honesty with which I am tackling each page of this book. The simple truth is by doing so, I would hurt a great many people I love in the process. Moreover, I would also have to retell certain stories and leave big gaps and glaring omissions. Shrouding them in such a veil of vagueness would undoubtedly protect some individuals from discomfort but I would also be going against my stated ambition and promise for this book. Hell, I would even be making a mockery of the title: I could not claim to be 'only being honest'. Rather I would likely be sinking into the realms of being deliberately dishonest – and that I will not do.

I will address that time and those issues in the future (I promise) but not right now. What I will relay though is a tale told to me when I was working on late-night radio for BRMB in Birmingham. We were talking then as I am talking now about the effects of drugs on their abusers and the families caught up in the ensuing vortex. The caller was a father who knew nothing at all of drugs until the day he had to confront the heroin addiction he never knew his daughter had.

The daughter in question was a young girl blessed with a full house of talents. She excelled in everything – academically, socially, in sport and she was the apple of her family's eye. Her parents were understandably brimming with pride when-ever they reflected on their angel's achievements and they had no doubt hers was a future that would be paved with gold. They thought nothing of agreeing to her taking a gap year before she resumed her studies at one of the Oxbridge colleges twelve months later. They thought this would broaden her cultural horizons and provide her with yet more strings to an already mightily impressive bow.

They became a little concerned, as I guess all parents would, when they started to hear less and less from her. Still, they reasoned she was intelligent and sensible and was probably just throwing herself into her gap year with typical commit-ment. They did not for one second consider that she was falling in with that ubiquitous 'wrong crowd' but a further retreat from contact and family life over successive months heightened their alert status from mild concern to open worrying.

The girl did return eventually, some months later, but to these parents it was as if only half of the daughter they knew had come home. Although they did not know what to look for the only thing that could make sense of what they saw before them was the prospect that their daughter must be on drugs. She was. And she was hooked.

It transpired that this particular 'wrong crowd' had introduced this gifted youngster to heroin at some party and she had instantly succumbed to its seduction. She had moved about from place to place with this group of urban nomads and developed a liking for heroin that had become addiction in no time at all. By the time she had returned home she was well schooled in the dark arts of the petty criminal and was facing a custodial sentence for the crimes she had committed to feed her habit.

Her father spoke to me so graphically about his plight and I understood his every word and emotion. Although he knew his daughter was 'on drugs' he did not really know what that meant and had not the faintest understanding of what he should do to help or even get through to his daughter. He felt impotent, helpless and that it was all his fault. He felt to blame for something he may have said or done – or not said and done – in the past but he could not work out what. He could not work out why. He went on to explain that he contacted myriad helplines and drug agencies to try and get his daughter help but to no avail. His friends could not provide him with the key that would unlock the mystery of this puzzle for him either and so he took the decision to take matters into his own hands.

In the end this man rented a country cottage in Wales, far away from the family's inner-city home and then pretty much kidnapped his own daughter! Once at the cottage he set her up in a bedroom and then locked himself in it with her and waited for the drugs to flush out of her system. He was there for anything up to three months and went through the whole vile process with her and was absolutely immovable to all of her desperate pleas for him to help her in a way that would only lead back to drugs. She went 'cold turkey' with him but emerged and later went on to build a successful life for herself, one that was free of drugs because of the bravery and desperation of one man. Her dad.

Now of course I am not advocating that anyone in a similar situation now goes around kidnapping their kin and forcing them through cold turkey. That would be ridiculous. I am merely telling this story to highlight the way certain drugs can lay waste to even the most talented minds. I want it to show just how divisive and destructive drugs can be for whole families (trust me, I do know what I am talking about on this one) – not just the desperate abuser at the centre of the problems they create. I was blown away by that man's dedication and his bravery in taking the decision to intervene as he did. Had I not worked on the show, had I never met Graham and been made aware of all that can be done to get a person off drugs and into recovery, I fear I might have been forced to do something similar if a daughter I loved was in the grip of something destroying her.

I find myself wondering, what would I do if Hattie, my eighteen-year-old, came back from her travels like this man's daughter did. At the time of writing this she has barely dropped me an email in a month of antipodean adventuring. I took this to be positive and figured that she was far too busy out there having fun and exploring all the world has to offer to get back in touch with her old man. But stories like the above do make you wonder and I suppose that is why most of us parents will always be worriers.

What would I do in that situation? I would worry that forcing the issue as that brave man did might actually push my daughter further into a drug spiral. Every parent knows how easy it is for their offspring to revel in taking the opposing view to Mum and Dad. If you disapprove of a boyfriend or girlfriend, chances are your son or daughter will then find them even more irresistible. If you tell someone they have a problem with drugs will they get so angry that they almost retaliate by taking more drugs and thereby become worse? Do you wait for them to hit rock bottom on their own or do you try and force them to find it that bit quicker? Do you stick around and watch your loved one destroy themselves or do you wait away at a distance? Do you lend a hand or cut off all ties after one final ultimatum? Phoning Graham is the only thing I know I definitely would do in that situation. I guess I couldn't quite explain what I would do from the range of options that would be available to me, that would all depend on the person involved, the drugs they were taking and the exact nature of the situation I was facing. All I can say, and with absolute certainty, is that I would do WHAT-EVER it took to get my child off drugs and into permanent recovery.

Of course, recovery isn't the end of any drug addict's story. I often find myself telling my show's guests that 'the hard work starts now', but many think that it is just the physical withdrawal, the actual giving up of drugs that will be the difficult bit. It isn't. Once the drugs are out of an addict's system the real struggle begins. Staying off is much harder than getting off drugs, because it requires a lifelong commit-ment, whereas getting off, via a chemical detox, can realisti-cally take as little as five to ten days. Staying off drugs means never dabbling ever again.

On the show, Graham always tells guests that it is not just

a case of reducing intake, it is avoiding intake altogether. Forever. End of. After all, addicts come to us after using substances they have proved they can't control. If anyone shows that they can't control their consumption of anything, be it alcohol or whatever drug, then the only sensible recourse is never to consume that substance again. That can be quite a concept to take on board. If for years your life has centred only on the buying and taking of drugs, sobriety's chief challenge for you will probably be distracting yourself and filling the hours that were previously given over to life on the drugs. Whole social networks have to be re-engineered and whole patterns of behaviour have to be reworked. The very boundaries within which any recovering addict lived their whole life have to be redrawn, and that can be quite scary. Relationships with friends or family have to be rebuilt.

I have seen how hard it is for some people to acknowledge the pain they have caused loved ones by repeatedly spurning them, lying to them, manipulating and using them to sustain a life on drugs. It can be hard to remain humble and as perennially apologetic as some feel they must, but it must be equally hard to once more trust someone who has abused the love you have shown them year after year. No one said giving up was easy – for any of the people caught up in one person's addiction.

Their fears mirror those of so many of the parents who come to the show pleading for me or Graham to help get through to their own drug-addled offspring because they no longer know how to. They too are paralysed by a mixture of fear and guilt. They see their kid's drug problems as their own failing, and are crushed as a result. Moreover, they fear that standing up to that same kid might send him or her hurtling back out of the family home and back into the arms of the local drug dealer. Well, that is just manipulation from someone who is failing to own up to the responsibility for the decisions they took to pump that toxic shit into their system.

I'm sure we could all do more at some level, but we surely have to reach a point where we can look at even those closest to us and say: 'Do you know what, I've done all I can for you now. You are taking the piss and you are hurting the people who love you the most. Stop taking us for a ride, stop blaming us for your own failings and stop expecting us to take responsibility for your problems!' I have met hundreds who want to say the same but fear what will happen if they do. Having written this today, I get that more clearly than I ever did before, but I am determined not to be held to ransom by this fear, guilt or manipulation ever again. Telling guests on my show this is one thing, but applying it to my own family will be quite another. However, from this moment onwards I will be bloody sure to try!

Much like alcohol abuse, drug taking is not confined to one particular class or section of society. Drug addiction is no respecter of wealth or status, but it is probably true to say that the areas of most concern are those defined by deprivation. Drug taking is for some an escape from the crushing realities or hopelessness they perceive in their own lives. Even though drug addiction can grab anyone from any background, some people flirt dangerously with the lifestyle to prove some point, and can often end up succumbing themselves. Such selfish indulgence infuriates me – more because it is so needless. I have seen it up close with my brother, of course, and am still no nearer to learning why it had to be so. It is far easier to understand how someone might want to escape the misery of an existence with no job, no money, no family and no prospects. I understand why those people living on the most hard-pressed estates, where there is unemployment, crime and poverty at every turn, are far more likely to be tempted by drugs than I ever have been. Who wouldn't want an hour off, or a week away, from the sense of foreboding that comes with taking your life in your hands every time you lock the front door of a house you can't afford, on a street you've learned to fear, in a community falling apart? I understand people would want a way out, and even that the way out offered by drugs is easier to access in such places, but I still can't see a reason to buy into it. After all, once the drugs have worn off, how much closer is the drug user *really* to getting away from the pressures that made them seem so appealing in the first place?

Most of the people I meet on my show have (bizarrely, disgustingly and unfathomably to me) put their weekly drug intake right at the very top of a list of priorities that has also to include the feeding, clothing and schooling of their own children. I have lost count of the number of parents I have had to reprimand and remind that their weekly stash of weed is nothing compared to the importance of everything else they should be doing for their children. I never cease to be amazed at how some don't see a problem with being stoned around their children all day, or can't see that the £20 a day they blow away as smoke might have been better spent building a secure future for their families.

I understand that many people in poorer communities just feel bored. In those areas where deprivation prevails at every level, and local services or resources have diminished under successive governments, people have turned to drugs. I will never understand why someone chooses to get off their face whilst their children are forced to live in squalor, but the fact is it happens. It's a reality. People that feel they have failed in or have been failed by school begin to see the rest of their lives marked out along similar lines. As a result they opt out, preferring reckless fun and the prospect of getting 'fucked up' to anything that might give them the stake in society they will all crave at some point. It is that short-sightedness that really angers me in those who then come begging for help. The fact that they can't see how truly fucked up it is to compound a poor background and poor schooling with the poor personal choice that leads them into a life monged out on whatever drugs they can get their hands on. These people, I understand, have come from tougher backgrounds than anything I am likely to face, but that surely is even more reason to try that bit harder to improve oneself in order to break out. At times I feel a bit like every taxpayer must do when asked to bail out another failing bank.

People come to me and brazenly admit that they have done nothing but take from the system for twenty years. They haven't put a penny towards any of the kids they have sired and have instead taken the state for all they can. Then one day they see the light and realise that they have pushed it too far. They are no longer in control of the substances they have been only too happy to pump themselves full of for as long as they have been able. It is at this point they come, cap in hand, demanding more help, more money and more treatment to get back on track. Of course it is my duty to help on the show, but I do understand the anger of most in the audience who think it unfair that someone who has done nothing but indulge them-selves at our expense is then bailed out with another chance at redemption, no further censure and another shot at life, again at our expense. What I see day-in, day-out, are people who have fallen at the first hurdle and then never bothered to try and pick themselves up. Maybe it wouldn't be so bad if just one person opted to choose drugs over life, but the people I see invariably have two or three kids in tow. It angers me that these people will then re-create the very environments that they say have been so damaging to themselves for the people they should cherish and adore above any other.

★

I'm afraid that poverty is a fact of life in this country and all around the world. I applaud and admire any attempts to 'make poverty history', but have to reasonably assume that there will always be people who have more money than others. There will always be people who are or feel poorer than their peers. What we have to do as a nation and society is really get to work on fixing those bits of a person's profile that cost absolutely nothing at all. It is reckoned the average drug addict costs the taxpayer at least £827,000 in their lifetime, whereas self-respect, a sense of responsibility, decency, hard work and ambition – all the things that even an idiot like me has drawn on to make something of himself – all come at a cost of precisely nothing.

It is also reckoned that if we successfully treat a drug addict before they are twenty-one, that would shave more than £730,000 from that earlier figure. That's a lot of taxpayer's money to be put back into the communities where these problems are so prevalent. That's a lot of people contributing to the improvement of society and their families from the age of twenty-one onwards, who might otherwise have been content to waste away their lives at our expense. It seems to me that if we redouble our efforts to get into the minds of these people early, before the drugs and before popular prevailing thinking tells anyone it is OK to become benefit dependent, we might just have a chance at reversing trends that at the moment seem to me to show no signs of slowing.

We might never get through to everyone who wants to experiment with drugs, but we must surely do more to show another way to those who give themselves no chance at all by their dependence on them. Moreover, we need to get them off our collective sick bill and back into a world where they will pay their own way. People have always experimented with drugs and people always will. While it is still wrong and criminal and all the rest of it, there is a part of me that can't be *as* bothered with those people who use certain drugs the way *most* of us use alcohol. If they pay their own way, are honestly earning their own money and would rather spend their weekends living like a vegetable in front of the TV, so be it – we've got more pressing problems to concern ourselves with. More worrying to me is that a whole generation of people are already preconditioned to give up at age sixteen. Doing drugs and having children is all that these people seem to see as available to them, so they play at both, a lot, and the cost, in every sense, is getting ridiculous.

Drug dealing for others offers an altogether different escape. Many see fortunes to be made and seek to shortcut the system in order to access riches they feel might be beyond them if they stuck to the same rules as the rest of us. I have more sympathy with these people than I ever have for those who wilfully waste their lives before giving themselves a chance to succeed in it. As much as I'll never condone drug dealing, it can at least be argued that they are doing *something* to improve their lot, which is more than can be said of those who wantonly waste every talent, privilege and advantage they have through drug taking!

I never thought I'd have much sympathy with drug dealers, but I do kind of understand where for some, a need to break the law comes from. I can't fault anyone for wanting more than they were given, or wishing for a better hand than they were dealt. I have met some thoroughly deplorable creatures on the show, drug dealers who prey on innocence and naivety. These people perpetuate misery and some seem to have taken a cold and cruel delight in every bit of hurt or hardship they have wrought on their communities. However, I did meet one who harnessed his intelligence and 'street smarts' to cultivate a life for himself that just would not have been on offer via the traditional routes of school and an average nine-to-five job. Who can blame anyone for wanting the fast cars, flash cash and beautifully bejewelled girlfriend when every advert or music video aimed at us is promoting just those things?

When I first read about this drug dealer, whom I would be encouraging to change his ways, I thought he would be like those hard-nosed social parasites I'd met a thousand times before. When I actually met him, I admit I was a little stumped. I told him he should be concentrating on his two kids and on the parents who worried for their little boy. He understood it and got everything I was trying to impart, but the cold reasoning of his retort was hard to resist. 'Everything I do, I do for my kids,' he said. 'I make a thousand a week dealing drugs and I couldn't make that anywhere else'; 'I've bought a nice house, I give my family nice things and I've got out of an area where I used to see stabbings and muggings and shootings every day. If I gave this up now, I'd have to go to the job centre, sign up for forty-five pounds a week benefits, give up my house, give up my kids' future and have them go back to exactly where I came from. I AM NOT PREPARED TO DO THAT!' He added that he would gladly go to jail for a couple of years if it meant his kids could live in some comfort and be spared the violence, insecurity and deprivation that so defined the area in which he was raised.

And that's when it struck me. There is no point trying to instil a universal doctrine in everyone because in society one size will never fit all. This guy was adhering to everything I have ever preached about supporting family, earning his own money to provide himself and his family with better opportunities. It just so happened that this guy, someone I warmed to and found decent and sincere, was a drug dealer. There was nothing I or society could offer him that would better what he had built for himself already. By his own admission, he would rather not be mixing with the sorts of people his 'business' obliged him to, but there was no way he wanted to go back to the deprivation of his upbringing either. He did not want to function in everyday life as a criminal, but 'decent society' hadn't really offered him the means to make the best provisions for those children he was determined to do right by. In a world where I am telling everyone to make better personal choices, here was the exception that proved the rule.

That man felt he had achieved a status in society through supplying drugs. He felt empowered by the money he made and emboldened by the respect he said he felt on the streets (whilst feeling no compunction for the misery he might be perpetuating in the lives of those he supplied: in his belief system, his needs outweighed theirs). But it's obvious that this is not the way we would want our children to go, so what we have to do as a society is get back to providing our young-sters with alternative ways out. I'm sure some members of the government are quite happy to know that thousands of junkies are holed up indoors somewhere and not troubling them for extra community resources and new school playing fields or whatever, but the truth is that the lack of investment in our youth is coming home to roost sooner and sooner for the vast numbers of people now sinking into drug depend-ence. In the meantime, of course, the rest of us are forced to pay to support them.

I have been involved in some amazing inner-city projects such as the United Estates of Wythenshawe in Manchester. I will cover this one in greater detail a little later, but in essence it is a project that has seen a community reclaim control of its streets. It put some pride back into the commu-nity, with everyone pitching in and taking responsibility for those things that cost a person nothing. Crime has gone down, kids are getting off drugs and spending their time in the local gym instead. More importantly, young people coming through are seeing that their life does not necessarily have to be dictated by their academic ability. Good luck to those who do well at school.

I actually think we should return to the grammar school model ditched some years back. The promising and talented in life should always be stimulated by greater challenges so that they can get the best from themselves in a way that will surely benefit society as a whole on some level. I've never understood the argument that the most able should be kept back or have their progress slowed just because others struggle to meet their level. Surely we should cater for every talent at every level?

Similarly at the other end of the scale we should get more vocational training into schools earlier. I feel sure that some of the kids I meet on the show would have benefited more from double mechanics than ever they did from double maths. I mean, show a young lad how to fix his dad's car and back that up with the basics on how to build and craft a business and we'll all benefit. The kid gets a sense of achievement, a reason to enjoy and want to go to school and the means with which to start a business when he leaves school. His family get someone they can be proud of, the school get credit for helping build a life and the local town gets a handy young mechanic to fix their car and contribute to the upkeep of the community via his taxes! Little initiatives like that will surely be more helpful than repeatedly obliging a kid with little confidence to keep banging his head against the brick wall of a history exam he'll never quite grasp. By all means teach the basics, give everyone a grasp of the fundamentals, but by a certain age we all know whether someone's talents are going to be more brickwork than biology. Some won't say it, fewer want to hear it, but we all know the truth, and we all know that not everyone is cut out for a wholly academic education. Why can't we recognise that, cater to these people's needs and start to send more people

out into the world with a school education that has properly
equipped them to make a start for themselves in whichever
trade or business most suits their talents?

I particularly like reading about what Ricky Hatton and
Amir Khan are doing for their communities too. Investing in
gymnasia and having kids get fit, preaching a creed where
drugs aren't cool or even acceptable is great. And icons like
them will get the message through far more successfully than
ever a boring, middle-aged man like me will. Councils and
the government should get behind these projects. There is
too much money wasted on think-tanks and unnecessary
surveys. Too much time spent on trying to get 50 per cent
of people into university without ever creating options for
those who would never want a university education anyway.
We were in Wythenshawe for a week getting our hands dirty
and it was obvious what was needed to help that particular
community. I listened to the locals and was left in no doubt
at all. There was no bullshit, no convoluted bureaucratic
process. We went in; they said, 'We need this,' told us why,
and in six days a community had the means to help itself
feel a whole lot better about the world! We've got to trust
these people to do the right thing by themselves, for themselves. After all, that's what taking and giving responsibility
is all about.

It is to be hoped that the message is indeed getting through.
In 2005/2006, 10.5 per cent of adults had used one or more
illicit drug in the previous year. That is down from 12.1 per
cent in 1998, but it is still more than a tenth of the population! For younger adults aged 16–24, drug use fell in the
same period from 31.8 per cent to 25.2 per cent. Again, nice
that it is dropping, but there's still a QUARTER of young
adults admitting to drug use.

Most people I meet of this age also report smoking cannabis
as an everyday event. Of all the drugs I have spoken at length

about to guests, cannabis is the one that perplexes me the most. Figures show that 10.1 per cent of our school pupils use this drug, but no one has yet convinced me of any significant benefit it brings to their life. I meet a lot of people who are frustrated by their inability to get on in life. They bemoan any number of circumstances that have 'conspired' against them, but never see weed as any part of their problems. From what I can see, smoking weed is a great way to waste a day. If you want to do not a lot more than sit around the house, watch TV and endlessly snack like a zombie with worms, it really is the drug for you. I have always been a bit fascinated by what it is about it that keeps people going back for more. It is not recognised as physically addictive, so what does it do to compensate you for substituting the very zest of life with unremitting lethargy?

As I say, the people I meet come to me with marriages and whole family futures on the line, but they can't see that the weed has helped bring them to the brink. They repeatedly waste whole days, without apparently realising that added together those days will soon read as a whole life wasted. It really does not need to be this way. Bad habits can be broken and good habits can be got into. With greater investment in our communities at government level, greater catering to the talents of the populace at an educational level and greater responsibility taken for our development at an individual level, there is no reason why drug taking can't release its choke-hold on particularly the poorer parts of this country. If we provide more alternatives to drugs, as well as better guidance as parents, teachers and citizens in our communities, they won't seem like the glamorous escape they are now.

I'm glad that junkie is still such a derisive label. We need to puncture that bubble of glamour attached to certain drugs and drug takers. We certainly don't need to be continuing to fuel the drug trade with government benefits being wasted on users paying for their next fix. Just imagine a world where even some of the least able kids came home from school excited about their prospects of becoming a builder or plumber, instead of just 'needing a spliff' to get over the stress of school work they hate. If that started to happen for one person at a time, might there be a trickle-up effect for the rest of society? Might we one day see a time where communities like the one in Wythenshawe will largely go about fixing their own problems according to their own needs?

Drugs needn't be the all-consuming problem they are in society today. There will always be some who rebel or experiment, but there just is no need for whole generations – as they are doing today – to tune out before they've even given life a chance. I can't physically remove them from the streets, but everyone has it in their power to say no, and perhaps to do so they just need to be made better aware of the alternatives. Failing that, I guess people like me can always be old and boring and just go back to bleating about the consequences.

7

Get a Job!

'KYLE, YOU WILL ACHIEVE ABSOLUTELY NOTHING!'
As I sauntered into the exam room for my sixth and final
attempt at securing a maths O-level, it was hard to discount
the testimony of the latest tutor charged with making silk
from this particular sow's ear. Here I was, eighteen years old,
queuing up for another crack at an all-too-familiar nemesis
(maths), standing in line with a bunch of fifteen-year-old kids
who would no doubt breeze through a paper that seemed to
mock my every attempt to grasp it. The fact that I was now
permitted to carry a calculator where once I had been obliged
to use only a slide rule did nothing to ease my worries; it
only served to remind me how long I had actually been trying
to get a pass in this godforsaken subject.

But I'm nothing if not a trier, so I ante'd up and re-sat
the exam, buoyed by the fact that this Herculean task was
now about to be made all the easier by a newfangled contrap-
tion's ability to actually do the sums for me. I was determined not to be bested by my maths O-level this time. I was
sure it would be different this sixth time because I had technology on my side; it had to be the key to cracking this
subject. And do you know what? That poxy bloody calculator made not a blind bit of difference – I messed it up and
failed again!

I can't really blame that teacher for saying what he did.
He must have thought I was deliberately setting out to make
his teaching look bad. I mean, six fails in one subject is not

very good by any measure, is it? I see now that he was only being as honest as I am each day to the various people I meet who seem similarly unable to master those fundamentals of 'The University of Life'. I see people who look as though they've given up, can't be bothered, and are happy to let the likes of me and you soften their existence for them. I sometimes think – sometimes can't help but think, despite the help we always offer many a directionless delinquent – that they too will achieve little more than the label of 'burden on society'. I don't want to think it, I fight against drawing that conclusion with every bit of optimism I can muster, but sometimes, just like my old maths teacher did with me, I can't ignore the evidence of my own eyes.

Lurking in the shadow of my infinitely more (and apparently effortlessly) successful older brother did not help, of course. Continually failing maths exams was similarly confidence-sapping and no great incentive to start chirping up from the back of whatever class I might be in. I studiously avoided any attempt to gain recognition of any sort, so convinced was I of the likelihood of failure in most of what I attempted. I didn't even have the balls to make trouble! For so long it just felt as though I could not find any respite at all, anywhere I looked in school. All around me I saw people who were better, more confident, more accomplished – it was as though they were more at ease in their own skin than I ever thought would be possible for me. And being so painfully shy (unbelievable I know) as to be almost mute in English was bad enough, but nothing compared to the shame that awaited me in my first feeble attempts to get by in a foreign tongue . . . I think I am right in saying that at 3 per cent my French mock oral exam result still represents the worst mark ever 'achieved' at Reading Bluecoat School.

Now, I am not reliving some of these hastily buried and

long-forgotten memories to entertain. Nor do these painful reminders serve as any kind of post-traumatic therapy for me. No, I am highlighting some of my own deficiencies precisely to lump myself in with those so quick to opt out or be written off; those who see a lack of classroom aptitude as sufficient excuse to lack application in all other areas of their life. I want to show everyone that success can be achieved if you are prepared to put your mind to achieving it.

What I managed to do was make something of myself by working hard and investing time, effort and determination in my own options. I think it's about time quite a few more people in this country did the same.

Little did Chris Grayling MP know when talking of his 'Jeremy Kyle Generation' that, socially at least, Jeremy Kyle himself could well have been considered one of those he deems 'ill-equipped for adult life'. I won't pretend for a second that I was in any way as disadvantaged as so many of the people Grayling is actually referring to. I was blessed to come from a loving and stable background with parents who thought nothing of sacrificing themselves for the sake of the opportunities they might provide for their two children. For the best part of fifteen years, my mother and father set aside a large part of their annual earnings so that my brother and I could chance our arms in private education. They never complained, never bemoaned the lack of foreign holidays that resulted from their financial sacrifice, and never did anything but love, support and encourage me to do better than I had done the day before. They scrimped, saved and adopted an almost wartime sense of thriftiness to ensure the bills were paid and we could continue with the education they passionately believed in, wanting to give their sons even the slightest head start in life, always making whatever savings they could in order to pass on the proceeds to me and my brother. I have always been eternally grateful for the foundations such selflessness allowed me to build on.

I model myself on my parents and seek to provide for my family just as they did. No matter what new opportunities have been passed my way, the one – the only – factor I will ever consider before saying 'yes' or signing a contract is: 'How will this affect my ability to provide for my family's future?' If it is not right for them, it won't be right for me.

I meet some guests who sit there and sneer at me for having made something of myself. They think it came easily and that it was somehow just chance that saw me get *given* my rewards, whilst they have had to put up with being short-changed in some way. It's almost as if they believe that fate determined I was in a more fortuitous place in the queue when life's riches were being handed out. They don't get that I struggled at school and had to work bloody hard through several different jobs, striving day and night to prove myself in each one, and to leave behind the memories of my earlier childhood failures. They don't get that I have had to fight and scrap my way to getting everything I've wanted in my professional life. They don't see that I, just like millions of other mortals each day, have to get up when perhaps I don't want to and work hard when perhaps I'd prefer not to. I've worked in jobs that were not fulfilling in the slightest, around people that only made thankless tasks all the more hideous and unbearable, but I kept at it, just like those millions of others do each day, because it is right to earn your own keep and pay your own way in this world.

Even today there are times when I'd rather be anywhere but in a television studio, 250 miles from my wife and children. I am often at a loss to explain just why there is no light that switches on inside the heads of those with no compulsion to work. Why are there no flames of passion flickering in their hearts, and nothing within them that seems to want to make more of or for themselves than they started with. Such people never seemingly think about what it might take to get ahead. They never take an honest look at how *they* might go about improving themselves and *their* situation. No. They wait in line, take whatever they're given and slope off to get in the next line, all the while bemoaning only the 'bad luck' that got them to this point.

It is that sort of attitude that so regularly riles me, as it sums up everything that is going wrong with vast numbers of people in twenty-first-century Britain. The growing dependency culture in this country, combined with the ever-decreasing propensity of some Britons to take responsibility for their own lots and paths in life, has led some to the absurd conclusion that it is ONLY a question of luck as to where their lives end up. Are we really so used to queuing up for the next hand-out that we can no longer see the correlation between application and achievement? Why can't some see that hard work will always help improve anyone's circumstances, provided they work hard enough for long enough? It seems some will never get it, if the abuse both I and my team tend to receive from certain guests on a fairly regular basis is to be believed.

Let me be plain. I know I was the product of a privileged upbringing. I thank my lucky stars each and every day (usually at the conclusion of each of the daily calls I make to my parents) that I was born into a family that abundantly catered for every financial, familial, emotional and social need a child could have. I could not have wished nor wanted for more – but that isn't it. That on its own does not explain every reason behind any success I have had, any more than one can explain a person's failures as *only* being the product of a disadvantaged background.

Some of my colleagues on the show, and a great many

people I have met through the show, have turned very unpromising beginnings into very successful and fulfilled lives and careers. Equally I know of those, in fact I am related to one, who blew every advantage their own 'privileged upbringing' had given them. The law of averages will undoubtedly point to more people from 'better' backgrounds making more of their lives, whilst I can't ignore the fact that someone from a disadvantaged background is statistically more likely to – in some way – perpetuate the cycle and live (and create) a disadvantaged life themselves.

But, even if you are taking this from an ex-problem gambler, trust me when I say that these odds in life are there to be beaten. Tell me now that I probably can't do something and I'll redouble my efforts to make sure that I absolutely bloody well can. There are no hard-and-fast rules, only possibilities and probabilities, which any of us can overturn if we work hard enough at it. In twenty-first-century Britain it surely can't boil down to a case of which side of the tracks you were born on? I will never buy into that theory. No matter how bad things are, you can improve them and, equally, no matter how good things may one day seem, you will always retain the power, through your own actions, to make an absolute mess of them.

There simply is no room in today's Britain for the kind of mealy-mouthed bleeding hearts who continue to give credence to those who want to make sure no one ever has to take responsibility or face up to the harsh realities of poor personal choice. The same sorts of people who, through the Nineties, tried to ban competitive sports in schools, just so nobody ever lost a race, are helping prop up and exacerbate a culture that can– unbelievably – encourage people to sit in and do nothing instead of go out and work for a living. No one loses at Sports Day and no one loses in life!

Well, I'm sorry, but that is horseshit! These people and

these attitudes encourage benefit scroungers and fraudsters to take what they can, regardless of their entitlement. And while they do their best to give away all they can, the beneficiaries are simultaneously mocking them for their benevolence. They don't realise that in some quarters they are being laughed at by street-smart, work-shy dropouts who know exactly what they are doing when openly exploiting a system put in place to help those in genuine need.

I recently had the misfortune of meeting a young man on my show who at nineteen appeared to be nothing other than a spoilt, grasping little boy. But it wasn't his parents who had spoiled him. No, it was the state and, more specifically, the social welfare machine he deliberately and systematically abused for his own advantage. I normally credit people for at least being honest when they meet me, but I think on this one occasion I would rather he had lied. That he didn't, that he was happy to blurt out on national television to an audience of nearly two million people that he wilfully takes the taxpayer for every penny he can get actually just shocked me. I know I have met a lot of people who might have cheated the system, but this was the first time I had met someone who was so open, so blasé and so self-satisfied about it. He arrived at the show, knowing he had cheated on his girlfriend, mother to one of his three children and pregnant with a fourth (he abandoned the other two because, in his words, he 'couldn't be arsed to be a dad at sixteen'), but still quite determined to put her through an ordeal he seemed to have orchestrated purely in order to wound her in as public a way as possible.

I could not believe his lack of compassion. This boy's front was unbelievable. Ostensibly he had sought our intervention with what he described as 'some anger issues and a bit of a drink problem'. His girlfriend concurred that these were problems affecting their relationship and that they needed addressing for the sake of everyone in their young family. That was the script I was to follow and those were the topics I intended to address. It was only when I questioned him on the amount he drank and the way he funded it that his true colours were revealed. He smirked and laughed his answer, pointing at me and the entire studio audience when he gloated, without any hint of irony, that: 'Yous lot all pay for my beers and I think it is fucking hilarious that I can sit at home and get pissed every day and not have to pay a penny towards it.' The harsh words of rebuke I had for him were not nearly sufficient to convey the absolute disgust everyone was feeling for this boy. Worse, he actually seemed to be enjoying the fact that the conversation had reached this inevitable revelation. He used his time on stage not to build bridges with his partner, but went on to brag (as she wept) that he had repeatedly cheated on her. He didn't make any attempt at acknowledging the horrors he was subjecting his youngest and unborn child to. And he did not once seek to address the underlying issues that played their part in causing such misery to all he came into contact with. No, far from seeking help to redress his failings as a father, partner and human being, he actually wanted to use my stage to stick two fingers up at the mugs he knew were picking up the bill for his daily piss-ups: you, me and every other British taxpayer.

It is that targeted, wilful and unchecked abuse of a system that should only be there for those in need that really gets me, for I can see no current end to the culture that allows it to happen so freely. How as a society did we get to this point? When did we all become so distracted that we allowed ourselves to take our eyes off the ball so catastrophically as to allow people free rein in this way? Instead of encouraging – forcing even – people into a job that would benefit them and their families whilst also unburdening society of one more unnecessary drain and statistic, we are instead sending out daily signals and weekly cheques for some to party in perpetuity.

Are the people that sanction this hand-over-fist funding of delinquency really aware of the consequences of their actions? Can't they see the effects of what in this case was little more than state-sponsored alcoholism and a licensed abdication of all personal responsibility? Perhaps we are all too caught up in the pace of modern life to really give a damn. Maybe chucking a few taxpayer pounds at the likes of that guest helps us absolve ourselves of the need to really make a collective effort to take the tough, affirmative action required. Are we throwing a pound in the collection box to buy ourselves peace of mind instead of throwing ourselves into the efforts really required to fix the problem?

I just wish those who – completely well-meaningly – try to help that lad through endless giving and blind support could see the effects of such indulgence with their own eyes. Blindly, naively, they hope they are doing 'the right thing' to help those less fortunate – but they so patently are not! This system is not right, it is wrong, and our country will truly go to the dogs if we don't wake up, get a grip and revert to a common-sense system that is there only for those in need and not just for anyone who wants money but does not want to earn it despite being perfectly able to do so.

It really is crunch time in Britain now. Unemployment numbers are rising fast as the credit crunch, recession and anticipated depression takes a hold. Good, willing and able workers who have done nothing but work hard and contribute to the system year after year are finding themselves out of work through no fault of their own. Those people are perfectly entitled and should feel perfectly at ease with taking what help the government can give them through a difficult time that was not of their making. How galling it must be for them too, then, when they get to see examples of the system being wilfully abused by those who don't deserve a penny!

What this young man and so many like him need is not another hand-out, not another fortnightly free pass to the bottom of a bottle, nor the endlessly willing and overly benign indulgence of a society propping up some to the extent that they never need stand on their own two feet. No, what they *need* – really need in so many ways they don't yet realise – is the self-esteem, the kick-start and self-motivation that comes from earning one's own crust. In short: GET A JOB! But why would they? What possible incentive is there for them to think seriously or work hard at anything when so much is just given to them without condition or contract?

This lad struck me as the sort who might just have struggled as I did in the classroom. He probably left school with no qualifications and squandered what talents he had whilst pursuing other pleasures. He wouldn't be the first, but what worries me about these sorts of people is just how motivated they might ever be to make a decent life for themselves and their families. At school, despite many setbacks, he probably thought he would be OK. Many from his estate always had been (this I know because he told us) and lots more always would be. He, like so many of his forebears and contemporaries, knew that the Great British Taxpayer would be there to bail him out. There was no need for him to do well at school, for he knew that at sixteen he could leave and have society dance to his tune. Have a couple of kids, get given a house and free money to spend each week on booze and partying (and not the young children who had, in part, facilitated his passport to such riches). I'll not address the lack of parental guidance or the willing acquiescence of those all around who may have endorsed or encouraged such limited ambitions. Here I will concentrate not on the families who fail individuals but more on the system that sickeningly sponsors such failure. A system that has been telling him for years to pick a bottle over a job.

So on the one hand I can hardly blame him for his lack of ambition. To a misguided sixteen-year-old, I'm sure the two stark options he faced were very clear and very easy to choose between. On the one hand he could work hard, sweat and toil all day for a reasonable amount of money. On the other he could sit around, do nothing but party and be given the same amount of cash by the government each week to go and play with. On top of all this, Option 2 might no doubt come with the added allure of a free house, around which he could invite every like-minded soul who also thinks getting pissed and having sex each day sounds far more fun than actually working for a living. It's no wonder he laughed and sneered at me. I mean, on paper there isn't a choice to make. Working hard to get less *net* than you are guaranteed to be given for doing absolutely nothing. It's just a no-brainer, isn't it?

In June 2008 the government's own claimant figures for the jobless in this country stood at 840,000, up 15,500 on the month before in the biggest monthly increase since 1992. The credit crunch is biting hard, and these jobless figures have pushed past 2 million (with 3 million widely predicted to be just around the corner), as I write this, I doubt whether the likes of that misguided boy are feeling the pinch quite like the rest of the country. After all, he was content to do nothing and pick up the freebies in the good times, and a change in fortunes for the rest of the nation won't change his habits in a hurry. Nearly one million people on this island are claiming unemployment benefits, but the total number of unemployed in June 2008 was 1.62 million and rising. Beyond that I read that there are 4.5 million people in this country currently being propped up in some way by state hand-outs.

I've read the stats and I've met people on my show who have proved to me, beyond any doubt, that taking place in this country is an almost gluttonous rape of our tax-funded resources. Perhaps unsurprisingly, a system so ripe for abuse is systematically being targeted by sprawling pockets of the population who by now should have been told NO! If you believe that all of the 4.5 million people currently relying on state help are actually genuinely entitled to it, then you are living in Cloud Cuckoo Land. I see with my own eyes what most only read about in the papers. I see families every morning where successive generations are content to stay on benefits for life. They don't even conceive of another option or any way in which they might better themselves through actually earning what they get each week. I'll repeat that I know there are a great many people who are fully deserving of the state help they receive. But I also believe there are a great many more conning the system, prefer-ring to be spoon-fed for free while the rest of us pick up the bill.

I dread to think how much money has been wasted by successive governments on benefit scroungers who should simply have been told, 'No, GET A JOB!' Some figures I have read suggest that the annual cost of paying just Incapacity Benefits has reached £16 BILLION! SIXTEEN BILLION – that's more than it will cost to stage the bloody Olympics, and a figure that only covers this country's costs for ONE year of supporting those 'on the sick'. That doesn't even take account of the extra millions doled out by the state via the Jobseekers Allowance to some I can't see as anything more than an undeserving scourge badly in need of a stern lesson. One government think-tank estimates the number of jobless in this country to be about 3.1 million but, tellingly, even they acknowledge that it should be possible to get approxi-mately 1.4 million of those off the benefits bill and back into work. If that's what the people usually charged with massaging the figures into something more palatable for the electorate are saying, what other conclusion is there to draw?

One proposal being put forward to combat this festering problem is that private firms should come in and take responsibility for the long-term unemployed. In essence they want the private sector to take on the 'risk' associated with funding the long-term unemployed in return for the promise of a juicy payout if they achieve the currently unthinkable and get them back into work. I read that the companies taking part could expect a hefty fee for getting someone off benefits and back into work for any period of longer than three years.

I'd be up for that on the one hand, letting the private sector have a go where the public purse and government policy is obviously failing, but to be honest I don't really think it goes far enough. I agree that something radical has to be done, but I think the people in Whitehall either ignore or just can't fathom the wanton opportunism of those who are fit to work but simply choose not to. Can they not see it, or do they choose not to believe such an attitude exists? They think the system we have at the moment somehow imprisons people on benefits. Government advisor David Freud asserted that ours is a 'system that sends 2.64 million people into a form of economic house arrest and encourages them to stay at home and watch daytime TV'. He goes on to say that we 'do nothing' for these people, before proposing the public-private partnership outlined above. Well, I'm sorry, Mr Freud, but the reasoning behind what is actually a very good idea is acutely flawed by a lack of awareness of the true nature of some of the sorts of people he wants to help. Far from being imprisoned in their homes with their forty-two-inch, flat-screen, wall-mounted televisions, I think Mr Freud needs to realise that a great many of these people are *willing* 'inmates'.

The majority of the guests I have met and berated for defrauding the system that the rest of us fund are not chained to their sofas by economic misfortune. No, some choose to be there because getting a job is literally too much like hard work, and the wages they might earn would not nearly begin to cover what they can 'make' for signing on and then lazing about the house with a can in one hand and a fag (or joint, if some of my guests are to be believed) in the other!

Mr Freud's idea could provide part of a solution to a small part of the problem, but he misses the point completely if he thinks private firms should 'take responsibility' for the prospects of the long-term unemployed. They should bloody well take responsibility for themselves, and we should all take responsibility for the overhauling of a welfare system so geared to help those who show no inclination to help themselves.

We need to reinvent the welfare system so that this country's citizens might reinvent themselves and, by turn, reinvigorate the ethics, morals and values so rapidly being eroded. If I were in charge, I would not just hand benefits out, I'd make any claimant work for what they were given. I learned long ago that 'you don't get something for nothing', and I think today's tranche of undeserving benefit recipients need a long lesson in the same. If someone is genuinely physically or mentally unable to work, fair enough. They should be given their entitlement whilst being regularly assessed until such time as they are able to return to the workforce. For those unemployed with no illness or condition that prevents them from working but job-seeking all the same, I would give them their allowance but only on the condition that they work for it. Why should we all have to hand over ever-higher proportions of our wage packets to people unwilling to lift one finger for the privilege of getting money? If you are able to work and yet can't find work, you could still perform some civic duty of benefit to your community. Whether it be helping deliver meals on wheels, picking up litter, mending broken fences or painting the gates at the local school, I think that those taking from the state should be obliged to put a little something back. Don't just sit about and expect me to pay you for nothing, get off your backside and make some contribution, in whatever way you are able, for the resources you continue to drain.

I guarantee that if you confronted some that I have challenged on the show with such a proposition, they would soon change their tune. And everyone would benefit, even and especially them. Let's look at my young friend from earlier again. If he knew throughout his schooling that there was to be no pot of gold at the end of the dropout's rainbow, he might, just might, have thought twice about squandering his education. If faced with the prospect of being forced to pick up litter, scrape up chewing gum or remove graffiti for his fortnightly benefit cheque, he might have begun to consider the other career paths available to him. If everyone was obliged to work in this way for minimal benefit payments, the penny might drop and more out there might think: 'Hang on a minute, I'm working anyway, so why don't I get a proper job, a proper wage, a proper life and a proper future?' As things stand, he is better off financially not doing or attempting anything, and society, not to mention his partner and children, suffers as a result.

Just think of the improvement to everyone's circumstances if the above model worked as it should. One young man gets his self-esteem, self-respect and sense of self-worth back by earning his living and providing for his family. That family get back a father and a role model to replace the arrogant drunk with the roving eye they are currently stuck with. They would have more money and more options to make better provisions for their own children. The cycle would be broken, there would be more money going towards the improvement of the state through his taxes, less money being drained from the state via his benefits, and even the local community would have benefited from all of his hard work with paintbrush in one hand and bin bag in the other as he considered other career options whilst still claiming.

There are millions currently being wasted on state dependants who have neither been told nor encouraged to follow a path that might lead them away from a life where handouts are a family's only source of income. The system seems – as ever – weighted in favour of those who want to do nothing, and the policies currently in place are just being taken advantage of by so many who simply can't be bothered. I think those millions could be better spent on schemes which help the underqualified – those who want to work but have genuinely fallen into a rut from which they are struggling to emerge – back onto the ladder via training and education initiatives. Training or educating someone whilst they look for work is surely better than solely throwing money at them? With the right skills and learning in place, the chances of a return to work being a permanent one must surely increase, and that can only be to the benefit of everyone, can't it?

To accompany these various ideas must come the serious and thorough checks required to police them. I read recently of a government proposal that would oblige all claimants to face a compulsory medical, to properly assess if they are fit to work. I can't believe there have been objections in some quarters. This is just common sense, pure and simple. If I said I could not work because of some illness or condition, I would have no problem having that checked out by the authority I was asking to keep and support me whilst I was out of work. It would be the least I'd expect to do.

I also agree with a proposal to take back hand-outs from the drug addicts who shoot every benefit payment they receive straight into their arms or into their crack pipe. Far better to put that money towards treating their addiction than blindly continuing to subsidise it. Obviously it might be some time before any addict can return to work, so they will need supporting. But why give them further temptation to return to drugs with free money when we could instead implement a voucher scheme that would at least see their food needs covered? Food stamps might sound a bit draconian, but guaranteeing someone food in their belly has got to be better than giving them the means to go out and score again.

And why not make better use of private recruitment firms to match currently unemployed but suitably qualified candidates to whatever placements they have on their books? I'd go further and force people to take the jobs they were qualified for if they had been out of work for long enough. If they didn't and there was no good reason why they could not begin a life of work away from benefits, then I would stop the benefits altogether.

All of these measures and the hundreds of others that spring to mind are all well and good. They would undoubtedly have an impact, and I believe we would soon see the drip-drip of cultural and societal change in this country as attitudes changed and people's lots began to improve. I look at people of my parents' generation – indeed I receive hundreds of letters from the senior citizens whose values should form the moral backbone of this country – and they continue to be aghast at how far everything they fought for in a world war just sixty-odd years ago seems to have slipped away. They have noted the greed and indolence that has taken root over the past three decades in particular. They regularly complain to me, and rightly so, that they put their very lives on the line to fight for a certain way of life, and yet all they see now are kids who can't even be bothered to fight for themselves wreaking terror in the streets. They see the freedoms they paid such a high price for being squandered by wasters who can't even bring themselves to get up, go out and find work. Sheer shame, these brave patriots tell me, would have prevented them from giving up on points of personal pride so easily.

My own epiphany happened shortly after my fourteenth birthday. That light bulb suddenly went on in my head and I decided that I no longer wanted to be an also-ran at school or in life. Gradually it dawned on me that I had to find my voice, and I had to attack each day to see what it might bring for me. I did not have the prodigious talents of my brother but being quiet and reserved in class had proved no great template for success, so I resolved to scrap as hard as I could for whatever was out there. I soon psyched myself up to tackle every day at school with a gusto, purpose and determination to not be beaten. In short, I got competitive. And, bit by bit, things improved for me.

I soon learned that those who so regularly ridiculed me were just as fallible themselves. They had faults too, and each provided a comic seam I could mine for myself. Every time they took the piss out of me, I thought I'd just take the piss back. And I did. Awkwardly and clumsily at first, never particularly wittily, but always I answered back those who sniped at me and gradually I forced myself to the edge of social circles that had previously been closed to me. I gained recognition and some acceptance purely on the back of standing up to be counted. I fought fire with fire and tried my best to win in any situation. I made an effort, worked hard, stopped taking the easy way out – and it paid off. I continued to be awful in French and maths but I could feel a difference within me. I had a fire in my belly that has sustained me through every job I have ever had, and still drives me today.

Having eventually scraped the qualifications I required to enrol at Froebel College in London, I threw myself into student life. I decided to work hard and strove to make the best of whatever talents I could bring to bear on any assignment. I wanted to make something of myself, and I also wanted to reward my parents with something tangible for the investment they had made in me and my education. Pride played a part in the decisions I took, as much as the drive that carried them. I did not want to let Mum or Dad down and I had no wish to return to life as the shy, quiet underachiever too scared to attempt anything with his life.

For every modicum of success I achieved, my spine straightened a little. I could puff out my chest a little more, walk a little taller, and feel a little less guilty when talking to the parents who always had such high hopes of me. That pride and drive is self-perpetuating. You taste a little success, you make someone a little proud of you and you want to do it again. That is what I try to get across to all those who show no inclination to do anything much more than sit around, scrounge and procreate. If they just gave themselves a chance, just backed themselves and made a little effort, they too could buck the trend and start finding themselves getting 'lucky' in a way that so many of their peers will never understand until they begin to lift their own fingers too.

That desire to scrap for every chance I got was the thing that evolved into the work ethic that spurs me on today. The need to fight for every opportunity soon morphed into a willingness to work for every penny. My first-ever job had seen me working each Saturday in Marks & Spencer for £1.75 per hour. My ambitions were not lofty, my duties were not complex and my status was not exalted in any way (I was in charge of bananas!). But I was sixteen, employed, and I took a good deal of pride in how I stacked and presented these bananas in that shop each weekend. After university and a pretty predictable 2:2 degree in history and sociology, I was all set for the world of permanent work. I had wanted to take a sabbatical at Froebel and stay on in an administrative capacity. I had really started to find and enjoy myself by this point, and I ran for election to the Students Union. As with all things in my life, I was desperate to win, and when my place was confirmed and the £5,000 salary that went with it assured, I naturally wanted it. But my parents were not so enamoured. They had already seen one son waste his talents and eschew the world of work, and I'm sure they thought history might repeat itself if I allowed myself to linger too long as a student. And so it was that I headed into the world of work, armed with only average qualifications but certificates that nonetheless 'guaranteed' their holder a far greater chance of finding work.

Apparently, in 2003, 88 per cent of those with a degree were employed whilst 50 per cent of those with no qualifications at all were unemployed. Now, I don't think that those of us holding degrees necessarily make better bets for prospective employers. Some jobs or vocations just don't need fifteen years of hitting the books as a prerequisite for suitability or success. What they will need, though, is a level of commitment that is commensurate with those invested by students up and down the land every day. I think that the 88 per cent 'lucky' enough to be in work in 2003 were there as much by dint of their personality as by virtue of any qualifications they possessed. Most will have been prepared to start anywhere and work their way up. They would be prepared to work long hours for low pay without wanting, far less expecting, any of the benefits doled out to those who do nothing.

TV is almost entirely made up of people who worked years for free whilst also holding down other jobs as waiters, tele-sales agents or call-centre operatives to pay the bills. They worked two jobs, day and night, just to gain experience whilst waiting for their break, and they stuck at it because of a passion to be better that should beat in every one of us. It is not a question of luck that they stuck it out, making tea and being ignored for month after month without even having the consolation of a pay packet to fall back on, it was their attitude and application that saw them through. I will always acknowledge the real luck and privileges that have played their part in my own success, but since the penny dropped for me at fourteen it has been the hard work I have invested on a daily basis that has made it so much easier to accept that perhaps I have earned just a tiny amount of the undoubted good fortune that has come my way. Certainly those I work with have done more for their own fortunes than anyone who thought better of schooling or working as a way forward. And anyone who scraps for every penny they earn is surely fulfilling far more of their esteem needs than anyone content to just take what they can from the rest of us.

I fervently believe there is passion and ability in everyone. Somewhere inside all of us there is a talent too. We just have to be prepared to put the hours in to harvest it. Some don't find it until they're forty, but it is in there somewhere. Lucky I may have been, but it didn't seem that way when I was washing cars on a car lot at sixteen or bored out of my mind as a filing clerk during one particular summer holiday at British Telecom/Yellow Pages. I stuck those jobs out because I knew it was the right thing to do and that it was important to be earning my own keep in society. I knew instinctively that I had taken enough off my parents and that I didn't want to take any more from them. I wanted to start putting something back, or at the very least leave them to keep everything they earned for the first time in their lives. I dreamt of earning and being more, of course, but I would never throw in the towel and live off state charity just because going to work isn't always a bed of roses. It wouldn't be called work if every day was a holiday, so sometimes we all just have to get our heads down and get on with it.

I meandered and drifted through many jobs that just weren't right or just weren't me. I spent just a matter of weeks at Bain-Clarkson the insurance brokerage and even less time at Billiton-Eindhoven, the commodities brokerage based in Fenchurch Street. They basically traded a variety of things from precious metals to everyday food products. I remember feeling very important as I flew around the City dressed to the nines in a sleek suit, Churches shoes and crisp Thomas Pink shirts, with a coronation chicken sandwich in one hand and a leather pouch in the other. In truth I might have been having the time of my life but I was merely a lowly runner who didn't ever really understand what he was supposed to be doing! I guess the bubble burst when the boss called me in one morning and unceremoniously dumped me, when I ignorantly asked, thinking that everything a brokerage traded must be kept somewhere out the back: 'So where do you keep all the gold then?'

Thank God I then found out that I was actually very good in the world of professional recruitment. I always know that, should all of this end tomorrow, I could go back and carve a decent living out for me and my family by finding jobs and then helping companies to fill them – not that anybody seems to be recruiting right now! Peter Thompson signed me first for Newman Personnel on Aldgate High Street. This was an unbelievable time for me and one that perfectly suited the competitive zeal I had now trained myself to bring to each day. It was most definitely a work-hard, play-hard environment, and it felt as though we worked twenty hours a day before partying for eighteen hours each night! I worked there for three years and made a lot of money placing people in jobs. It was there I got a real feel for working with people. I enjoyed the face-to-face nature of dealing with someone up front, and avoided the phone if possible. I took it upon myself to walk people to their interviews, always keeping spare pairs of black socks in my desk for those days when candidates would arrive, expecting to go to the appointment I had just made for them in horrible white sports socks!

I moved about the recruitment industry, eventually ending up in the West Country, determined to show them that I would be their best recruiter yet by dazzling them with the techniques I'd learned in London. Maybe I got lucky here too (I know I worked bloody hard as well), because in my first week I filled five jobs. Whereas others sat about, filled forms and waited for the phones to ring, I attacked what was needed to be done to get things moving. I feel no shame in admitting that I wanted to beat the colleagues around me. I wanted to be on top of any leader-board there was and, knowing just how average my academic successes had been, knew I probably had to work twice as hard to achieve it.

This led to a quite lengthy and, I might say, successful career in sales; one in which my competitive instincts would always serve me well. From radio sales I eventually moved into radio presenting and then TV, both industries where I would need that sheer will-to-win just to survive. But more of that another time.

Obviously I am not advocating that everyone should follow my own career path. What I am urging, though, is that everyone should look within themselves and challenge themselves as I did at fourteen. It is unrealistic to push for everyone to go to university, despite the fact a degree will apparently improve the holder's chances of getting a job. There will always be low educational achievers, but there will also always be jobs that do not necessarily require their incumbents to be the next Carol Vorderman.

It is true that young people who do badly in school *tend* to do badly in the fight for worthwhile work. However, the point that most needs addressing here is the fact that not enough are fighting for work. Not everyone in this world is going to be a high-achieving student. Similarly not everyone in life is cut out to conform to the nine-to-five lifestyle of office work that is fine for many. Some talents are more suited to vocational choices, and this is what I try to get across to those who complain to me that being poor in the classroom means they won't ever have a chance to really make something of themselves. I try to impress upon them that they can achieve all they want to by being the best possible postman, milkman, butcher or whatever.

For those with a spark but no guidance, I always say there is nothing to stop them becoming the next entrepreneur or budding millionaire. This country has plenty of hugely successful businessmen who all failed at school but have since gone on to make fortunes with their own businesses. But NONE of them ever did so by sitting on their backside and waiting for opportunity to come knocking on their door. They found what they were good at, worked at it, and kept on slogging until they got their rewards. If they suffered setbacks on the way – and we all do – they learned from them before picking themselves up, dusting themselves down and starting all over again. With each attempt and each new working day they got a little better and felt a bit more pride in themselves. I know this because I did it myself. I just wish I could do more to light that spark in the vast swathes of wasted talents out there who are not even bothering to give themselves a shot at their own dreams.

Nobody had particularly high hopes of Jeremy Kyle, least of all Jeremy Kyle himself. That did not change until I decided to make an effort. The change in me was not instantaneous, but it did bring its rewards. One teacher, Mr Firebrace, once said of me that 'Kyle acts and then he thinks!' That propensity to jump in has only done me a few favours but the accompanying competitiveness which always burns so bright in me before rational thought kicks in, does tell me one thing at least: I know I'll always be prepared to act. I got where I am by having the guts and summoning the courage to act. I fought hard to change my circumstances for the better, and that hadn't always been the case. I only wish a few more of the people I talk to could one day look in the mirror and resolve as I did to give the life they have the best shot they can. I mean, if I can do it, surely anyone can.

8

Put Something on the End of it . . .

How I'm not the poster boy for Durex, I'll never know. Perhaps they think that plastering my mug all over their packets might put any potential punters off having sex altogether. That can be the only reason they haven't yet sought out my agent, because I am yet to meet anyone who bangs on about the need for contra-bloody-ception as much as I do. So regularly do I bang this particular drum that apparently there are students out there who have created drinking games based around the amount of times I will chide some feckless individual or other for not having considered contraception before sex! I am told that our 'overworked, underfunded' academics, the future backbone of our great nation, will sit and watch my show with twenty-four cans of lager in the corner. If I say 'contraception' or 'put something on the end of it', the players of the game are obliged to immediately take a lusty swig from their can! They say there's nothing like hard work and, trust me, that is nothing like hard work, but I guess it at least highlights the regularity with which I am forced to fall back on the same, simple message. What does it say about the amount I have to repeat myself when the few students not in bed at 9.25 in the morning see a middle-aged man ranting about contraception as a convenient excuse to begin a breakfast drinking binge? 'Sod the dissertation, make mine a bowl of Stella and I reckon we'll be pissed before the pubs open!'

The message that the University Fraternity of Fledgling

Future Alcoholics might use to kick off that morning's bout of binge-drinking is probably just as applicable to them as it is to anyone I am confronting about their own ignorant stupidity on my stage. For as long as I have breath in my body, I will forever preach about taking precautions and the practising of safe sex, because I see far too many of the consequences for those who've had a roll in the hay with nothing but a thought for the moment. I'm no killjoy, but it seems to me that every house party or pub car park is full to the brim of people throwing themselves at each other before catching the last bus home. And I'm not just making this up. Oh no, I'm told this each and every morning by someone seeking my help because they've had a baby or caught some hideous infection they don't much want.

I've already spoken about my particular problem with kids having kids. If they were the only problem we might have a chance, but the big picture suggests that everyone's at it, with no one seemingly bothered by the simple scientific possibility that casual, unprotected sex might lead to something far more significant than another notch on the bedpost. I am regularly stunned by the research notes I read for the show. Some of the 'parties' being held every weekend by teenagers up and down the country sound more like orgies. The rampant, thoughtless pleasure-seeking that is prevalent among those who give themselves so little chance of a proper stake in society apparently knows no bounds. There are no rules, conventions or social courtesies that can't be broken at these parties. They sound like the sort of 'anything goes' bashes the Romans used to be famed for, though the specific indiscretions, not to mention the prolific promiscuity, that my guests regularly talk about might even have forced a blush from Caligula himself!

My eldest daughter is eighteen and so about the same age as many of the people who come to my show having got themselves into some bother on the back of sexual encounters they neither planned for nor cared about until sometime after the night they took place. Shock just wouldn't do justice to the fears that would grip me were my daughter to tell me that she too was indulging in the sorts of vices that seem so commonplace and 'normal' to so many of my guests. Young girls of sixteen, seventeen and eighteen talk to me without any hint of shame or embarrassment about the fact that they have been regularly having group sex. Not even a flicker of discomfiture passes through them as they detail on national television how they were passed around two, three, sometimes four blokes on what was just an average Saturday-night house party on their estate. There is none of the awkwardness or resignation I would feel if I was confessing to the world that I had thoughtlessly contracted some pretty disgusting sexually transmitted infection. And I am still stunned when such people look up at me with seemingly no care in the world, only offering a shrug of the shoulders when asked: 'Do you know who the father of your baby might be?' Might be. Not, 'Do you know which of these two men is the father of your baby?' No, I am talking about people I meet every day who see nothing particularly surprising or abnormal about the fact that their progeny's paternity must be decided by the DNA equivalent of a lucky dip. People who put it around so willingly, so thoughtlessly and with such little self-respect that they must phone and get a television-show researcher to help them sift through myriad sexual partners and possible fathers, searching for the truth like a couple of cowboys panning for gold.

I mean, for God's sake, I can understand that some people of whatever age will get too pissed or too carried away by the moment to properly 'stop, look and listen' before crossing the road to sexual congress. I'll never stop that, but I've never met any friend or colleague who can't actually remember how many people they might have slept with the night before. I've met a few who can't recall the specific name or job title of their previous night's conquest, struggle as they might through the crashing cymbals of a brass-band hangover, but never have I known anyone who nonchalantly forgets the NUMBER of people they slept with the night before. Am I living on another planet, or is that just not normal?

Again it may seem as if I am banging on about a particular section of society, a problem that does not affect the rest of us. However, the truth is that the problems associated with people having casual, unprotected sex are on the rise all across the country.

I am not proposing anything radical in what I say each morning to the latest mum with a fatherless child they barely want, or to anyone who thinks that their contraction of another STI was down to mere bad luck. No, I chime precisely with all government advice and basic common sense on this one. The Health Protection Agency spells out the patently obvious when it advises sexually active young people to 'have fewer sexual partners and avoid overlapping sexual relationships'. In a victory for all lager-swigging students with a penchant for daytime TV everywhere, the HPA also advises that such people 'use condoms when having sex with a new partner and continue to do so until you have both been screened'. You see, CON-TRA-CEP-TION, I'm not just making this stuff up! One of the HPA's final messages to sexually active young people is to 'get screened for chlamydia every year and whenever you have a new partner'. It is that final piece of advice that is causing me some concern, because it is advice that is not getting through until far too late.

Some of the people I meet could probably benefit from a mobile GUM lab on permanent twenty-four-hour standby. Fearing, as I often do, that at forty-three years of age I may just be too old or out of touch to truly grasp what is going on with the youngsters who seem so careless in the face of the very real consequences of casual sex, I asked around my office and more than a few friends. Most of them had barely heard of the GUM (genitourinary medicine) clinics that I so frequently learn my guests have been obliged to patronise. They, like me, got themselves 'checked out' some time ago and have since settled into monogamous relationships. I am also happy to report that those who told me they were still enjoying the single life were very much in the habit of practising safe sex. The message has got through to them, but then I guess they would tell me that, wouldn't they?

Before I go on to explain the importance of contraception and enlighten everyone as to just how prevalent the problems following unsafe sex are in this country, I must first risk being labelled a hypocrite with what some may consider a quite shocking confession: I NEVER USED TO WEAR A CONDOM! There, I said it. I am not talking about the experiences that have spawned me three children, nor am I talking about the monogamous sexual relations that have taken place over the course of my two marriages. No, I am referring to the times when I, just like a lot of the guests I meet on my show, was a young single man with far too much testosterone in his system to resist certain temptations on offer. I have been in situations where, as my guests so often tell me, 'one thing led to another', or one drink led to one night and a condom never made it onto the agenda. I know what it is like; I even understand the argument put forward by some blokes who say that wearing a condom spoils the fun because 'it feels different' or 'takes the feeling away'. I get all that, and indeed bought into all that for a lot longer than I should have, but something made me see sense in a way that no rant from any confrontational TV host/authority-figure lecture ever could: HIV-AIDS.

I surely don't have to tell anyone what impact the killer

disease HIV-AIDS has had on the world in the last twenty
or thirty years, and we all watch with concern about how
HIV-AIDS is ripping through Africa today. The HIV-AIDS
campaigns doing the rounds in the Eighties were sufficient
to grab my attention and curb my carelessness. Seemingly
out of nowhere the issue came to prominence and I was as
compelled as anyone by what I was being told. Despite having
been keen to view myself as some irresistible lothario, the
whole AIDS phenomenon stopped me dead in my tracks.
The more I learned, the more convinced I became of the
need for contraception with any future sexual partner. I was
once so paranoid (and more than a little drunk) that I even
thought about 'double-bagging' myself before a certain sexual
encounter. Double-bagging was how one particularly attain-
able and sexually prolific ex-colleague described his preferred
ritual of wearing not one but two condoms before he insti-
gated intercourse. Even he, a man with the morals of the
most wild and stray of alley cats, knew he could not go about
his quasi-gigolo lifestyle without proper precautions in place.
And trust me, if the message could get through to him, I
have to believe it can get through to anyone!

Nowadays, if I was a single young man and the opportunity presented itself, I wouldn't dream of having sex without
putting something on the end of it. As I keep saying in this
book, those who know better, do better, and those Eighties
HIV-AIDS ads told me all I wanted to know about carrying
on the way I had been to that point, thank you very much.
I just wish that I could be as effective at getting the message
through today as the advertisers were back then.

Perhaps it is the fact that HIV-AIDS is not a new issue
any more. We've all been living with its potential peril for so
long that perhaps some of the fear has just evaporated. Is it
a bit like the terrorism threat we face? When the Twin Towers
came crashing down, or when the 7/7 bombers struck in

London, everyone thought twice about boarding a plane or any form of public transport. If the news is to be believed, the same level of threat remains but because we live with that threat every day, the actual fear that once drove us to stop going about our daily business has rescinded. As Graham always tells me, the logical part of our brain has regained control of the emotional part of our brain and we are once more persuaded of the safety, if not just the necessity, of boarding whatever means of transport we need to get to work or go on holiday. We are acclimatised to the dangers and no longer put off by them. Having lived with the threat of HIV-AIDS for so long, but maybe without having lost anyone close to it, perhaps today's young think that this killer won't get them. Worse, maybe they just don't care. Maybe certain lives are so miserable or meaningless that the short-term gratification of having sex is worth the risk of playing the percentages. Thank God for marriage and monogamy because, if the stats are to be believed, it's not just HIV-AIDS that the single, sexually active and/or promiscuous have to worry about today.

By and large, the message seems to have got through to people of my age and slightly younger. I would also fully expect that people of my parents' age are sufficiently well informed or otherwise motivated to not still be putting themselves at risk! Obviously the older you get, the more likely you are to approach sex in a mature way. The chances are that people of pensionable age are not running around having kids or spraying nasty diseases about the place with the ignorant abandon typical of most sixteen- to twenty-four-year-olds I meet – the British rock music establishment notwithstanding, of course.

The statistics bear that out. According to the figures, sixteen- to twenty-four-year-olds are still the group most at risk of being diagnosed with a sexually transmitted infection. They accounted for 65 per cent of all chlamydia cases, 50 per cent of genital warts and 50 per cent of gonorrhoea infections diagnosed in UK GUM clinics in 2007.

The most commonly sexually transmitted infection in young people is genital chlamydia. Of the 270,729 screened under the age of twenty-five in 2007, 9.5 per cent of women and 8.4 per cent of men were found to be positive. A further 79,557 diagnoses of genital chlamydia infection were made among young people in those same GUM clinics, a rise of 7 per cent on the year before. The statistics are shocking, if not quite as worrying as the upward trend for infection in our young. That said, what is most worrying for me is the attitude of the young that seem so regularly to get themselves infected. I can't even hold the government to account on this one. I can't claim that the word isn't being spread: it is, as are the diseases – it's just that the message isn't getting through.

From my experience I can see that people hear the words or even see the consequences but they just don't care enough to take note. Last week I met a young female guest on the show. She said without any hint of humour or irony that yes, she had had a few STIs in her time but 'that the only one she had right now was chlamydia'. That wasn't so bad in her world because she'd had it before and besides, 'Everyone round ours has it at some point.' What do you do when you hear that from someone? I'm ashamed to say I had to stifle a laugh because what she was saying was almost too ridiculous to be true. It was as if she was in complete denial, living in complete ignorance.

That this young woman's atrocious attitude to personal protection had been allowed, almost encouraged, to develop as it had by family or society is another matter that goes to the heart of the problem. However, for those who are still unsure as to what an acceptable or unacceptable STI is, let me be clear: THERE ARE NO ACCEPTABLE STIs. We should never get to a state where we just accept that people are going to pass around potentially killer diseases without taking any personal responsibility to stop their spread. That is just wrong. For those still labouring under the misapprehension that chlamydia is in some way a lesser infection, one more palatable or permissible to contract, perhaps, let me just point out the following: chlamydia's bacteria can infect the cervix, urethra, rectum, throat and eyes! Doesn't that sound lovely? In women, symptoms include abdominal pain, bleeding after sex, bleeding between periods, unusual vaginal discharge or pain when passing urine. And all that is just from something some people are apparently happy to announce to a whole nation that they have, whilst also offering their thoughts on the harmlessness of it! To be frank, just reading those symptoms makes my stomach turn – it certainly couldn't make anyone feel sexy, could it?, but beyond those distinctly unedifying physiological possibilities is the harsher reality that if you did catch chlamydia, you might also have caught something far worse.

Let's consider something else. Beyond chlamydia there's the delightfully descriptive infection of genital warts, which surely leave little to the imagination. These were the second most commonly diagnosed sexual contagion among young people in UK GUM clinics in 2007. The 49,250 cases of genital warts detected in the sixteen-to-twenty-four age group also represented an 8 per cent rise on the 2006 figures. These fleshy lumps, all gnarled and knobbly just where you might want to be looking your most impressive, are not just found around your genitals. Oh no, these little things often spread to the fingers, mouth and throat. Perfect for Hallowe'en and anyone wanting to dress all green and Grotbags, but maybe not so appealing when thrown into profile by the romantic candlelight of any first date. From first glance you'd know that taking things further would lead to a sharing of much, much more than the bill.

As if to prove my earlier point about the fear of HIV-AIDS fading away in our young, it was also reported that 702 young people were diagnosed with HIV in the UK in 2007. Eleven per cent of all new HIV diagnoses are made up from those in the sixteen-to-twenty-four age group. That stuns me. How can such a significant proportion of today's young have escaped the warnings that so petrified me way back in the Eighties? Why hasn't that message been passed on by parents from my generation? Why hasn't it been listened to and heeded by the young people of the next generation? How much time and how many lives have been needlessly wasted? That is probably the aspect that frustrates me the most about these entirely preventable statistics: the sheer waste of it all. I often feel as if I am wasting my time trying to get the message across to people who just do not seem as though they will ever care. But me daily banging my head against a brick wall is nothing compared to the loss and what-might-have-beens being needlessly suffered by families up and down the land. After all, I only stand to lose my patience.

I have highlighted the worst, or at least the most common STIs being passed about like a ball in some sick game of catch. It really is like being back in the playground. Back in my schooldays, the age-old game of 'it' or 'tag' was spun to incorporate new levels of jeopardy for those playing. We used to play 'You've Got the Lurgy'. The rules were the same, the only difference being that when you were made 'it', everyone knew you had the lurgy – an unimaginably horrible disease, only fathomable to the muckiest of children's minds, that the recipient felt obliged to get rid of at the earliest opportunity. If you were the last one to receive the lurgy before lessons resumed after 'playtime', you would have a stigma, an almost tangible whiff of nastiness about you (think how a cartoonist would make a pile of dung look smelly by drawing those wavy lines above it and you'll see what only us kids playing the game back then could see when someone 'got the lurgy'). The lurgy infection came with an almost perceptible odour that hung around you and would last until you were released back to the playground, once more free to pass the lurgy on to someone else. That's what today's young are doing now. They are just passing on these different 'lurgies' with the same ease and frivolity as kids in a playground playing 'it' – and none seem to know or care about the consequences that WILL catch up with them eventually.

But it is not just the young. Sixteen- to twenty-four-year-olds are by far the worst age group, but I get regular calls to my show from many a thirty-something demanding their partner take a lie-detector test after apparently contracting an STI despite never having cheated – an 'immaculate infection' until a polygraph proves otherwise.

The infections I am talking about are rife. They are everywhere and offer further compelling evidence of how standards are slipping in a society that ostensibly demands more from its supposedly progressive citizens. That irony has not been lost on me as I sit here wading through reports on STIs. Aside from chlamydia and genital warts, there were also reported increases in gonorrhoea (682 cases per 100,000), with rates still a third higher than in 1998. Gonorrhoea?! Didn't that die out in the Renaissance, when men ran around in tights with wigs and make-up? Gonorrhoea, for the record, is a particularly nasty infection that can also cause infertility and long-term pelvic pain. Men can develop painful erections and secondary infections in the testicles and prostate gland. Inflammation of joints can occur and, if you get a particularly pungent dose, liver disease, meningitis, or even a life-threatening inflammation of the heart might be diagnosed. I note the recent resurgence of men in tights and metrosexual males wearing 'guyliner' or 'manscara', and wonder if we might not be coming full circle. In some of the people I meet, there certainly seems to be that same sense of hedonism that was so rife in the moneyed homes and whorehouses of 250 years ago.

I had to look a little deeper into this research just to find something positive that might quell my increasing anxiety – and there is some hope. People of Great Britain, I am proud to announce that in 2008 reports of SYPHILIS are down to six cases per 100,000 – way down from 1998! Joy and rapture unconfined! Well done, everybody. In 2008 we have finally managed to reduce rates of something that I thought only randy sailors from Lord Nelson's era were ever really troubled by. Syphilis is down, and in some corner of London penises are no longer dropping off – fan-bloody-tastic, what progress!

The stats show that it is young people who are, as ever, disproportionately affected by STIs. I guess that figures. The people having most sex with most partners are the ones at most risk of getting the crabs and critters that are being passed around! But with young people accounting for only 12 per cent of the population and yet for nearly half of all STIs diagnosed in UK GUM clinics, isn't it about time that some of them please listened to me? Whether Durex sponsors me or not I really don't care, but something needs to be done to spread the word (and not the diseases), because people out there just are not protecting themselves from some pretty abominable potential consequences. Thinking about some of those STI symptoms is enough to make me want to head for the shower; they make my very blood itch. If I were to have my time over and condoms did not exist, I think complete celibacy might be a very real lifestyle option.

There's no great fix to this problem, of course. Getting

the warnings out there and hoping they might be heeded is all any of us can do. As ever, I hope that parents and teachers impress upon their families or classes the need for safe sex. Pull out the most horrific pictures of a genital wart or the lesions on a syphilitic penis and see if that has an effect. Talking about it clearly is not enough – maybe we need to shock people with the truth nowadays. Prick that teenage sense of invincibility with the realities of what will go wrong and maybe then some will sit up and take notice. A fear of dying was plenty to get a message through to me; maybe just a fear of dying with embarrassment will be enough to get through to a population increasingly obsessed with every label, look, lump and bump – all of which have to be just so, nowadays. Everyone knows the young and adventurous walk around with an air of invincibility as they start succeeding sexually. However, we have to do what we can to promote a bit more respect and responsibility; a little bit of thought to complement attitudes that will always be a little cavalier in those who've just discovered how all of their bits and bobs work. Good education is a must: it will provide a cornerstone and permanent historical reference that can always be topped up with future warnings or updates. Beyond that we just have to get over our coyness and outdated sense of reserve or embarrassment in discussing anything affecting the (sexual) health and wellbeing of the nation.

In Australia, Cyprus, Spain and all around the globe, something as simple as the proper application of sunblock is taught in schools from a very early age. Such nations can barely believe what they are seeing when each summer the next wave of invading Britishers come to turn themselves lobster-red on their beaches. The natives of these countries go about their business, apply their creams and walk home every night still basking in the glory of their golden tan. We Brits waddle off to the nearest bar, skin pulled tight and blistered after a sustained bashing from the sun, and sink the multiple beers required to make the pain go away. After two weeks we return home, liver pickled by pain relief, skin peeling and being shed like a snake, one step closer to skin cancer but still no nearer accepting the advice of all those who said: 'Cover up, use some factor fifteen.' Well, where sexual health is concerned we need to wise up and get with the programme – and quickly. As I say, let's shock today's kids with the reality of what might happen. Everyone is into the immediate and visual gratification offered up by the likes of YouTube, etc. so surely our teachers have to be given the tools that can get the message across in their preferred medium.

Sexual health isn't the only reason I want more people to wear condoms, though it is certainly reason enough. The other big problem – literally born out of the perpetual practising of unsafe sex – is babies. Unwanted babies particularly, or offspring I just know won't be raised or cared for in the way that every innocent child deserves. Would that it were only the 'kids having kids' that I had to convince to stop breeding! Again I find I am increasingly called upon to supply DNA tests to people who really should have known better. Beyond that, I have also noted a growing number of parents contacting the show to get back in touch with children they wilfully neglected or abandoned twenty or thirty years earlier. You'd be forgiven for thinking that the numbers of people admitting to past abuse or neglect of their children might be relatively small, but on my show they are large and growing.

The Jeremy Kyle Show office has to filter the vast number of calls that comes into it. The research team has to subdivide the thousands of calls we get into functional working categories to help keep a track of everyone it is in touch with. You won't be surprised to hear that there are always vast piles of numbers siphoned off under requests for 'DNA Testing' (feel free to scream 'CONTRACEPTION!' at any time), and there are obviously a high percentage of lie-detector enquiries, family feuds, neighbourly disputes, etc., that come into us. However, in the last eighteen months of filming I have noticed an inexorable increase in the amount of people calling in to complain of their abuse at the hands of parents that simply did not seem to care about the lives they had created. They call in hoping to build bridges ultimately, but the children in these types of situations are united in their desperate need to know the answer to one question: why?

I, like them, can't understand why anyone would decide to have a child only to then deliberately hurt, hinder or humiliate them. My children are THE most important things in my life, and I often struggle to comprehend even the most penitent of parents seeking to make amends. I just don't get how anyone could knowingly allow any child, not even necessarily their own, come to harm. If you are anything like me you too will find the behaviour of one mother I met recently every bit as deplorable as I did.

Lynn came onto the show to be reunited with three children whose childhoods she ostensibly admitted to having ruined. I say 'ostensibly', as there seemed to be no real acknowledgement or appreciation of the horrors she had subjected her children to. The right conciliatory words were coming out, but there was none of the emotional or spiritual connection with them that the children sitting next to her needed to hear. As so many in her situation seem to on my show, she wanted her apology or partial admission of wrongdoing to be the end of it and for everyone now to play happy families. That is clearly never going to happen, is it? If I subjected you to countless beatings, locked you in the house against your will and painfully humiliated you over a number of years, disappeared and then came back, trying to close that chapter with only a footnote that went, 'Sorry, but I was in a bad place back then, I'm OK now and I want us to be friends again,' you would likely feel inclined to punch me in the face. It's just not on, is it? How can anyone really expect to have not just their sins, but also the devastating effects of them, absolved and wiped away via one half-hearted apology that doesn't even come with a full admission of what really went on?

Most of the children on the show in that situation expect an apology as the very least their wayward parent(s) might proffer. More important to them is a proper recognition of what they had to endure at the hands of those who should have been their chief protectors in life and, moreover, of how these past events still continue to affect them in the present day. I remain positive that even from the most unpromising of beginnings, reconciliation is possible – even when on first reading the stories it seems as if there will never be any common ground on which to reconcile the participating protagonists. But forgiveness can surely only be given when someone first comes up with a meaningful apology, a confession laced with a true understanding of what really went on. People don't want to *hear* you're sorry, they need to see and feel it.

The thing that so angered me about Lynn's story was not just the abhorrent regime she forced her children to grow up under. The specifics of the tyrannical reign of terror she subjected her family to was easily enough to fill me with revulsion on their own, but what angered me even more was this woman's decision to keep having children. Again, like so many of the people I am referring to in this book, she viewed getting pregnant and then having children as something predetermined by the fates. She seemingly could not conceive of how any decisions she took might influence or lead to a certain outcome. Getting pregnant was not down to poor personal choices or an abdication of responsibility on her part. No, it must be down to dumb luck. Even if I could buy Lynn's protestations of ignorance or carelessness with her first pregnancy, it would certainly not excuse the subsequent repetition of the choices that led to yet more kids being conceived whom she had no intention of doing anything with other than exploiting as some form of cheap, Third World sweatshop labour. Why don't some people learn? It's simple: thoughtless sex minus proper precaution equals more babies I can't cope with. That is not too hard to work out, is it?

On the show, Lynn admitted to an amphetamine addiction that had (conveniently?) blurred in her memory most of the horrors inflicted on the only three children she had left who were sufficiently curious or forgiving to attempt a reunion. She had forgotten, apparently, about how she had stopped her children going to school, preventing them from getting a proper education by locking them in their room for days at a time. She would tie rope from the upstairs balustrade to the bedroom door to ensure her children could not escape, leaving them with no food or water and only a bucket for a toilet. During this time she would lock herself away in her own bedroom, imbibing as many drugs as she could until her stash had run dry. Once recovered from her session, she would allow the children out of the bedroom. They would dress themselves each morning for school, but Lynn was having none of it. She wanted her children to go out and steal! With the only money coming into the house being wasted on Mummy's drug intake, no food was ever on the table for anyone to eat. Rather than get off her backside and seek a means of providing for her family, Lynn instead exploited her young family, forcing them to go out and rob whatever they could from the local shops and community, literally dragging them down the stairs by the hair and exploding with rage until she got her way and the kids followed her sick, twisted diktats. The children were also forced to witness and endure acts of horrendous violence. As well as being beaten themselves, the children also had front-row seats for their mum's latest pummelling at the hands of whatever lowlife, lover or disaffected dealer was passing through.

I could write reams on the wilful, sustained and systematic abuse perpetrated by this woman on her family; the children – who amazingly could still be bothered with her – filled my researchers' notebooks with page upon page of abusive acts meted out by their mother, any one of which I would previously have considered to be unimaginable in its cruelty. The one that stood out for me was the story of Lynn's young son who, at the age of eleven, was forced – not asked, forced – to go and collect her latest fix from the local dealer. Could you ever conceive of any set of circumstances in which you might consider it acceptable to send a defenceless eleven-year-old boy to a drug den to remonstrate with the violent, shady criminals lurking within? Through working on the show I have begun to understand something of the all-consuming nature of addiction, but there will never be an excuse that justifies sending your young son to barter with drug pushers just so you can get high all over again. Go cold turkey, sweat it out, go without or – if you really need your fix that bad – get off your fat arse and go and get the bloody stuff yourself, any of those options has got to be better than sending your young boy into a situation like that, hasn't it?!

I meet a great many people who claim that their every problem has been born of the terrible upbringing meted out to them by cruel and uncaring parents. There can be no denying of course that parental failures do account for quite a few of the issues that spawn some of the social and behavioural problems I am discussing throughout this book. However, it is equally true in my experience that a great many of those who accuse their parents of orchestrating an unbearable upbringing are guilty themselves of doing the same to their own children. Worse still, some are so reluctant to take responsibility for the children that they have created by refusing to countenance contraception that they then deign to dump those kids on the very parents they said were so terrible to them! That just doesn't make sense, does it? I mean, if your mother or father was some terrible ogre and a danger to children, you wouldn't very well choose to leave your children with either of them, would you? Well it seems, at least on my show, they do!

The fact that so many of my guests so readily claim that their parents were the very epitome of bad parenting, just prior to dumping their own children on them indefinitely, tends to tell me all I need to know about most people's situations or motivations. Most find that having a baby is a lot harder to deal with than they first thought. They certainly soon see that it goes way beyond trying to prove some infantile point to their parents. No matter what the circumstances that precede their arrival, children are a permanent fixture; the ignorance of certain people irritates me until the reality dawns that another life has been brought carelessly, needlessly into the world. At this point I just get sickened. I will never understand the ease with which anyone can desert their own flesh and blood – a poor, innocent child, who had no wish to be born in the first place – at the first sign that they are rightly going to need a touch more attention than their mother.

The free and easy way in which so many children are gracelessly dumped on family members, or worse, the state, is perhaps an indictment of the disposable society we are all caught up in. We are all being urged to buy into the fact that everything is now temporary, or at least can be changed at one click of a button. Breasts too small? Get them enlarged. Don't like your nose? Change it. Just realised getting pregnant was a bad idea? Dump the baby on your mum! No one seems to recognise that certain things in life are meant to be permanent. People see it as their right to change absolutely everything about their situation without ever considering the consequences involved.

In this day and age I applaud how cosmetic surgery can improve the lives of some, but having a baby is a whole other commitment and one to which, as parents, you are reasonably expected to be signed up for life. And, as I keep pointing out to all those who have apparently just been 'caught' pregnant, not getting pregnant is pretty bloody easy to achieve if you really don't want a baby. Nobody I knew ever got 'caught' pregnant in the way so many of my guests believe they have. Most people get pregnant by having unprotected sex and then letting nature take its course. The wind doesn't change direction, the music doesn't stop and pregnancy doesn't just happen to someone unlucky enough to get caught. The sooner people realise that they are in control of their own basic bodily functions, the sooner we might see an end to the needless and disturbingly unfair creation of life.

To finish my thoughts on this subject I'll add not one, not two, but 45,000 reasons why people should wear proper protection before having sex! Forty-five thousand is the number of children born every year in England and Wales without a father on the birth certificate – seven out of every 100! That figure, I am sure, is reached in part through some men trying to dodge their parental responsibilities, others trying to keep affairs secret, or some who just can't be remembered nine months down the line. Surely any one of those reasons is reason enough for any lust-struck young pairing to consider contraception? However, the most frustrating influence on that statistic comes from a problem I see all too often: new mums playing God. I am absolutely fed up of trying to explain to young mothers that they have a responsibility to name their baby's father on its birth certificate. I have met hundreds of young mums who have decided to omit the true identity of their baby's biological father on the strength of nothing more than a desire to be with someone else. Some mums even talk themselves into believing that their baby might be someone else's, rewriting history and biology whilst ignoring the stark bloody truth of what actually took place when they conceived.

Now, I don't think I am proposing anything particularly radical merely by asking mothers to start being honest. I fully accept that relationships may break down, that situations might change and that a mother might end up raising her child away from the man who fathered it. However, the breakdown of a relationship, the need – or even just the desire – to move away from a certain man is *no excuse whatsoever* for denying your child a fundamental truth about its identity. Every human being on earth deserves to know who his or her father is, and at least some of the circumstances that led to their being conceived in the first place. Nobody does women a greater disservice than those young mums I meet who try to lie and tell some poor sap that their baby is his just because he might be a better bet to provide stability and security. I suppose it is good and admirable that a light switches on in some and they belatedly realise the need to be, do and provide more for their children – God knows I meet enough who couldn't give a damn – but it is just plain wrong to make up a kid's history to achieve it. We're not talking here about a white lie on a CV; this is the very first piece of information given to and on behalf of your child. How bad is it to start what should be a lifelong relationship with the person you should hold closest to your heart with a deliberate, self-serving lie?

I understand that in some cases, where horrific acts of violence or rape have occurred, such information has to be carefully controlled, sometimes concealed and only ever revealed at the right time, but I am not referring to those rare and tragic cases. Many I have met have made this stuff up just to get ahead, regardless of the consequences.

There are few things I hate more than the grasping, opportunistic way some girls play the game to get a better feathered nest for them and theirs. I have had guys on the show who have sworn blind that they have never even slept with the woman sitting opposite them. DNA testing has often proved them right, but the results I give can never claw back the money they have been drained of, nor can it compensate them for the hassle they have been caused by women who knew perfectly well they were lying in every conversation they had about kids they should not have had.

I've been told by people working in the industry that, before the advent of DNA testing, anywhere up to 30 per cent of 'fathers' in this country were raising children they thought were theirs but biologically were not! That figure may be an exaggeration, and would certainly include some genuine mistakes. Equally though, it will have been bolstered by the manoeuvring of someone being deliberately dishonest: a woman whose craven pursuit of selfish gains ranks just as deplorably in my mind as those men who wantonly spread their seed before patently dodging their responsibilities. Lying in this way is not a million miles away from those who falsely cry 'rape' when trying to bleed money out of some innocent and unsuspecting man. To not know the identity of your baby's father is one thing, to make it up with money in mind really is quite another.

I am pleased to note that the government seems set to follow my lead on this. I read with interest how Work and Pensions Secretary James Purnell wants new laws passed that would order DNA tests to end any disputes over paternity. We've been doing DNA tests for the entire four years I have been presenting *The Jeremy Kyle Show*. I have to say that

DNA testing is by far the best way to cut through the bull-shit and establish the true facts. Try as some people bizarrely have, you just can't argue with the science of a DNA test. They prove paternity with 99.9 per cent probability, and that conclusion is arrived at via foolproof analysis of the genetic matter that forms the very building blocks of each human being. There is no point in arguing with the science informing a properly accredited test that proves you to be the parent you might so have wanted to avoid becoming. Many have sat with their head in their hands and struggled to compre-hend the enormity of their new realities and how a few silly decisions changed their life forever.

And do you know what rankles the most? It is that nagging little voice in the back of your mind, the one that haunts you over and over as it reminds you that things need not have turned out like this. It gets through far more succinctly and successfully than I will ever manage to, because it is a little voice that is yours and yours alone. It is a little voice that cruelly mocks with the constant refrain: if only I'd put some-thing on the end of it!

9

Raise the Bar!

Never in a million years could I ever see myself taking a lie-detector test! That is not to say that I don't believe in the veracity or accuracy of the tests we so regularly carry out on the show: I do. 'Well, you must have something to hide!' I hear you all scream. I don't. It's not even that I would be reluctant to put my relationship's fate in the hands of a test, which I am told is 96 per cent accurate, which is a pretty good score by any estimation. If I could access horse-racing tips with 96 per cent accuracy guaranteed, I might still be tempted to regress from today's occasional flutter to the serious gambling habit that so consumed me all those years ago! No, the reason I wouldn't subject my marriage and my family's future to the professional probing of even the most revered polygraph analyst is because it would mean the basic trust required as the foundation of any successful, loving relationship just was not there in the first place. If I were obliged to sit a test by a partner who did not trust me, that would probably be sufficient for me to walk away anyway. If the person who is meant to be closest to you no longer actually believes you, it is probably time for the dreaded chat that signals the death knell of most adult relationships; the one that begins with one or other of you saying: 'We need to talk.'

Of course, I am only talking about my situation. I am a person who needs to believe that the people closest to me are 100 per cent, foursquare behind me. From my wife to the colleagues I work with, all the way up to the people in power at the broadcasters who employ me, I need to feel their support. On matters of personal trust and belief, I am not big on proving people wrong. I would always prefer to prove right those who show faith in me. Relationships with those who publicly or privately doubt me have tended to fade quite quickly after that initial detection or declaration of their confidence in me waning. On matters of professional pride I am an altogether different beast. If someone challenges me to do something they believe might be beyond me, I am only too happy to try and prove people wrong. Sometimes there can be nothing more satisfying than a victory against someone who thought you just weren't up to much. This competitive instinct is the legacy of my previously discussed schooldays, where not a lot came easily to me. I am not ashamed to admit that even today I take a great personal delight in beating anyone anywhere, from the golf course to the go-kart track. The sweet taste of victory is undoubtedly made all the sweeter when the vanquished opponent is someone who previously dismissed the threat I posed or openly mocked the abilities (s)he thought I might bring to the table. I am always happy to prove such people wrong.

Surely the key to a successful and loving relationship with your partner is your ability, desire and determination to live up to every good thing they see in you. If your partner believes you to be kind, caring and completely trustworthy, don't you have a duty to live up to that billing and prove them right in their beliefs every single day? I can't imagine living in a relationship where I was forced to prove my partner's every doubt or fear wrong. And yet, that is precisely what I come up against on the show all the time. I could conceive of situations where I wanted to clear my own name and prove a point to any doubters by way of a lie detector. That is different, and indeed we feature a great many people who want to nail the rumours that destroy reputations or skewer the whispers that can make lives so unnecessarily miserable. I have known times where everyone has been talking in hushed tones about me, re-forming their opinion of me on the basis of some rumour over which I have had no control. At those times, in an instant, I would leap at the chance to sit a lie-detector test just to shut some people up. However, for those people who somehow seem to have been emotionally manipulated by their partners into sitting such a test, I often struggle to see the point. If they don't trust you, they just don't trust you.

Most of us, through no fault of our own, have been hurt, let down, betrayed or even abused by a partner whom we latterly come to realise was never deserving of our affections in the first place. Unfortunately it is hard to ignore the scars inflicted or discount the baggage we then become saddled with when braving the first few steps into a new relationship. However, all too often I see people's worries about what might happen to them at the hands of their latest partner as the only barrier to a successful relationship with that partner. A lot of people really do need to take an honest look at what they have and where they have come from before throwing around the sorts of wild accusations that lie at the heart of most 'relationships in crisis' I encounter when filming *The Jeremy Kyle Show*.

Most of the people I meet in this situation base all of their doubts about their partners on rumour and hearsay. Frequently I am left aghast at the sheer paucity of evidence on which people base the rows that threaten the futures of whole families. I am amazed at how readily some will want to believe the shit-stirring of a neighbour they have known five minutes over the protestations of a spouse they have been wed to for ten years. It is also always interesting to note how someone wronged or scorned in a previous relationship will then seek to dominate their next relationship. The persecution complex feeding their insecurities does not diminish as you might expect it would once another lover has been found. Instead, it feeds the insecurities exposed or exacerbated by the last bad experience and the latest partner then becomes the victim of all sorts of accusations they can neither understand nor disprove. These poor souls are the ones dragged along to the show before being made to sit lie-detector tests by their partners, their only comfort coming when they pass with flying colours and can put the ball back in their loved one's court and demand, with some justification, that they take a longer, harder and more honest look at themselves.

More often than not, the arguments I am asked to referee are ones that have been repeatedly, subconsciously engineered by the very people who claim to be suffering most as a result of them. Typically someone will have been cheated on in the past before then going on to accuse all future partners of having done or being about to do exactly the same. Sometimes it takes a lie-detector test to point out that they are the ones with the problem, not their partner. A test used in this way is as much about identifying the real problem as it is about giving someone the platform to prove their innocence.

I understand why so many would want the proof that can apparently be provided by a polygraph analyst or lie detector. I can empathise with the jealousy, doubts, worries and paranoia that persuade so many to pursue polygraph testing as their only means of grabbing onto something they can trust. But that to me is the very essence of it. I have to be 100 per cent committed to any relationship I am in and I would expect only that my partner is 100 per cent committed to me in return. No conditions, no caveats, no contracts. I'll put my faith, love and trust 100 per cent in you. I'll give you the means to manipulate and destroy me if you so choose.

There will be no corner of my heart you can't explore, no door or drawer in my life that will be locked to you. I'll give you my heart and show you my every weakness and insecurity. I'll show myself to you sometimes at my worst, sometimes at my best – but try at all times to be true. All I ask is that you do the same for me. One hundred per cent. Not 96 per cent.

You see, to me, proper adult relationships – and I'm not talking about flings or casual encounters – have to be 100 per cent if they are to have any chance of going the distance. I can only put my faith 100 per cent into someone, and it is that blind loyalty, trust and hope that makes it work in my world. If you give yourself to your partner as I give myself to Carla, you do so with the full knowledge that they have absolute power over you and, with your consent, have the means to level you completely. In return you have the same power over them and you share in the responsibility to make every bit of that partnership work as well as it can, with the needs of both parties consistently met and catered for. It is for that reason that I could never consent to pushing my partner towards a lie-detector test that only afforded a 96 per cent certainty. I would rather put 100 per cent trust in someone and get it 100 per cent wrong than enter into any relationship knowing that one or other of us was holding back even just 4 per cent of themselves.

Please don't misunderstand me here. I am not doing down the lie-detector tests we perform, but sometimes I just can't get away from telling people that it is not lie-detector results that will change their relationship, only the amount they are prepared to invest and give of themselves to that relationship. I've lost count of the number of people I've met who you can just tell in an instant are completely innocent of all the charges laid at their door by those who should be their most trusting companions. When the inevitable results are read out and they are exonerated of any wrongdoing, what else can I do but implore that the accuser take a long, hard and brutally honest look at themselves. If they don't, you can be sure that I will get another call four weeks down the line with those same jealousies and paranoias resurfacing and their partner accused of cheating because of the way (s)he reacted to a stranger on the street or even a character on the telly (trust me, it happens. A lot!).

No, I stand by the testing we do and the results we give. Aside from the science of it, which I don't really understand, it is the reactions of people after filming that give the greatest indicator as to whether or not the results we read out are in fact true. I have seen more than my fair share of guests who protest wildly that the results are wrong or that they are among the 4 per cent of people who may fail a lie-detector test without actually having lied. On more than one occasion, I have been moved by someone's on-stage protestations of innocence after giving them results they screamed were false, only to hear them confess all not five minutes after filming has finished. I have seen tears, and bought wholeheartedly into a sob story in which the show is cast as wrongdoer whilst the person with an acknowledged track record for cheating somehow becomes the victim. I have sat alone in my dressing room wondering if we have done the right thing, only to then get told that the person in question admitted everything the minute they came off stage.

I have even seen it with my own eyes. I have chased someone who stormed out of the studio while the cameras were still rolling, apparently apoplectic at the injustice of being served a wrong result. I myself stood in the corridors with that person, trying to console them and plot a way forward as the tears streamed down their face and they blamed me for 'making them lose everything'. At times like that it is hard to remain balanced or unmoved by such an emotional performance.

But performance it was, because the minute the cameras disappeared back into the studio, the ostensibly devastated recipient of deceptive results then confessed to me that they were guilty of everything they were being accused of! You'd be amazed at some of what goes on backstage, and I never cease to be astounded at the sheer front of those who willingly take a lie-detector test whilst knowing they will be found out.

I am frequently asked why anyone would come on a national television show and sit through a test of that type if they knew they were going to be portrayed as a guilty, cheating, bare-faced liar to the world. My answer is simple: they don't have a choice! Think about it. You've got a history of cheating, you may even have cheated on your current partner, and you've been caught out getting up to some very suspicious behaviour whilst out and about. Your partner, understandably fearing the worst and suspecting she'll get nothing but lies from you, issues an ultimatum: 'Take a lie-detector test to prove your innocence or I'll leave you for good anyway!' If you want to be with that person despite knowing that you have cheated on them, you can only really go ahead with the test – privately or via shows like mine.

Most people in this situation follow distinct patterns of behaviour once they have signed up and are committed to seeing a test through. They typically start to look up on the web how to beat the test, whilst simultaneously waging smear campaigns against polygraph testing for the benefit of their partners. Having repeatedly claimed how inaccurate they are whilst also studying how to beat or at least produce an inconclusive result when sitting the test, they then set about providing their partner with a plethora of excuses that would explain their failure of any test once completed. Hundreds of guests report to my researchers how their loved one returned from the test looking sweaty, nervous and full of pre-emptive reasons why the result given on the show the next day might not be the one they had promised their partner. Many at this stage then choose to bolt from Manchester before ever getting to the studio; others issue a desperate counter-ultimatum that basically boils down to 'back me or sack me', whilst the ballsy few resolve to ride out the result, take what's coming on the chin and salvage the relationship in any way they can – probably with yet more lies.

It wasn't until I had been in the job for quite a while that I saw the truth of the lie-detector results we reveal. That encounter in the corridor and several more backstage like it led me to believe that some will come for a test knowing they will fail precisely because they know they can still claw back the affections of the partner they have betrayed. Deep down they know they are in control for they, in most cases, have been taken back and forgiven for such unfaithfulness in the past. Pouring scorn on the accuracy of a lie-detector test is all part of a well-rehearsed routine that starts with feigning disbelief, moves quickly on to manufactured anger and a mock sense of injustice before calming quietly, once the cameras are gone, to acknowledgement, a begging for forgiveness and a promise to be better in future. At times like this it is possible for a fractured couple to temporarily unite against a common foe, *The Jeremy Kyle Show*, and once more play at happy families until a partner's wandering eye goes a-roving once again.

More often than not, the people who call into the show requesting lie-detector tests for their partners are people who have been cheated on by those same partners before. Anyone in a relationship with someone who already has a track record in cheating on them surely needs no further proof of their partner's unsuitability for a full-time, full-commitment, full-on loving relationship, do they? I have sat before couples where one party has cheated ten or twenty times and yet still the other wants to know if (s)he did it one last time. Of course they did, and that's why they can sit there so brazenly, knowing that another guilty verdict is heading their way! I find myself pleading with such people to please: RAISE. THE. BAR. 'Make yourself Everest,' I hear myself repeating, 'make someone work hard for your love and affection.' But the message invariably goes in one ear and out of the other.

In some cases I am convinced that they know their partner has cheated, know they will be found to be lying on the test, but come along anyway just to see me stand up to their partner and give them the bollocking they can't bring themselves to deliver. I guess they figure that me admonishing their partner is as close as they'll get to their pound of flesh. They bask in this temporary flash of their partner's penitence and try to enjoy the most Pyrrhic of victories, one that just encourages their partner to carry on philandering as they settle back into the same old routine. In this situation I just can't help but wonder why people don't demand more for themselves. Have more self-respect, have more self-belief, foster a greater sense of self-worth – RAISE THE BLOODY BAR! – and if you continually choose not to, stop bloody moaning about it.

Each day you get up in the morning you have a choice about whether you remain with or seek an escape from whomever you're with. It is to be hoped that you get enough reminders in the course of any day, week, month or year of just why you love the person you're with. If your faith in that person is tested, you can choose to endure the rocky patches we all do and put up with setbacks in the hope that things will be all right in the end. Nobody says you have to: you make that choice and you have to live with that choice whilst also knowing that you alone have the power to change that choice at any time you so wish. We will all go through bad times in a relationship and our survival of them will only set us in good stead for the future. However, if you are betrayed by someone and they have broken your trust in them beyond repair, you have no one but yourself to blame for continuing to be in a relationship with them. It may well be their fault that the trust was broken, but it becomes your choice to stay in a relationship where there is now no trust!

I suppose it is too easy to blithely insist that others raise the bar for themselves without considering why they set it so low in the first place. Invariably the process of bolstering someone's belief that they are entitled to more from a partner and a relationship is a slow one, especially when considering the backgrounds that some have come from. The poor personal choices that can adversely affect someone's schooling and subsequent attitude to work can only really be applied in part here. In school, work or life there are a lot of people who choose to opt out, despite being aware of what else might be on offer if they applied themselves. Unfortunately, in terms of relationships, some people just latch onto whoever is nearest who might help them escape from a broken home.

I've met countless young women who have dived into a relationship at the first signs of affection being shown to them by anyone who seems to present a contrast to the over-bearing, argumentative or downright abusive men they have left behind. Such people put the real issues they need to address on hold as they hop from one heartbreak to the next, in the forlorn hope of finding a happiness they probably would not recognise, far less trust, were it to land right in their laps. I could list countless examples of people I've met who have immersed themselves in a relationship that is patently wrong for them, just to escape an earlier one that was margin-ally worse. A lot have decried my attempts to get through to the guests on the show, and one even went so far as to say that I end up telling more people to split up than I ever do to make up! How can anyone really advise someone to go

back to a relationship that makes them unhappy or – worse
– is abusive? My plea for people to raise the bar in these
cases is all about getting people to realise that they really do
have it within themselves to be happy on their own. I want
these people to know that there is nothing to be scared of in
living an independent, single life. In fact, if you were to ask
more than a few of my married friends, they might even say
that the single, independent lifestyle they had twenty or so
years ago is something that they occasionally crave! Part of
that is human nature of course, it will always be the case that
some people want the exact opposite to what they have got
at any given time. By that same token, I also know of a great
many singletons who crave the steadiness and stability on
which my loving marriage is built.

Of course, what I am talking about here is not the same
as when parents belly-ache that the latest suitor their hor-
monally charged young offspring has brought home is 'not
good enough'! That schism will always exist for as long as
there are worried parents and even slightly rebellious children out there. I have fallen foul of this trap myself, and no
doubt will do so again as I steel myself to play the role of
father of the bride at least once for each of my three daughters. So far I have only negotiated this potential minefield
with my eldest daughter. Initially, as is the right and prerog-
ative of any middle-aged father (!), I had overly protective
paternal concerns about the beau she spoke so adoringly of
from the age of about seventeen. For once, though, I let head
rule heart and followed my own advice. I didn't register a
protest or even indifference. I tried to put aside all thought
of this young lad taking advantage of my little baby (only
fellow fathers of teenage daughters will truly understand the
horror of meeting the young lad you know will lead your
first-born daughter through her first sexual experiences!),
and was as outwardly supportive as I could be. I backed her

all the way whilst resolving to be there if they split up. But to date they are still together and apparently in love a few months into their year of backpacking in Australia and the southern hemisphere.

I'll no doubt have a few more heart-stopping encounters with the future boyfriends all my daughters bring home, but I can do no more than be there for advice and support, in good times and bad. If you come down in judgement, as I see all too often on the show, you only run the risk of clouding their own clear thinking on the subject and pushing them further away as they seek to make a stand against you on principle – if not true love – for the latest Mr Right (or is that Mr Right Now?) in their life.

I have no problem with my eldest daughter. She knows what she wants and certainly knows how to get it (if her wrapping of me round her little finger is anything to go by). She will be fine. Of greater concern is the huge percentage of guests who seem to be settling for so little when they appear on the show. I just wish these people could see how deserving they were of a proper shot at a proper relationship and the happy life that all adds up to a real future. Not long back I met, for the third time on the show, Donna. She was the perennial victim of some naive choices she had taken to try and make her life better and she couldn't see until the end of our third meeting just how much she was short-changing herself. Her first two appearances on the show revolved around DNA testing. She was adamant that one guy, and subsequently another on the second show, was the father to her young child. She was absolutely insistent both times before being proved wrong. I took her to task over her demands that these poor sops should continue to provide financial and emotional support for a child they knew was not theirs. I begged her to set about building a life that at first should only include herself and her baby. She ignored my advice and came back a third time to insist her latest partner take a lie-detector test because she suspected he was seeing his ex of seven years. He was – and the ex admitted as much too. In fact he only told the truth after first denying it and then, predictably, claiming he was the victim of a wrong result!

This time Donna required no advice or prompting to do the right thing. She took off her engagement ring (they had been together twelve weeks!), told him where he could stick it and finally, at very long last, decided that she would start all over again but this time without any new man in sight. Good for her! And about time too! Our aftercare team are determined to help her do just that, as now she seems to have seen the light and grasped the importance of raising the bar for herself. No more men taking advantage, no more selling herself short in the hope of finding her perfect man at the end of a false rainbow. No, this time she said she only wants to concentrate on herself and her baby. If she sticks to that, if she makes herself a proud prize that will be hard won by any suitor, I guarantee that she will reap the rewards that she has for so long sought in all the wrong places. She'll no longer have to make do, she can now look forward to picking and choosing, safe in the knowledge that she can say 'no' without fear of losing or missing out on anything at all.

For Donna, raising the bar would allow her the means to regain control of her life and the ability to live it on her terms. Fortunately, she was still at a stage of her life where it was relatively easy to point out certain distinctions that would help her grasp what really needed to be done to effect the positive changes necessary in her life. For some I have met, though, things have gone too far, and a spiral that started with poor self-esteem, and possibly a lack of guidance, has deteriorated into a far more sinister set of circumstances.

Unfortunately my office is still in receipt of hundreds of

calls each week from couples struggling to survive horrendous acts of domestic violence. Nine years of hosting confes-
sional talk shows on the radio and the occasional heated
barney with my own wife had not really prepared me for
what I was to read and hear once face to face with victims
of domestic violence. I have now spoken to literally hundreds
of people, the majority female but some, almost more shock-
ingly, male, who have been the victims of sustained physical, sexual or psychological violence from their partners. I
suppose I was slightly naive at first, but now I can see the
patterns of coercive and controlling behaviour that form the
blueprint for those on the path to perpetrating these heinous
acts of violence. I have sat with guests and tried to help them
see how they came to be so battered, bruised and miserable
at this point. Being in the middle of an unending and
deteriorating nightmare, they are typically unable to plot the
subtle but inevitable shifts that see a once-charming (in most
cases) boyfriend turn into the uncontrollable, volatile and
savage monster capable of almost unimaginable acts of
violence and cruelty. What starts as a perceived neediness
or craving for attention so often leads to something altogether more menacing, sometimes even culminating in
murder. It is as much my job to listen as it is to point out
the symptoms and cycles gone through before domestic
violence manifests itself with that first slap or punch. Beyond
that, it is just a battle to break through and make the victims
see that none of the horrors they are daily subjected to are
ever their fault.

In the UK, domestic violence accounts for between 16 per
cent and one quarter of all recorded violent crime. The police
in this country receive an estimated 1,300 calls each day –
over 570,000 each year! – from members of the public looking
for assistance to help deal with a violent domestic encounter.

Apparently, one in four women will experience domestic violence from a partner in their lifetime, whilst *more than* 10 per cent of women experience it *daily*. I am sorry to say that I have sat backstage and heard tales from people too terrified to speak out, but desperate for us to help negotiate any kind of escape for them. I have heard, time and again, how what started as a boyfriend's petty sulking to get his own way, has somehow – and almost imperceptibly – moved on to a dismantling of someone's entire family or social network. Control is seized as the boyfriend bans contact with friends then family, normally whilst continuing to go out socialising himself. Then the lies start. Boyfriend comes home late so girlfriend asks where he's been. The story does not add up and at any rate looks a little suspect considering the smell of perfume and the lipstick on the collar. Persistent enquiry leads to raised tempers and threats. Girlfriend needs to get away for a while so goes to get dressed up for a night with her long-neglected friends. Boyfriend kicks off and so the insults begin: 'You're not wearing that, you'll look like a slut!' 'You're not going out until I say you can!' From what I have heard it is normally at this point that the violence first erupts, just as girlfriend tries to push past and make for the front door. It could be a slap, punch or a pinning to the ground, but a line gets crossed from which it is almost impossibly difficult to return.

From this one incident, ultimate control is established by the perpetrators of domestic violence, and from this moment on the victims I have spoken to tell me that the physical attacks become more regular and generally more destructive. Many guests of the show have reported receiving broken noses or ribs on a fairly regular basis. Some have said they have been tossed about the room by their hair, or smashed into windows and dressers, whilst at least three others explained how they had been repeatedly punched and kicked in the face whilst lying unconscious on the floor beside a young child.

No one surely needs me to spell out all that is wrong with scenarios such as these that are so commonplace in today's society. But the thing I really struggle to get my head around is just how someone could even curl their hands into a fist and then unleash a full-blooded punch into the face of a woman. Am I sounding old-fashioned, or am I just from a different time and place to? I mean can anyone out there actually imagine what it must be like as a fully grown adult male, probably twice the size of your partner, to actually explode in violence in such a way? I simply can't. I just cannot imagine any situation in which I would become so enraged that I might slap, punch or, God forbid, kick a woman – nor can I conceive of any part of my brain that would allow that. I have an almost morbid fascination with the warped reasoning of men who can be so violent, as what they do is complete and utter anathema to me. Part of any success I have in getting through to some and impressing upon them the need for change is all born out of my ability to connect and build a rapport with them. In short I have to be able to get onto their level. If I haven't actually been through a situation like theirs, I am left to make an imaginary leap, bolstered of course by the advice and research conducted by the show's production and aftercare teams.

When dealing with life, it is not too hard to recall a certain time where one felt angry or even compelled to retaliate with violence. There have undoubtedly been times in my life where I have wanted to lash out and smash whichever bully was picking on me at the time, squarely in the face and with all of my might. I get that just as I get how jealousies, stresses and strains at home can make a relationship seem like a pressure cooker about to explode. But never in my life have I ever even come close to punching a woman. I just do not know how anyone could. How exactly could a man deliberately break the nose of a woman and then follow up with a flurry of further blows to her already limp and unconscious body on the floor? It really does beggar belief in my world, but apparently that represents something like the norm for those in domestically violent relationships. Others I have met say the need for control leaps to a whole new level in what are the most extreme and disgusting acts of one person abusing and humiliating another I have ever heard.

One lady told me how her husband's violent sprees and dominance of her had developed to the extent that she was punched and kicked severely on an almost daily basis. Her face was permanently puffed up purple with bruising, and she had not been allowed to leave the house for anything more than the weekly shop for five years. In the house, even her own children had been brainwashed into insulting her regularly in a vile and aggressive manner that perfectly aped their father's brutal mocking. This guy had apparently cavorted with a string of other women in the marital bedroom whilst she was forced to listen from downstairs.

At family meal times, this woman was forced further into her hell of humiliation as she was made to eat her dinner from a bowl on the floor whilst her husband and children looked on from the table above. She was literally being treated like a dog! Words failed me, tears did not. I pestered Graham for weeks after I heard her story, trying desperately to find an answer that might explain acts of cruelty that I could barely bring myself to believe were possible in this day and age. Was it mental illness? Was it drunkenness that provoked this sustained and systematic campaign to reduce a woman to absolutely nothing? I mean, I understand anger and the full spectrum of human emotions, but I just could not, still *cannot*, comprehend what the perpetrator of all this sickening abuse ever got from it.

Of course mental illness, drunkenness, drug addiction, jealousy, paranoia – or even the worst day at the worst office in the worst part of town – can never excuse any act of domestic violence. Abusers can be violent with or without the aid of any added stimulus, and they alone are responsible for what they mete out to their victims. That said, I get all the more frustrated when I meet perpetrators of domestic violence who acknowledge their wrongdoing without ever addressing one of the root causes they themselves have identified as acting as a catalyst or trigger to their violence. About seven out of ten wife-beaters (is there really any other name for them?) I meet tentatively hide behind the excuse, 'I was drunk,' before seeking to put further distance between themselves and accepting responsibility with the added disclaimer: 'I blacked out and can't remember a thing, but if she said it happened then it must have.' BLOODY HELL – WHAT DO YOU HAVE TO DO TO GET THROUGH TO SOME PEOPLE? Drinking before being violent is the most flimsy of excuses, especially if you yourself have recognised the link between your own drinking and the punches you throw when drunk. It really is quite simple: if drinking ten pints leads to a fight in the street or punches being thrown at home, STOP DRINKING TEN PINTS – IN FACT, JUST STOP DRINKING! I would suggest that the problems go far deeper than alcohol consumption, but giving up drinking is at least a start: no one needs a counsellor to point out the blindingly obvious.

It is hard to impress upon the perpetrators of these heinous acts of unprovoked violence that they must raise their own bar. I am often at a loss. All I can do is offer to expedite their joining of whatever counselling, support group or domestic violence course is most appropriate to their needs, and ask that they try to behave more like human beings and less like animals. But what of the victims? It is not appropriate to implore them to raise the bar, because usually they can't do this without external help. Whereas so many people in so many of the situations I attempt to resolve on stage merely need to re-evaluate where they are and what they want from life in order to raise their own expectations, victims of domestic violence invariably need a professional intervention – started by Graham and his aftercare team but continued and supported by one of the many wonderful organisations that are out there to help. Sufferers of domestic violence invariably lack a confidence, belief and trust in the world, which has to be painstakingly put back together over months and years. Social networks and family support systems have to be rebuilt whilst the individual also begins to truly deal with the psychological legacy of what they have been through.

What is needed here is for society rather than the individual to raise the bar. We have got to stop the culture of walking on by, of not lending a hand when we have the capacity to do so. I'm not advocating a nanny state, but there is no longer the neighbourly concern for one another that would surely help promote a sense that someone could reach out and ask for help before they took another pummelling.

The total cost of domestic violence to society in monetary terms in this country is estimated to be £23 BILLION! The cost of treating the depression, distress and mental illnesses that result from domestic violence alone is £176 MILLION! And yet still the perception persists that it is a private problem that should remain behind closed doors. That sort of attitude only helps create an environment in which the sick pigs who beat up their partners are allowed to continue unchecked.

I was stunned to learn that a study conducted as recently as 1998 showed that one in five young men and one in ten young women still think that abuse or violence against women is acceptable! That is just frightening. It shows just how

widespread the roots of a problem that claim TWO
WOMEN'S LIVES PER WEEK really do go in this country.
It also highlights just how widespread our approach in tackling this scourge on civilised society has to be. Alas, it is a
root-and-branch philosophy that needs to be adopted. One
policy here or there won't even make a dent in these sorry
statistics. We have to attack the culture that makes it OK in
the minds of some to hit women. We have to instead hit *them*
hard, with long custodial sentences and rehabilitation orders,
to be completed whilst being removed from decent, civilised
society. We have to do more to help the refuges and charities that give these poor victims at least some means of
escape. No more walking on by: the cost to everyone in society,
even down to the pounds in our pocket, is far too much to
bear. A society-wide approach is required because it is a
society-wide problem, affecting huge numbers regardless of
class, background, wealth or privilege. This, allied to the need
for more individuals to take more responsibility for their own
lives, might, just might, lead to a gradual raising of the bar
across the whole country.

   If everyone were to raise their own standards and expectations even slightly, I swear this country would be trans-
formed. If every girl blindly dating and selfishly procreating
with some drugged-up, whacked-out waste of space actually
took a step back and thought, 'No, I'm worth more than this,
I want more than this; my children deserve more than this,'
then maybe some of the depressing cycles perpetuating social
injustice and social immobility in this country would be
broken. We might not see an immediately obvious upturn in
the country's fortunes but, bit by bit, everyone in this country
would begin to *feel* that much better about themselves and
the society that spawned them. There would be higher hopes
and higher individual expectations.

   I think we almost need to re-inject that sense of shame

into society, the one that persuaded me it would be just plain embarrassing to get caught in trouble by anyone on my parents' street. Parents in this country should be better able to receive guidance as well as give it to their offspring. People now are too determined to leap to the defence of their offspring, even when they know they have done wrong. I would much rather see a society where Mrs Miggins from Number 42 could give my kid a clip round the ear if they were being rude or misbehaving than the situation we have now where kids see it as honourable to get given ASBOs.

At work I am surrounded by people who are every bit as motivated and ambitious as I am. Some have come from very tough backgrounds and most could recount traumas and personal tragedies far worse than anything I can claim to have been through. Many I know have made mistakes, and more than a few have been tempted at some point to throw in the towel and take the easy way out when all was seemingly going against them. But they didn't. They wanted something more and they scrapped and fought and worked for it, just as I did. They strove for something better than they were given and now refuse to settle for anything or anyone that doesn't match up to their standards. They don't come to work or indeed go out in life with any sense of divine right or entitlement. They put in the hours and send off their CVs with everyone else. They have taken numerous knock-backs and used the disappointment of rejection as motivation to come back stronger or even better prepared next time round.

A lot of the people I work with didn't go to university. Some are dyslexic and I'm sure quite a few did not get the best of grades at school. The series editor of *The Jeremy Kyle Show* is someone who left school at eighteen and spent whole summers apparently dressed as a chicken on the pier of Great Yarmouth! I have met a lot of people guesting on the show who wouldn't stand the perceived indignity of such a role; people who wouldn't lose face in front of friends or family, but who might crazily think it cooler to sit on life's sidelines and do little more than take drugs or hand-outs, or both, each day. Well, I applaud my series editor and anyone like him who knew that their job at the time may not have been the best in the world, but at least they were prepared to do it to begin improving a life lived on their own terms.

Seriously, it's as if we're not allowed to cast aspersions on anyone these days. I can see that there are a thousand apologists for every one of society's failures, but I do think it high time that we got back to having much more demanding standards of ourselves, and the people we mix with. There is nothing wrong with a disapproving look or harsh word to anyone who has let themselves down. There is nothing wrong with being disappointed that all has not gone as you'd hoped. Use these feelings to motivate others or inspire yourselves and please, don't just rely on the rest of the world to bail you out. There is nothing so depressing as having to run cap in hand to someone when you have been given all the tools you need to make a success of yourself. Make it clear that you will accept nothing but the best for yourself. Don't expect anything to be given, but do be prepared to bust your balls with hard graft to get the things you want. In relationships, don't be a pushover. Don't give of yourself too easily and don't be scared to call time on those relationships where you are making all the running. If you're putting in all the effort, paying all the bills and being left with nothing but fears that your lazy layabout partner may be up to no good, ask yourself if you really need to be with them. Either they shape up or you ship them out! Likewise, don't get too lazy yourselves. Be attentive to someone's needs, understand them as a person and start a life together as an unbreakable team. Build from an equal footing, invest in each other's needs and you'll not go far wrong.

Basically, if you start trusting yourself to do what's right, you'll know exactly how to deal with any situation. You'll know your standards, you'll know what is acceptable behaviour and you'll let everyone know exactly what you are not prepared to tolerate. If the people you invite into your life don't seem to be matching up, *you'll* know the time might be right to move on. You'll know this because the bar will be raised higher. You'll know yourself and you'll know you deserve more . . . and do you know what, you won't need a lie detector to prove it!

10

I Can't Just Wave a Magic Wand!

I am not so sure that I suffer from Obsessive-Compulsive Disorder, but increasingly I get told that I exhibit many of its symptoms.

I have always been rather wary of labels, particularly in the modern age. I struggle to balance the increased sophistication with which we can articulate every known condition in the twenty-first century against the fact that most of our ancestors muddled through to this point more or less OK and without being stigmatised by syndromes unknown to them. I hopefully won't be too facile about this and I certainly don't want to denigrate the good work being done everywhere to advance the study of mental health issues. However, my contemporaries and I grew up on the cusp of overlapping generations, with very different appreciations of the things that affect our minds. My parents knew nothing of OCD, depression, Borderline Personality Disorder or any of the other more modern diagnoses with which their grandchildren will probably be familiar. Anyone depressed in *their* youth would likely be written off as 'down', or 'blue', or 'just having a bad day'. Nowadays, teenagers up and down the land are being medicated for stress, anxiety and being dosed up to the hilt for clinical depression. We must all be grateful for the great strides being made in the diagnosis, treatment and public awareness of mental health issues, but I do sometimes wonder if things are now starting to swing too far the other way. Where my parents' generation were maybe not clued-up enough, are my children's generation now going to be overly familiar with the jargon of modern mental health medicine? Where too many people previously had genuine problems ignored, are today's and tomorrow's children now going to have too many problems thrust upon them?

I don't know. I only ask because of the way I am being badgered into thinking that I am suffering from a problem I never knew I had. I have got to know myself pretty well over the last forty-three years. I know all of my little quirks and idiosyncrasies and I know how I'll react in most of the situations likely to be thrown at me each day. It wasn't until I started meeting genuine sufferers – admittedly rather extreme examples – of some of the syndromes above that I was forced into a bit of a rethink.

In the earlier days of filming *The Jeremy Kyle Show*, there seemed to be a lot of callers coming through to seek help with more extreme cases of OCD. I remember the helplessness I felt when first speaking to a lady who washed her hands to the point of drawing blood after each little task she undertook. Every time she made a cup of tea, each time she switched on the television and every time she touched her own door handles she would have to go out into the kitchen to begin a scrubbing ritual that had become progressively more extreme over the years. She told me she had started by simply cleaning her hands just a little more often than most. Later she came to claim that she could see specks of dirt all over her that were imperceptible to everyone else. Hand soap ceased to be of use to her and she went on to using bleach and scouring pads for fully ten minutes each time, to rid herself of the stubborn stains she alone could 'see'. I have met others like this lady who have almost become prisoners of their own mind, slavishly adhering to complex rituals and regimes that scarcely make sense to the rest of us.

I would never claim to have anything so serious as the condition described above. As I have said, I never considered myself to have any real problem at all. I have always thought of myself as a bit pernickety, and tight organisation is very important to me, but I never once considered that I might display symptoms of OCD. However, the more work I have done alongside people with OCD, the more I have had parallels pointed out to me. I am not sure my personal peccadilloes qualify as a disorder as such, but I can't really deny that I am both obsessive and compulsive.

For as long as I can remember, I have always been a very ordered and tidy person. I have always placed great emphasis on regulation and form. I always thought I needed a structure imposed upon my life and I'm sure I'm not the only person who recoils at mess. I know I am not alone in seeking to write a 'to-do' list at the start of each morning. I like routine, the more regimented the better, and I don't like too many deviations from an already published schedule. Once I am told I am filming on a certain day, it is locked in my mind as permanent. When unforeseen events force a change in the timetable, a deep feeling of uneasiness sweeps through me. Why have things changed? Why couldn't we have known sooner? No bad has ever come of any calendar being rejigged at the last minute, but still it feels to me as if someone has deliberately thrown me off balance. I can't explain why, but my sense of equilibrium just becomes skewed. The 'to-do' list I have begun mentally making for the rest of the year goes into disarray and for a time my mind becomes too noisy and messy for me to properly concentrate. In essence I don't mind problems because I can always find solutions to them. What I don't like are bloody surprises!

I have always subscribed to the security my lists bring to my life. I like to know where I am supposed to be, when I am supposed to be there and exactly what is required of me when I arrive. This need for order I have always linked to a need to make sure that I never missed an opportunity. I curse myself to the point of insomnia whenever I fail to tick off something on my list for that day. If for some reason I have not written down something I later remember needed to be done, I will become restless and agitated all night long. It will have been another opportunity missed, another failure in my mind. I'll envisage myself once again falling behind a pack of more talented peers which is no good for a man who likes to be fifty yards in front of everybody!

I guess my need for an ordered approach to life began as a coping mechanism. Or perhaps it was merely a means of ensuring I made the best of what I had. I guess I always saw myself as some sort of underdog. I was West Ham and everyone else was Man United. They had more money, better players – and nine times out of ten would be expected to beat me. However, I knew, as every football manager knows, that even the big guns can come unstuck against a compact, well-drilled side from the lower reaches. Organisation is the key. To kill the metaphor, I was never going to be as lavishly gifted as any Ronaldo out there, so in life I set out to ensure I was as fit and well trained as I could possibly be. I knew if I organised my life in the right way I could cause an upset and break through. Organisation and relentless determination would ensure I always had the best possible day I could. This, by and large, has always worked for me, but the need for order has stealthily crept its way into other areas of my life, without me even realising.

When you look in the mirror each day it is hard to notice each new wrinkle that creases its way into your face. Likewise with my rituals and routines. I hadn't noticed how many little quirks had crept into my life, until I joined ITV and had them pointed out by a whole new set of colleagues who had never known me before. All my friends and family had become as used to my habits as I had. There was nothing out of the ordinary for anybody to consider as, to them, Jeremy was just being Jeremy. However, new colleagues soon became friends and then they started to ask about certain things they came to know as my little tics.

The first instance came during rather an important briefing with Lucy, my show's executive producer. She was giving me chapter and verse on a whole raft of important new legislation I was to take on board before recording began that week. She became increasingly agitated before exploding at me, 'Why the bloody hell aren't you paying attention, Jeremy?' she asked. 'This is really important stuff!' I could only apologise for annoying her with a distractedness I just could not disguise. Moments earlier my mobile had rung. It was on silent and the incoming call caused it to vibrate. This meant it had shaken itself off the arm of the chair it was resting on and onto the floor below. Instinctively, Lucy had kindly bent down to pick up the phone. The ringing had stopped and she'd placed it back where it had been resting. Ever since, though, my eyes had been flicking towards it.

I wasn't worried that I'd missed a call (I was). It didn't bother me that I still didn't know who had rung (it did). What was driving me to distraction was the smudge her fingerprint had left on the screen of my phone. As soon as Lucy had broken the ice, I let her know what was bothering me. She seemed confused that something so minor would play on my mind as it had. I picked up my phone, licked the screen (as is now customary), and dried it with a wipe on my trousers in much the same way that a cricketer shines a ball before bowling. I couldn't explain to her, as I can't explain to you now, why I always feel so compelled to clean my phone in that way. All I know is that I do it every day after every call I have made or taken on it. I don't know when the habit started, but I know it won't end anytime soon.

Phone licking isn't the only thing you can pin on the Jeremy Kyle Wall of Weird! I have exactly the same fixation about cleanliness over, wait for it, my golf balls! Regularly, during each round of golf I play, I *have* to lick my golf ball and clean it properly. (The reason I lick my balls in this way is probably more strange than the licking of the balls themselves. It does not lend any discernible benefit to my game, it's just that cleaning my balls on the pristine, white towel dangling from my golf bag might in turn make my golf towel dirty. And I most certainly could not have that, I really couldn't!) That said, if I don't clean the ball my brain feels out of balance and I'll feel like I have cursed my round or even my whole day. Is that just sporting superstition, or is that more akin to OCD? I know of a great many footballers who succumb to all sorts of superstitions before they play. Paul Ince, the first black captain of England, had to exit the players' tunnel last, never pulling on his shirt until well clear of it. Bruce Grobbelaar, the old Liverpool goalkeeper, apparently wouldn't leave the dressing room until he had turned out the lights by kicking a ball against the switch. I won't take a shot before I have licked my golf ball clean. There is no reason to do it, but I just feel compelled, as if something bad will happen if I don't. How ironic then that something quite bad often follows when I do . . . On more than one occasion I have been stuck fast to the toilet seat the minute I have returned home from the golf course. There are a lot of pesticides used to spray certain courses and, through licking my balls (!), I average about eighty servings of the stuff with each round I play! Not good for anything other than rapid, painful weight loss, trust me!

At home I am fairly obsessive about cleanliness too. A day with the kids can leave me feeling more stressed out than most, such is the chaos that the Kyle clan can bring to my ordered sense of things. I don't moan at the children, though. I don't think I complain and I always pitch in with whatever game they are playing. However, once the debris has been cleared and they have gone off to bed, I have to go around the house once more and ensure everything is cleaned, tidied and put away with military precision. Carla thought me strange at first, but I think she now accepts that this is the way I am. She has just got used to the way my little obsessions work their way into certain areas of our life together. I'm sure she must tear her hair out to wake up and find me downstairs mopping the kitchen floor at two a.m. in the morning, but if I can't sleep I find the whole process very therapeutic. Mopping the floor helps me unwind; not mopping the floor leaves me wound up – so what can I do?

I am not so anally retentive as to need all the tins in the cupboard lined up and looking like a scene from *Sleeping with the Enemy*, but I am quite a stickler for sorting out the dishwasher. Everyone in the house knows that filling the dishwasher is my responsibility. Every plate and piece of cutlery has its own spot on one of the shelves and I can't help but check that its cargo is OK before the cleaning cycle commences, especially if anyone else has dared lend a hand to fill it.

I ensure all of my towels are always folded neatly away. I hoover around the house repeatedly, and mini-mania inexplicably grabs me if the gravel from the driveway has spilled onto any patch of the lawn! I have often been known to rake the gravel on my driveway because to see it displaced and undulating after the comings and goings of a variety of vehicles leaves my mind screaming at me to sort it out. I need everything back to nice and flat and calm and even. People play on it to wind me up, kicking stones this way and that just to see if they can get a reaction. I don't give in there and then, but it plays on my mind until they leave. And the minute they've gone, I'll be out there restoring things to how they should be!

I'm sure I must annoy Carla. In fact I'm sure I must annoy everyone around me! You could set your watch by my movements in the morning. At 6.50 a.m., I'll be straight up and out of bed. I know I need ninety minutes to get ready each morning. Yes, ninety minutes. If at work I am morphing into my dad, then at home I must be turning into my mum! I take longer in the bathroom than even my wife! I have to shower and shave and have to read a paper too – generally in the quiet sanctuary that is my own toilet – before leaving the house. I'll have spent hours doing the ironing the night before, just to make sure I am as well presented as can be. I don't do this for vanity; for me it is like lining up the pieces and getting everything tidy in my mind before I leave the house to take on the day. I have even been known to iron my driver's shirt – just to get things exactly as they should be!

I feel slightly embarrassed to have revealed all of that. As I say, I have never thought of 'my little ways' as anything more than personality traits I am well used to living with. I can't even remember when they started, and it is only writing them down now that I realise how many of them there are. And I haven't even scratched the surface . . . I haven't even mentioned the stripes on the lawn, the need for someone to pick up their phone the second I call them, and the fact I'll keep calling if they don't. I could go on but I think you get the point.

When I was growing up with Mum and Dad, there was a man who lived down the road from us and he was definitely an OCD sufferer and he became something of a local talking point. Every time he returned home from work he would wait outside and go through a ritual before entering the house. He would remove his gloves, shoes and socks. Then he would scrub his feet and hands thoroughly in a bowl of disinfectant. Only then could he go through his front door.

His behaviour was looked upon as something of an oddity; he was shot some of the same looks that I can sometimes detect nowadays, from those who see some of the things I do as a touch, well, weird. More than one producer has given me the raised eyebrows when we have been reading research notes together and some of the OCD traits discussed seem to mirror my own. I can see the link and concede that there must be some truth in what people say, but I am just not sure that I can be labelled as a case study for OCD.

The label in itself does not bother me, and I am certainly not fearful of any negative connotation that might in some quarters be applied to it. (I wouldn't be writing about it now if I was scared of being labelled.) No, I just keep going back to wondering about the labels that exist now, how widespread they are and how easily people will reach for them to self-diagnose problems that perhaps aren't that bad. I remember talking to some lads in the pub a few years back. One of them was a footballer for a Sunday pub team. He explained that he couldn't turn out for his team that week because he had 'done his cruciates'. He had undoubtedly had a bit of a fall and had probably twisted his knee somewhat, but the mild limp he sported as he gamely shuffled to and from the bar was not commensurate with cruciate ligament damage. My suspicions were confirmed when, right as rain, he was playing pub football the following week, thundering around the pitch like a bull in a play-pen. The diagnosis he had given himself had, I suspect, come on the back of a wave of high-profile cruciate ligament injuries, like the ones once suffered by Alan Shearer and Paul Gascoigne. Because my friend had read about them and was familiar with the terminology, he assumed the little tumble that kept him on the sidelines for a week to be the same injury that typically keeps inter-national footballers out for seven months!

That incident with the footballing bullock illustrates in

microcosm what might, just might, be happening in terms of far more serious issues in other areas of this country. I note the rise of 'cyberchondria' – a new phenomenon where people are researching their every ache and pain online and falsely diagnosing themselves with diseases where one symptom in ten matches what they believe they are suffering from. I'm sure every family must have had a similar figure in years gone by, like the determinedly ill aunty who declared herself practically dead each week, and all on the back of her reading another chapter of the medical encyclopaedia she'd been bought last Christmas!

Not so long back I was filming amongst the community estates in Wythenshawe, Manchester. During one of the few breaks I got between painting, moving furniture and trying to install a kitchen as part of a project to refurbish the local community centre, I was approached by two teenage mums, each aged nineteen. Both had heard we might be in town and had come to see if we could make the *Challenge Anneka*-type deadline that had been set. One of them wanted to quiz me on something. She had apparently made a call to my show some weeks before but her request to appear had been turned down on the advice of our aftercare team. Apparently she had only just been prescribed a course of antidepressants and it was explained to her that we could not take another look at her request until at least a few months later, after she had stabilised on this course of new medication. She wanted to tell me that it was unfair and asked if I could help her cut any corners. I politely told her I could not. I was about to return to my chores when her friend then approached me about appearing on the show herself. What she confided next astounded me.

She knew she would not be considered to appear on the show if she disclosed to us that she had just been prescribed a course of new antidepressant medication. She therefore asked if her case would be strengthened if she delayed actually starting her course of medication until after any appearance with us. When I told her quite plainly that she should not opt in and out of the advice a professional doctor gives, she seemed a little shocked. She went on to explain that quite a few young people her age had seen their GP to see if antidepressants might help them along a little. She was quite frank in explaining that some of her mates had got 'signed off sick' with depression purely to escape work. Some had done it to hang around with (m)others the same age, but some, I was almost relieved to hear, 'were in quite a bad way and did actually need them [the antidepressants]'.

I left her some moments later, but I wasn't quite sure what was being said to me. Are there young people out there deliberately attempting to fool doctors into handing over antidepressants, just to escape the prospect of work – or, worse, just to follow and hang out with their mates? Do young people now know how to play another part of the system, or are there really increasing numbers of younger people who genuinely know how to spot the signs of clinical depression in themselves before then seeking professional confirmation? The truth lies somewhere in between, I suspect, but I was shocked nonetheless.

Apparently 20 per cent of people in this country stand a chance of suffering from depression at least once in their lives. That's one in every five; but one in every ten of us are likely to be suffering from depression now! Women are twice as likely to suffer from depression as men, and the only way it can be diagnosed is via an assessment of an individual's symptoms. There are no scans or blood tests that can provide any proof, only the identification of symptoms that typically include feelings of uselessness, isolation, withdrawal and an inability to derive pleasure from any of the things a person normally enjoys. And although depression is a stark reality for so many of us, there is still no consensus on what causes it. Genes can play a part, as can traumatic life events, stress, illness and recreational drug taking.

There was a time when I doubted if I'd ever know the difference between feeling really down or actually being depressed. There is a big grey area out there, with the potential for exploitation that might ultimately count against all of us. It seems there might be more than a few youngsters out there who know how to fake it, opting out of life as if they were getting out of PE.

I later asked Graham about all of this and he told me that he thought that a number of the people he had met in recent years had used false pretences to obtain antidepressant medication or similar. I would never claim to be an expert on this, but even I have seen some of the identifying symptoms of a true depressive illness. In some I've met there has been a list-lessness and lethargy that you would describe as completely out of character for that person. You can see that they just have no energy or enthusiasm, none of their normal zest for life, and often not even the desire to get out of bed for days on end. The girls I met that day showed none of the symptoms above, though of course I can't know what was really going on in their lives. I might just be getting more cynical with age, but I saw nothing in them that hinted that they were even having a bad day, let alone suffering from depression.

Many I have met only fuel my suspicions further by not seeming to display ANY of the symptoms usually associated with depression. However, even leaving my cynicism aside, the thing that infuriates me most is when people make no attempt to resolve their problems before they come on the show. Even worse is the flat rejection by some of all the assistance laid on to help them resolve whatever issue they came to address in the first place! That is the one bit of my job that really sticks in the craw. Sometimes I know that I am going to have an offer of help thrown back in my face, but I am obliged to put pride aside and offer it anyway. And then, not twenty minutes later, they are off, ignoring every promise they have made to me, their loved ones and themselves. Off into the distance, still blaming everyone but the one person their problem always begins and ends with . . .

One such guy was Peter Davies. He first appeared with his father. This was an elderly man desperately worried about the series of his son's addictions that had blighted their family's happiness. He told the story of how Peter, a rising tennis star from the age of eleven, had suddenly given in to temptation as so many young people do. Peter started hanging around with the wrong crowd, smoking cannabis and starting down a path of drug taking that culminated in a rampant heroin addiction that destroyed the very fabric of his family. His father came to us at a loss over where to turn next. He just did not know what more he could do to help Peter. Over the years he had watched his son lurch from one problem to the next as his drug problem escalated. Money had been stolen, feelings manipulated and relationships irreparably damaged as two kind and gentle parents were repeatedly taken to the cleaners by their own flesh and blood. He came to us to say 'enough is enough', but more than that wanted us to help enlighten him as to how one person could go so badly off the rails.

We tried to explain the nature of addiction; we gave Peter some much-deserved credit for finding it within himself to beat his heroin addiction. However, as can often happen, alcohol had gradually become the replacement for Peter's heroin addiction, and now his father had reached a breaking point, emotionally and financially. He didn't know what else to do. Peter by contrast – addiction or no addiction – knew exactly what he was doing. He had his parents just where he wanted them and he was milking them for all they were worth. He blamed them for his addictions, saying their lack of support was the thing that drove him further into the clutches of his demons. Peter's father didn't know how else to help his son stop drinking, but knew he could not continue to blindly support him with hand-out upon hand-out. Having seen how much Peter had fleeced him for in life, his father made the decision to cut him from his will, if only to protect Peter from his own worst excesses. Cue much screaming and the predictable self-pitying tantrums from the ungrateful little sod who could only see his father's belated wising up as the end of an indefinite meal ticket!

I had my say on the matter and didn't stop short of telling him how disgusting I thought his behaviour towards his father had consistently been. Nevertheless, I offered him the full weight of the show's resources to help him finally conquer the last of his addictions. I did it as much to spare his father any more heartache, and thought this might be the chance for a family to put the source of their recurring troubles behind them. What happened next should have come as no surprise, but it was shocking nonetheless.

Needless to say, Peter eschewed all of our attempts to offer him counselling and the community detox programme he had intimated he would willingly sign up to. He was a prime example of someone who had wanted the make-believe magic wand to be waved and for all of his problems to disappear in a puff of smoke without him ever having to lift a finger. Beating his addiction represented a path of hard work that he just could not find it within himself to commit to. He no doubt figured that at home he could wallow in his problems and continue to indulge himself at his parents' expense. Peter is not the first to have balked at the idea of fighting a battle to save himself when giving in was the easier option. He won't be the last, either, but he was certainly one of the most annoying.

There is not one particular issue I cover on stage where failure to accept personal responsibility is more prevalent than in others. It is right across the board. And it is that unwillingness in some to first recognise that they have a problem before then taking the necessary steps to address it that really worries me. Insofar as I act obsessively and compulsively, I know that I sometimes go too far. I can occasionally become a bit too demanding a bit too quickly. The compulsion can take over from time to time and my patience might be the first thing to give way. I am not sure that the television industry is the best place to keep any excesses of this nature in check. It is easy to let ego take over, believe your own hype and become seduced by the power of your position. If you host your own show you will always find more people willing to say 'yes' than 'no' to you, and for me that presents a particular test. I crave adulation, I have a desperation to impress and, if I am honest, a need to feel important. Add those elements to the obsessive compulsions I spoke of earlier, surround them with all of the ego-stroking that will always go on in TV (occasionally invited, I have to admit), and the potential for 'Me-Me-Me' celebrity diva-dom is massive. It is therefore incumbent on me to recognise my own weaknesses and make an effort to keep myself in check. I rely on the sound advice and guidance of those around me, of course, but the decisions I take to hopefully remain a decent and honourable human being each day are down to me and me alone, no matter what other forces might be at work.

Too many people in this country just are not taking responsibility for their own actions. They are not taking responsibility for their own addictions, relationship issues, or whatever, and they are certainly not bearing responsibility for the hard work required to fix them. People come to the show expecting that I will parent their kids. Others talk about drug problems they think I might magically make disappear whilst they sit there, almost detached from the conversation. Some almost expect you to believe that they somehow just woke up addicted to drugs or that they suddenly became alcoholic overnight. Mothers and fathers who have abandoned their kids for twenty years at a time look confused when it is put to them that the children they left behind might be harbouring a bit of resentment. I have seen some storm out of backstage counselling sessions the minute the first awkward question is asked about the life, and the mess, they helped create. What do they expect?

Maybe the fact that we are a television show is the thing that counts against us. Maybe people are conditioned to expect that Hollywood miracles are just going to be served up to them. Some must come to us in a state of denial. I'm sure they just expect to be whisked through the doors and be given some Cilla *Surprise, Surprise* moment that will lift every trouble from their shoulders. Well, I'm sorry to shatter any illusions, but there's nothing that goes on backstage but talk and an invitation for guests to begin working hard to turn their own lives around. When I tell people that 'Graham is waiting', a palpable sense of relief washes across any guest's face. What so many apparently fail to hear is the bit that always follows: 'THE HARD WORK STARTS NOW!'

Graham is my good friend and the man I call 'The Genius' for achieving the nigh-on impossible when helping some of those who *are* motivated to make the most of what the show can offer. I don't think a day goes by without me doubting whether certain guests really have what it takes to turn their lives around with our support – Graham or no Graham. Speaking frankly, I am confronted by too many who have become lazy and apathetic. Too many bury their heads in the sand and expect the help we offer to somehow be injected into them. They sit there passively, doing nothing to meet their challenges head-on. I have seen countless counselling sessions spurned and I hear each week of programmes we have set up not being attended by the guests they have been set up for. At first I admit I used to feel a little crushed, personally let down. That feeling never really goes away but I guess I am just a bit more used to dealing with it nowadays.

The minute I have any personal problems that start encroaching into my life I will seek whatever help is available and lap it up gratefully. If I find my obsessive-compulsive traits become worse to the point where they inhibit my own life or the enjoyment of my family's, I'll not hesitate to pick up the phone and speed-dial 'The Genius'. I would take on board his every bit of advice and set out along whichever path he pointed to. I would try to assimilate everything he said and then I would sit back and contemplate what lay ahead for a few moments. I'd take a pause and a very deep breath for I'd know THE HARD WORK WAS STARTING NOW. Not Graham's hard work, not my family's or anyone's around me. Mine. Why? Because my problems are my responsibility and only I can cover the ground and make the effort really required to sort them.

The saddest truth of all in this is that so many of the issues I try to help resolve each day are so eminently fixable. Openness, honesty and good communication are key, but the resolve to do whatever it takes is what will ultimately see any change through. If it's rehab or detox, the addict will have to face the sweating and tears and pain of withdrawal. If it's a relationship that needs rebuilding, it will be the couple in it who will have to endure the discomfort of giving then receiving some hard-to-hear truths about one another. What awaits any guest backstage is the chance to rebuild under the watchful eyes of some very experienced and appropriately qualified professionals. There is no magic involved and no

fairy-tale ending for anyone not prepared to write it for themselves.

So, please think long and hard before calling in and
expecting miracles. We will always be prepared to give it a
go, but you will have to match that and more. I'll always
applaud anyone who puts their hand up and asks for help.
That is the first and most important step but it is never by
any means the hardest – the most difficult are all the ones
that follow and only one person can take them. YOU. Graham
may well be The Genius, but he certainly ain't a wizard and,
no matter how large or small your issue, no one can just wave
a magic wand to fix it!

11

'You're Amazing!'

As regular viewers of *The Jeremy Kyle Show* may note, it takes quite a lot to shut me up! I have long suffered with verbal diarrhoea and I'm not apparently blessed with the inbuilt radar that points most people towards silence at an appropriate juncture. I am one of the world's worst for repeating myself endlessly or just talking to fill any gap in conversation. Maybe this is the legacy of a twelve-year radio career in which 'dead air' is *the* cardinal sin, one that must be avoided at all costs. Better the inane twitterings of a middle-aged man whacked up on caffeine than a silence that will see listeners desert in their droves, or so the Radio Rule Book goes.

I still seek a way of clamping my overworked jaws shut, but please don't be in any doubt: I have been bowled over by a fair few people whose courage has left me pretty much speechless. I consider myself supremely privileged to have shared a stage with a great many people whose stories of survival should shame those who seek to use my stage only to whine and endlessly battle over little more than juvenile trivia. For every ten dads who have tried to cast doubt on DNA results just to duck out of taking responsibility for the life they have created, there will be one guest who leaves me dumbstruck with the awe-inspiring tale of their triumph against the odds.

I never fail to be struck by the humility with which so many battle debilitating physical, social or circumstantial hardships to make the best of even the most difficult of starts. I have banged on plenty about what is wrong with this country and just how far we still have to go to break through into the consciousness of so many of our fellow citizens. For someone in my position, it is easy to become despondent about the future forecasts for this nation and yet still, about once a month without fail, I will be introduced to someone who can't help but inspire everyone they meet. I wish I could bottle the surge of optimism that rushes through me when I meet such people. I wish I could distil and distribute it to anyone who feels they are beginning to despair about the state of Great Britain, because, make no mistake about it, these people have it in them to make EVERYONE in this country walk a little taller.

Their stories can be heartbreaking but their individual response to whatever setbacks they have suffered truly is the stuff of legend. It is these people who prompt us all to puff out our chests a little more as we proclaim that they are one of ours; that they are the best of British. They are beacons of hope, examples to all the rest of us. I hope I can do them more justice here than I ever did on television, for when I saw each of the people I am about to mention, I could not do much more than keep repeating: 'You're amazing!'

Yes, the person reviled by many as the gobbiest, most cynically hardhearted man on British television has regularly been left flapping, tears in his eyes, as he searches for any word that might encapsulate all that the hero standing before him represents for so many. Leaders, inspirations, survivors – all manner of people from all walks of life; and each displaying a uniqueness of spirit that should be coveted and cherished and applauded by us all. I know what I felt when I saw them, I know what I mean when I talk of them, I am only sorry that 'amazing' is all I can offer when talking *to* them. The word itself somehow just doesn't seem to be amazing enough when weighed against the people I use it to describe.

There are too many amazing people out there to mention them all by name, and I don't mean this to read like some three-hour Oscar ceremony played out to an extended applause soundtrack. However, I feel it is only right that I should acknowledge the good that so many do in this country, even though it is sometimes hard to find the words to do justice to them. These are the people who have exactly the sort of attitude we need to start making right of so much that is wrong in Britain.

It is their indomitable spirit and positivity we should look to most when seeking to restore this nation to former glories and, more, to take it to previously unseen heights. As much as I am blown away by miraculous one-off stories, there is little that stirs up my pride more than those ordinary citizens who prove themselves extraordinary contributors to their community. They rarely seek recognition or reward, they are motivated only by a desire to drag their areas up by the bootstraps and improve them for the benefit of everyone living there. Of all the people I have met, nobody typifies this sense of mission and civic pride more than Greg Davies.

Greg is the founder of the United Estates of Wythenshawe, a project in one of the harder areas of Manchester that provides a credible alternative for young people who might otherwise get sucked into the sorts of criminal activity and antisocial behaviour now so prevalent in Britain. With no outside backing and not much more than the idea that he wanted to put something back into a community that had given him so much in his younger years, he set about creating a scheme that looks like being a beacon for everyone in Wythenshawe for years to come.

Greg told me of the despair he felt when he returned to Wythenshawe some years ago and saw for himself the disrepair it had fallen into at every level. Buildings were dilapidated and his hometown's community spirit seemed to be breaking down just as conspicuously as its architecture. The Wythenshawe he had left had never been blessed with financial riches, but it once had a pride and a sense of identity that had evaporated by the time he had returned. The church he'd attended as a child was also falling apart and congregations were down to single figures. That building had provided a meeting place and a focal point for the community in his youth, but it seemed it had lost its relevance in the twenty-first century. Greg wasn't having any of that, so he set about restoring it.

In the years since returning he has begged, borrowed and badgered all around to help join in his efforts to restore battered pride to Wythenshawe. The results have been truly astounding. The buildings have been overhauled and he has built a café, gym and dance studio that lies at the very heart of the community. His efforts and those of the team he has called to his cause have given his area a renewed sense of purpose. They have a sense of pride in their achievements that is self-fulfilling, self-promoting and encouraging for the next generation coming through. Greg would never say that he has created anything so uncool as a youth club, but the gym that forms the core of this amazing complex attracts teenagers from all around. Kids that once roamed the streets getting involved in violence, crime and drugs are now going to the gym and getting fit. They are taking a pride in themselves as well as their community, and all around people are once more discovering their own feelings of self-worth. Instead of joining those marauding gangs of miscreants so often written about in the press, Greg's personality and undimming positivity has compelled whole legions of teenagers to join *his* gang. He doesn't promise anything 'rock 'n' roll'. All he offers is the chance to 'refurbish old buildings, turn dilapidated churches into gyms and dance studios and maybe paint some fences for old ladies'. And do you know what, they flock to him!

He gets everyone involved and he has everyone invested in what he is doing and why. Greg rarely gets thanked for his efforts as he should be, but he says he needs nothing more than to see the positive effects of his project rippling through his community. That is thanks enough for him. Everyone is benefiting and the government are rightly adopting Greg's model for regenerating certain inner-city areas, such is his success in giving people in the area the respect, pride and self-worth that so many used to feel could only be found down criminal avenues.

I was fortunate enough to meet Greg and was only too happy to throw the weight of the show's resources behind his ongoing efforts to improve the facilities he provides for everyone to enjoy. We helped refurbish the dance studios, kitchen and community café that is the hub for the United Estates of Wythenshawe. We managed to secure £70,000-worth of charitable donations for the cause in just six days, and we managed to get a few more people signed up and investing in the promotion of their own area. Being part of that project gave me such pleasure but, more than that, it gave me such hope. It showed me that the poorest areas financially do not have to be written off. I saw for myself just how many good and giving people there were in an area that no one will mind admitting has had more than its fair share of bad press.

Historically it has always been the case that more crime, more delinquency and more problems with drugs, alcoholism and antisocial behaviour will arise in poor areas. However, men like Greg Davies and all of the wonderful people we saw getting fully stuck into the Wythenshawe makeover show me that it doesn't always have to be that way. Person by person, he helped restore some pride – to the point where doing the right things and having some respect for oneself and one another has become the 'cool' norm. Being an unruly yob is now the harder path to take. It is seen by too many now as unacceptable and uncool in Wythenshawe – at least while Greg Davies is in town.

Another who came to the show, this time with a message aimed at taking gangs and guns from our streets, was the inimitable Pat Regan. Again, amazing. Pat lost her son, Danny, to a shotgun attack. She did not shy away from the fact that Danny was a known drug dealer. She did not, as so many do, use tragedy to rose-tint her every memory of someone she loved in spite of his wrongdoing. No, she got involved with campaigning, pulling out all the stops until Tony Blair's government took notice of what she was saying. She gave the authorities a far greater insight than any focus group could into the problems that had led to her son's demise. She opened up my eyes, too, and dropped everything when we asked her to help intervene with a youngster who was threatening to make the same choices that Danny once had.

She got through to him as she got through to so many teenagers, steering them away from dangerous choices. She only worked on a shoestring budget but that did not seem to dilute her ability to make a huge difference. Anyone who met her was left in no doubt that poverty persuaded so many like Danny to the temptations of the fast money and flash cars on offer via drug dealing. She understood the temptation, but fought hard to educate people so that they might make a difference for themselves without taking an 'easy' way out that could ultimately prove fatal.

Pat tragically became a victim of violent crime herself. Almost unbelievably she was stabbed in her own home in 2008. I only found out when I walked into the office and found Kelly, the producer of Pat's show, crying. She told me the bad news and we all just sat around in a silence broken only by the occasional sob. I won't claim to have been Pat's best friend, nor even to have known her all that well, but I did see the impact she had on people's lives and I saw the guts and determination with which she went about each day, always committed to trying to improve the lives of others despite the tragedy of her own terrible loss. Overcoming the personal pain she had to endure when constantly invited to relive the moments that led to her son's death, she remained focused on the message she thought necessary to get across to whole communities, any one of whose members she feared might end up as Danny did.

I try to do what I can, but nothing I am ever likely to do will compare to the bravery Pat Regan showed. If I am ever able to make half the difference she did to people's lives, then I will die a peaceful, contented man. To that end, although Pat is no longer with us, I worked on a project with her other son that will hopefully further highlight the problems this country has with knife crime and, more importantly, what can be done to tackle it at a local level. He's a star in the making that one, just like his mum. We'll be doing what we can to keep her message alive; we can only hope that it is then taken on board by those who need to listen.

Bravery is a trait that I can only admire. I admit that, at times of personal crisis, during those moments when the very fibre of one's being is tested, I have sometimes been found wanting. There's no point pretending otherwise: Carla is the true strength in my marriage. If the press are at our door or our family is under attack in any way, she is the one who swings into action first – sometimes swinging for me on the way! She sets the tone of our response and she leads the charge to face down any accusers.

Of course you can never know how you might react in extreme, unforeseen crises. I was quite surprised at how calmly

I reacted to a recent 70-mph car smash. I might have expected to be a hysterical wreck but I was, even according to Graham, quite lucid throughout the whole ordeal. Courage can be summoned, even by the most unlikely person; it may lurk deep within, ready to surprise us in truly desperate times. However, I believe there is something special that exists only within a certain few that really marks them out as brave.

I can only be thankful that I have never yet had to prove myself like Jody, another heroic guest of the show, has. She is a remarkable young lady who became paralysed by a fear that she might become a victim of gang violence. She had witnessed the murder of her best friend since primary school, Tyrone. She watched him set upon by wild-eyed thugs and could do nothing as they beat, gassed – yes, gassed – and stabbed Tyrone to death. She was with him as his killers, a group of five evil animals, all brandishing weapons, approached. More joined them as they neared Jody, Tyrone and a few others. Panicked, people began to disperse. The gang gave chase. They caught Tyrone and began beating him with baseball bats and iron bars. One of the gang even sprayed gas into Tyrone's eyes to blind him and prolong his torture.

Jody had stopped chasing after Tyrone in order to help a little boy who had been felled by a brick hurled by one of the gang members. When she did finally reach Tyrone, Jody told me that 'he was in a right state', eyes rolling and almost unrecognisable from the injuries he had sustained. The ambulance crew that arrived could do little to save him and, by the time he arrived at hospital, Tyrone had died.

Jody knew that people in her community would be terrified to speak out against the notorious thugs who publicly preyed on everyone's fears. She was threatened by the gang and warned against admitting to seeing anything that might endanger their liberty. She was taken out of school, missing out on friends as well as the vital years of her education, such was the danger posed by some members of the gang she had shared classes with. Jody was told in no uncertain terms that, if she testified, she would suffer a similar fate to Tyrone's, only this time they added the chilling caveat: 'Tyrone was stabbed, you'll be shot!' She had seen what this gang could do; she had been told she would lose her own life and she knew these threats were not idle. Jody had seen this gang of up to thirty thugs control her streets for years, without any fear of censure from the authorities. Her faith in the British justice system was bankrupt but, do you know what? SHE STILL TESTIFIED!

Something inside her said, 'This is wrong, this has to stop', and she made bloody sure that she did what she could to get justice for Tyrone, not to mention everyone else who had been caught up in this gang's reign of terror. It was extraordinarily brave. I don't know that I could have done the same had my family's or my own life been so deliberately and sincerely threatened. But Jody stood up as the key witness at the trial and faced down the four people standing before her in the dock, despite knowing that she would live the rest of her days fearing reprisals or revenge attacks. I can only look up to and admire people like Jody. Their heroic deeds speak for themselves.

Those three people typify the sort of spirit that should be an example for us all. One person fighting hard to turn his whole community around, another turning personal tragedy into a mission to educate the whole nation, and an individual who refused to let the endangering of her own life get in the way of doing the right thing to see justice done.

I have met many more who have exemplified all that can be good in Britain and all that remains so remarkable about the human spirit. Thankfully we don't have to look too far to find a story of someone whose kindness and big-heartedness has won the day. Even though our media diets are sustained more by the negative than the positive – and I guess it is only right that we continue to highlight problems that we could all do more to fix – it is nice to hear the good stories too. Positive events like the Pride of Britain Awards do much to cheer the nation. I am now a regular at the event. We have featured many of the ceremony's champions on our show and I never fail to be amazed by their 'unbreakability'.

She incurred the wrath of her family by shopping her two sons to the police. I say, well done to her. She put herself through the heartbreak of condemning her own sons to jail, but her reasons were the right ones as far as I am concerned. She can have derived no pleasure from doing this; at one stroke she had to banish the two sons she adored to a life of incarceration. She knew her family, the very people she would need to support her through this trauma, would turn its back on her for doing so. But she did it and it is good she did. Why? Well, Carol's two sons had left their victim, Marc Parkinson, blind in one eye after beating him to a pulp. The attack was unprovoked and unjustified in every way.

I keep saying that it is parents who must take more responsibility for setting an example and leading the way. Well, Carol did that and more, by going against what must have been her every maternal instinct to protect and forgive her own flesh and blood. Instead she did what she knew was right, pressing ahead for the sake of Marc and every fair-minded citizen in our society.

The Pride of Britain Awards ceremony is in itself amazing, always leaving everyone who attends them so humbled. I am a man whose job leaves him prone to ranting and raving, but when I attend these ceremonies no words are needed: I find myself just clapping wildly in some places or watching in silent awe in others. Even in the image-obsessed world of show business, there is a tangible sense that even the most demanding of divas are checking in their egos at the door. Whatever quibbles, stresses or hardships some of us might be thinking we are doing well to endure, they just do not compare to the courageous stories told at these awards. Services personnel sacrificing themselves for their brothers in arms, smothering an exploding grenade so that others would be spared the full force of the blast. Lance Corporal Matt Croucher, you are amazing. As is Bernard Butler, the 'everyday lorry driver', who ignored his own heart condition to rush through a fifty-foot wall of ferocious chemical flames to rescue a complete stranger after a motorway smash. There were so many people there at those awards, as indeed there are so many people up and down this land of ours, who genuinely qualify for the title of hero/heroine. They show the right way for this country and, at the most basic level, provide us all with the motivation to be just that bit better as a person each day. For all they have contributed and all they have inspired in me, I can only say thank you.

Most of my work on *The Jeremy Kyle Show* does involve wading through many a difficult problem. But every once in a while I get to work on specific shows that are dedicated to the sort of awe-inspiring heroes and heroines who make up every Pride of Britain or, more specifically, Children of Courage Awards roster ever written. Not so long back I met the – yes – amazing Michael Weir and his amazing family.

Michael is fast becoming a bit of a regular on the media circuit, such is the effect he has on all those who meet him. He, his mum, Ivy, and his dad, Andrew, must be on the short-list for every award going. If there was one presented for Just Getting On with It, Making the Best of It and Teaching the Rest of Us How It Should Be Done, there'd be no contest. They'd win it hands down. And quite rightly so. Where bravery, courage, stoicism, determination and dedication to a cause are concerned, this family must be runaway favourite for most gongs given. Michael was born with Apert Syndrome and his symptoms include malformations of the hands and skull. He has never been able to speak but, from what I saw, he can communicate supremely effectively using the smiles and boundless energy with which he fills every room. Michael and his family resonated with me, particularly because they have survived the most vile abuse directed at them from members of the Great British public. Just because Michael looks different, he and his family have been targeted for vandalism to their property and the most vicious of verbal attacks. He knows exactly what is going on all around him, but for years he has been subjected to taunts of 'Devil Boy' and other insults from strangers who know nothing of this amazing young man who is just eleven years old.

Even more amazing to me than Michael, though, is his mum. Ivy Oliver was rather quiet and unassuming when I first met her. She was dressed normally, as anyone else I would meet in the studio might be, and there was nothing about her appearance that made her stand out as remarkable. She had the same cheeky grin and twinkle in her eye so evident in her son, but it wasn't until reading about what she goes through each day to look after him that I got a true perspective on just what a remarkable lady she really is. She didn't talk too much about her extraordinary timetable. She was typically self-effacing, and everything I put to her as being, well, amazing, she just dismissed with a shrug of her shoulders.

Michael is one never-ending ball of fun, whose zest for life is endless. We nearly had to give three researchers the day off after trying to keep up with him for just three hours. Boy, does he have an appetite for playing. The family's daily routine involves ferrying Michael to and from school across Manchester and then being run into the ground as he whizzes about playing football. His every movement, every second of the day has to be watched, since the slightest bump to Michael's head could prove fatal. Then he has to be shepherded through the taunts and guided away from the stares and the insults daily hurled their way. Money has to be found to replace the slashed tyres on their family car, and to keep both phone and car running, so that Michael can make the next of his endless hospital appointments. At the end of all that, the rest of the family will go to bed, shattered. Ivy, though, has to stand sentry over Michael's bed. If she drops off for one moment, there is a very real possibility that she might miss Michael choking or the valve implant in his neck becoming blocked and killing him. That responsibility to keep him alive as he and the rest of the world sleeps is hers and hers alone, but she does not shirk it and never complains about it. She steals twenty-minute naps here and there and does everything she can to provide Michael with every bit of happiness he can cram into each day. How she does it, I'll never know. How she can do it and still find time to have a laugh and a chat with the likes of me is completely beyond my comprehension. She and her family are just amazing.

I really could sit here all day and reel off a list of truly inspirational people I have met. With every name that springs to mind comes another heart-warming memory of a moment I was privileged to share. The best memories, I suppose, are when we as a show have been able to give a little back. From getting eight-year-old William Hardcastle, who was suffering from cystic fibrosis, a slot presenting the Virgin Radio Breakfast Show, to taking little Olive Kelly to Disneyland, it really is nice to play a part in making someone's wish come true. I'll never forget Martin Heald. He had bravely battled osteosarcoma for years. When I first met him he looked very ill indeed, but again he never complained of the obvious pain he was suffering. Instead he focused on the trip we'd organised for him, to one place he'd always wanted to go: Chester Zoo!

Now I am not a big animal fan, and certainly not a *big*-animal fan. I have been left scarred mentally and literally by an encounter I once had with an Alsatian dog as a child. I was minding my own business, playing about on the floor as young kids can, when this dog set upon me. It bit my face without warning or provocation, drawing blood from the wound it had opened on my forehead. I was soon scooped away and stitched up, but ever since I have had a terrible fear of dogs and some large animals. Zoos, therefore, are not where I feel at my most comfortable.

Still, Martin wanted to experience all that Chester Zoo had to offer as, deep down, he had always wanted to be a vet. I was meant to be there as his guide, but he was pretty much holding my hand as we were allowed access into pens with animals like rhinoceroses that looked anything but pleased to see us. One actually charged at us. It stomped ferociously towards the fence that I in particular was anxious to back away from further. Martin didn't flinch. He stayed there and just watched calmly as this 6,000-lb dump truck on four legs zeroed in on us at about 25 mph. I thought it would plough through the fence and trample us all to death. Thankfully, it didn't. It slowed and stopped right in front of Martin, who just looked calmly at this magnificent animal. You could have forgiven a kid in desperate pain with bone cancer for being a little perturbed, but I have never seen serenity like it. It was as though he had some sort of telepathic Crocodile Dundee-type connection with it. All of his problems and all of that bravery in dealing with them, all of his talents, all of his unique qualities – and on top of that the kid was a rhino-whisperer! Amazing.

That brush with the jaws of an Alsatian has reminded me of another incredible lady I met just a few weeks ago. Her name is Princess and she came to the show to offer inspiration to a couple of other guests who were struggling to come to terms with some facial disfigurements that had left them scared to leave the house. Princess's gesture was all the more remarkable as she was just twelve weeks out of the fourth of eight operations she will require to rebuild her own face. She too had suffered an attack by a dog. Her dog.

As Princess lay in her bed, the family pet was curled up beside her. They both fell asleep as they did every night together. The next memory Princess had is of waking up and thinking that a brick had somehow been dropped on her face! She knew something was wrong and so went to look in the bathroom mirror. She expected to see some sort of blood but could never have been prepared to see that half of her face was missing! Princess can only guess that her dog must have been spooked in the middle of the night. It must have awoken aggressively from a bad dream and set upon the nearest person to it.

The dog had devoured Princess's face, leaving a massive hole where her nose used to be. She went straight to hospital of course and, from the minute she arrived, began dazzling everyone with her sense of humour. From Day 1 and her first restorative operation she set about tackling this event with positivity. Instead of worrying about how things might be for her, she walked around the wards comforting any worried patients fretting about *their* forthcoming procedures. Princess suffered abuse in the streets too. People pointed, stared, and a group of young lads sneered as they asked, 'What's up with your face?' Princess replied deadpan with a message that more than a few of my guests on other shows could do well to heed: 'This,' she said, 'is what happens when you sleep with dogs!' Brilliant.

Princess blew everyone away with her capacity to cope and her enthusiasm for helping everyone else get through whatever was bothering them. She saw her ordeal as just another experience to deal with and got on with it without one word of complaint.

On that same show I also met two little girls who brought tears to my eyes. Hayley and Ashanti are the only two girls in the UK with progeria, a condition in which the sufferer's body ages at about seven times the normal rate. Hayley had been on a previous show with me to talk about this with her parents. In the wake of that show being aired came the call from Ashanti's parents. Ashanti, it transpired, recognised Hayley from a TV documentary that had been made about her. From the moment she had seen Hayley on screen, she became convinced that they must be twins because there was the only person who looked remotely like her in the whole world. She wanted to meet Hayley and so we set it up in the same way that we sometimes do surprise reunions. They met and there was not a dry eye in the house as they both sat with me on the steps of the stage and talked and laughed and made light of their differences in a way that also left me with a tear or two in the eyes. They are happily in contact now, and their families are united in moving forward, appreciating every second of every day they share with their children. Hayley and Ashanti are adorable and their families a revelation. I couldn't say they are anything but amazing.

Those are just a few of the amazing characters that exist on every street in this country. They are the ones that immediately jump out in my mind, but there are countless others who are equally deserving of mention here. Such as – and here's another one – Joan, who set up and continues to manage the amazing Tumaini Orphanage in Kenya. The work she does out there for some truly wonderful children is just breathtaking, and I was proud we could do our bit in some small way too.

I have mentioned everyone here (whilst being forced to

leave out far too many more) as much to thank them as to highlight the spirit they exemplify. They are exceptional people, whose qualities, I believe, can exist in all of us; they should spur us all on to try harder to display these qualities more. None have let unfortunate circumstances get them down or hold them back. There is no blaming of bad luck, no hiding behind bad starts in order to opt out of life. They get on with it, and I bet they enjoy each minute of their lives.

However, just as amazing to me are the amount of people who have turned their lives around. So I'd also like to salute every alcoholic who admitted their problem and then sought help for it. Every drug addict that owned up to their plight and then honestly saw through the help required to recover. The couples, the families, the estranged parents and daughters – everyone who dared to confront a problem and choose the often harder option of fixing it.

Most of those I have mentioned throughout this chapter will never need any of the support services offered backstage at *The Jeremy Kyle Show*. A great many do, though. I know it can't be easy to admit to problems, and the programmes we offer to those serious about getting help are only ever going to be tough to complete. There is nothing easy about seeing through the hard yards of rehab or taking the steps necessary to truly rectify some of the issues out there. It takes a whole heap of commitment and soul-searching that will always remain beyond some. But for those who can stick at it, there are amazing rewards on offer. And so it follows that anyone still standing to receive those rewards at the end of their journey through a personal hell must also be amazing too. I certainly think so.

12

Some People are Just Evil!

I admit I was angry. I admit I went too far. The minute I said it I thought my whole world would come crashing in on me. I was no longer capable of rational thought; the capacity to hold a civil conversation had deserted me. In full view of a live studio audience, with the cameras rolling and despite the protestations of the editor screaming in my ear, I lost it. Big time! I walked over to a diminutive little lady and barked with all of my might that she should have been sterilised at birth! Denied the chance to ever have any children!

I played the comments back to myself in slow motion as the whole studio momentarily ground to a standstill around me. What had I done? The silent panic that gripped me was punctured by a noise building around me that I only faintly recognised. Suddenly I realised: the noise was applause and I was being cheered to the rafters for voicing an opinion that surely only despots and dictators have ever gone public with! Had the mask slipped? Had the audience wildly clapping all about me taken a wrong turn into the studio whilst en route to a fascist rally? Apparently not. They had seen, just as I had seen, that here was a lady who did not just have a few failings. This was a woman who had deliberately allowed her own children to suffer almost unutterable cruelty. This wasn't a woman whose family endured tough but tolerable hard-ships as she herself struggled through hard times. She was, in truth, beyond help. Beyond reason, beyond logic; and lacking any of the basic thread of decency that runs through all the rest of us. She was evil, pure and simple. Some people just are.

That encounter was the first time I remember letting my emotions get the better of me during filming. I thought I'd be sacked. That day had begun like any other at the Manchester studios. It wasn't until I had read the research notes for that morning's show that things changed. The seriousness of what we were about to discuss seemed to be on an entirely different level to the usual disputes I had tried to sort. I hoped beyond hope that the accounts supplied by this mother's (and I use that term biologically only) two daughters had been in part made up, or at the very least embroidered for effect. Alas, as I was soon to discover, there was no embellishment. They hadn't exaggerated one word of the horrific stories they had told our researchers about their childhood. If anything, they had tried to play some elements of their abuse down.

I'll be honest now and I make no apology for the way I feel about this. Stories where young children are being hurt or have been abused are the ones that short-circuit my emotions more than any other. Stories of abuse, which in some cases amount to little more than sustained campaigns of torture – yes, torture – against defenceless toddlers move me to tears. There is nothing more important to me than my children. The words to describe the power of the love I feel for my own kids still fail me. There is nothing I would not do for my own children. Nothing at all. Everything I have worked towards, every struggle I have endured to get where I am today, has been for them. The most important moments of my life have been when holding my newborn children. From that moment, and every one since where I've cradled them in my arms, the responsibility of parenthood hits home absolutely. I have seen on countless occasions my three daughters look up to their daddy, not knowing what is going on in the big wide world all around them. It might be a giggle, a little wiggle of tiny fingers, or maybe just a pudgy smile on their beautiful faces that gets me, but get me it does, and get me it always will.

My commitment to the task, my resolve to see through this wonderful privilege and responsibility has been reinforced with every one of those moments. There is no harm I would knowingly let come to my children, and I would lay my life down in a heartbeat to spare any of them any of the upset I once swore blind I would do my best to protect them from. I thought all parents were like this, but my time on *The Jeremy Kyle Show* has taught me just how wrong I was on that one.

I was trying to get through, explaining what she needed to do to win back the trust of two daughters who, amazingly, still wanted a relationship with a mother who had so wilfully neglected them throughout their younger years. What was discussed on stage did not even scratch the surface of what had actually taken place in their home for the best part of a decade. Being a daytime show, broadcast at 9.25 each morning, we naturally can't divulge some of the more squalid details which are occasionally relayed to us beforehand. That might help explain why, on certain occasions, I might seem dispro-portionately angry with some of the guests I confront on stage. For obvious reasons, an exchange where anything too shocking, too sordid or unsavoury comes to light has to be lost, editorially, legally, sometimes even morally, to the cutting-room floor. Clearly the stuff that angers me most is also likely to be the most shocking stuff. We can't show everything we film, but that doesn't mean I can dilute how I feel on any given subject, just for the sake of the editors. If someone disgusts me, I'll tell them. If they have behaved abominably, I'll say so. If someone should have been sterilised to prevent her own children suffering as they did . . . well, you know what happened there.

The catalogue of horrors meted out to her own children

by this woman is just too extensive for me to go into in any great detail here. The social services files on this woman alone were enough to occupy a filing cabinet of their own! I am prevented from naming her in this book and that, to me, is just one more insult. She should be named, shamed, and held up as an example to everyone of why some people just should not be allowed anywhere near children, far less have any of their own. Beyond that, I honestly believe she should long ago have been incarcerated for the crimes she committed against her own children.

Her daughters told me that, from an early age, they were forced to fend for themselves. They would scavenge through the bins of their own house. Mum would be out; the cupboards would be bare. They were forced to try and cook the odd frozen sausage on a barely warm radiator or eat any crumbs they could find on the floor. Whilst Mum was shooting up next door, the kids would be locked in the bathroom. The bathroom would be chained shut from the outside so that Mum's drug bubble wouldn't be burst by anything so irritating as the need to nurture the kids she was only too happy to have whilst knocking about with the local riff-raff. Occasionally, when Mummy wasn't lolling about her pit in a daze or collapsing in an empty bathtub, the kids would be evicted from their usual prison and sent to a bare bedroom for three days at a time. No food, no way out. Unbelievably, they were forced to steal clothes, score drugs from the local pusher and on occasions, this mother would ply them with enough amphetamine to leave them as high as a kite for days! I understand that people in the depths of addiction can do things that the rest of us would find deplorable, unbelievable even. But the litany of failures, the never-ending list of deliberate acts which this mother must have known would lead to the harm or endangering of her offspring I just found disgusting. And more than that, evil!

These kids were left ignored, malnourished and unclothed, but for a few dirty rags they themselves had to try and wash in a sink of cold water. Successions of men came and went, adding a terrifying new twist to the torment as they watched their mum occasionally raped and pummelled as her search for drugs continued. The kids themselves were slapped, kicked and punched if they dared to try and help Mummy when the drugs had run out. They endured the worst of it until they were able to make good their own escape, but still they wanted a relationship with a woman who had not once been there for them. They tried to blame all of her failings on the drugs she had taken and hoped that deep inside was the mother they had always longed for. With our help they wanted to draw out the woman they needed to believe lived within the angry, hollow husk that sat before us. They needed an apology or, failing that, at least acknowledgement of what they had been subjected to. They got neither.

This woman refused to accept that she had been anything but a perfect mother. She admitted to a drug habit (not the rapacious addiction it actually was back then), but blamed her children for not being as supportive as they should have been towards her. She actually thought these poor defence-less mites should somehow have done more to improve *her* life. She saw them as a drain on limited resources, no doubt jealously viewing the few pennies she might have thrown their way each week as money that could instead have been put towards the purchase of her next stash. She said she had done all she could for them and that they should be more grateful. She disagreed with their version of events and every word of the reams of testimony social services had accumulated on her.

So it was then that I blew my top and told her exactly what everyone watching would surely be thinking of her. She still showed no remorse. I fought my natural instincts and tried to leave the door ajar. However much I did not myself believe she was capable of it, sitting next to this hideous excuse for a human being were two young ladies still hopeful of engineering some sort of relationship with their mother, twenty years down the line. I offered mediation. Graham was on hand to try and help find common ground away from the cameras and studio audience. I fought every instinct tearing away inside of me and was as conciliatory as I could be. I put it simply, and asked if this woman was prepared to at least sit and try and find a way to accept her daughters into her life. I promised we would work with her for as long as it took, told her we would take it slowly and plan for the long term. I wasn't looking for miracles, just a sense that she might want to try and be a mother in some capacity to her children. She wasn't interested. She again blamed her children for her problems, said they should have been there for her, not the other way round, and invited them to get on with their lives without her!

Although I have no direct experience of drug taking, I have met more than enough characters whose combustibility is in part defined by their history of drug dependence. I tried to give this woman the benefit of the doubt. If only to keep my own faith in humanity, I tried to reason that the pressure of being in front of the cameras might have made her react the way she did. She might have felt cornered, realised that her usual tricks of manipulation and lying were not working, and so bolted to the relative safety of a dressing room backstage. Strangely I found myself hoping that maybe she was still in the grip of an addiction and that her thoughts were too clouded by whatever she was taking to see the situation for what it was. Again I was wrong. This woman told me backstage that she was clean and perfectly *compos mentis*. She went on to reject her daughters out of hand and tell them that she would prefer to live out the rest of her days without them 'constantly going on at her and lying about stuff that happened years ago'.

How does anyone get through to someone who is clearly completely unaware of the basic rights and wrongs that are ingrained, albeit in varying degrees, in the rest of the world? I can offer all the aftercare help in the world. I could lock someone in a room for twenty-four hours a day with Graham and everyone else in his team, but no amount of counselling can untwist the twisted in some, can it? How do you cater for someone who, to me, just seems evil? I think it is their denial of wrongdoing and wholesale blaming of someone else for horrific, unspeakable acts that so repels me. If you want to be evil, at least admit it, acknowledge it. Sod it, if you're that evil, be sick and be proud of it – at least the rest of us would know where we stand! But to carry on, destroying lives, whilst taking no responsibility and accepting none of the blame, is just so wrong.

I can only presume that that woman was so deeply ashamed of the truth of what had gone on that she could not bring herself to face it. Looking at her two children each day might bring back the awful horrors she had inflicted on them, and maybe she decided that that was just too much to cope with. That is the only explanation I can come up with to explain that final rejection of two children, who graduated from injury only to find insult at the end of an awful journey spanning three decades.

I would love to say that this was the one stand-out example of unfathomable abuse that has been brought to me in the last three years. Unfortunately it is not. The sad truth is that the airing of one story of this type inevitably leads to our phone lines being jammed with tales of more, many of them just as bad. This wasn't the only tale of a mother turning her back on her kids so vindictively. I guess charities like the NSPCC wouldn't be around if such stories were isolated. I understand it can be hard to face past mistakes, especially ones that have caused so much torment to the flesh and blood we are all meant to love, cherish and protect above all others. It can be hard in the cold, sober light of day to reflect on all you have done that's bad. Seeing the people you have hurt might bring painful reminders of a person you have ceased to be. But it is still necessary. The hurt your pride will feel will be nothing to the hurt you have inflicted on those you are attempting any reunion with. It is never easy. The road is bumpy, at best, but it has to be followed diligently if anyone is to find their catharsis, and write their own happy ending.

Unfortunately, examples of parents completely failing to love and nurture their children are rife in this country. I remember it was a story of wilful abuse that first brought me to tears during a recording of the show. Maybe this particular show is so fresh in my mind because I have recently been wading through the tragic story of 'Baby P' in the papers. I feel guilty for having been compelled to read every last detail printed about that poor baby's demise. I felt like the worst kind of horror-whore as I slavishly devoured every morsel of information served up to me. I think my morbid curiosity was amplified to such an extent because I just could not believe what I was reading. The story represented the absolute worst example of human behaviour. I just could not comprehend how anyone could be so callously capable of meting out to Baby P what those cold, murdering, sadistic bastards had. I'm sure I wasn't the only person gripped by sheer disbelief at what I was reading, nor can I have been the only one whose faith in the human race was knocked in a way that it will never truly recover from. I had always liked to believe that all people, no matter how terrible on balance, did at least have the capacity for some good within them. The case of Baby P shook that and showed me more than ever that some people are just evil. The first time this was confirmed to me in person, though, was when I met a poor lady who went by the name of Sharon.

Baby P's abominable torture and death echoed a story I had heard about two years earlier. Sharon came to the show looking for help to come to terms with the almost incalculable loss of the two people she had loved most in the world. Sharon's life had already been shattered by the devastating killing of her daughter three years prior to appearing with me. Her daughter was another victim of an evil murderer whose actions no sane person could ever surely justify.

Sharon had built her existence around Elizabeth. She was loving and doting and wonderful – everything any mother could wish for. However, Elizabeth had told her mother that a strange neighbour had kept taking pictures of her. Two days later, with no more warning than that, Sharon was told that her daughter had been raped and killed by that same neighbour! Unable to bury her daughter for three months because of the trial, Sharon sought some sort of closure in court. The murderer spat in her face! How can that happen in a human mind? After ripping the soul out of someone, after raping and killing their child, how can you then spit in their face!? A life sentence, ten life sentences, just doesn't seem a high enough tariff. When a murderer has deliberately caused so much pain and suffering on the one hand, why should he be rewarded with shelter, safety, warmth and a good daily feed? Where's the justice?

I wish Sharon's troubles had ended there: they would have been plenty enough for all of us. She coped as best she could by trying to forget and deliberately keeping herself ignorant of the darker details of her daughter's ordeal. Now, though, she was occupied by an even more horrifying death of someone else she also cherished.

A couple of years after Elizabeth's loss to that vile pervert, her cousin Becky had given birth to a son, Aaron. Aaron had become a source of pride and joy, a means by which Sharon could escape her horrific memories, and a child into whom she could pour the love she still yearned to give. To some extent Aaron had filled a part of the void created by the tragedy of losing Elizabeth the way she did. That she was then to lose Aaron in even more horrendous circumstances seems cruel beyond belief.

Aaron was just one year old when Becky met her future partner, Andrew. Sharon hated Andrew from the moment she met him; she could just tell the guy was different in a sinister and chilling sort of way. Increasingly often he would be at the house when Sharon visited. She would see him blowing cannabis smoke rings into the child's face, but when she got up to intervene she was told to 'Fuck off!' in no uncertain terms.

Becky started to fall under Andrew's spell and was soon completely under his control. Sharon was denied visiting time with Aaron, but was aghast to witness his deterioration when occasionally allowed into the house. Andrew would refuse to be around if Sharon was there, but it was what he had done before she arrived that left Sharon crippled with tears and that tightening knot of despair that can make a person physically sick.

Aaron had started to become covered in bruising. As she told me this story when we were recording the show, tears were streaming down my face, even though I was meant to be the composed voice of calm and reason. She recalled how baby Aaron's ears were black from bruising caused by being picked up by the face and held too tightly. The child smelled constantly of urine but Andrew, who now ruled the roost with violent flashes of hot temper, refused to allow him to be changed. Sharon stood clutching poor Aaron. He clung to her, burbling 'Nana', as if imploring her to do something to save him. One night she tried.

She confronted Andrew and Becky at their home and demanded to see Aaron. When she saw the baby, though, her mouth fell open in shock. I am crying again as I write this and it is almost too painful, too incomprehensible for the words to come out in this order – THEY JUST DON'T MAKE SENSE TO ME. Aaron's patchwork of bruising had now completely covered his body. Around his tiny ankles Sharon could see the perfectly formed markings of Andrew's fingerprints. Evidently, Aaron had been swung around by his ankles and flung into a wall. Repeatedly. Sharon groped for explanations as she told me that it must have been Andrew's jealous rages that prompted such a sickening outburst. That said, she could not discount that he might have just done it to get some sick pleasurable kick out of it.

They fought on the stairs but Sharon was overpowered and forced from the premises. Bloodied and bruised herself, with cuts on her arms, markings on her face and very real death threats ringing in her ears, Sharon waited for news of baby Aaron.

She got a call the next day to say that he was at the hospital, on a life-support machine. Sharon went there. She saw her 'little angel' lying on a massive hospital bed. Its adult size swallowed Aaron whole and only made the framing of the picture she saw before her all the more unbearable. Blood was trickling out of Aaron's nose and ears, and his arm was broken. Sharon overheard the doctors intimating that Aaron must have been thrown about and 'had obviously seen the four corners of the wall'.

Methadone was also found in Aaron's bloodstream, which means that the people who should have been doing everything to care for someone so defenceless and innocent were also forcing drugs into his system too. As if the ritual beatings and the wanton slaughter of a child wasn't enough, as she stood over the bed and watched Aaron fade away, she looked up at

Becky and looked for some sense that she recognised the wrong she had allowed to happen to her own son. Apparently she just smirked and said: 'Life goes on.'

Disgusting. Absolutely bloody disgusting! How else can that be anything but pure evil at its most toxic?!

Now, what do you think happened to the two evil, hate-filled, drug-fuelled monsters who perpetrated these heinous acts? Sharon has in effect been handed a painful life sentence from which she might never truly recover. She no doubt replays all that came to pass, analysing over and over again just what else she could have done to prevent this sickening tragedy. I know she was racked with guilt that she did not do more sooner but she truly did not know the extent of what was going on behind the doors so viciously closed to her. She was not aware of the true nature of baby Aaron's decline nor his worsening toll of horrific injuries. Beyond that she probably feared for her own life if her benign attempts at intervention for Aaron's sake were misconstrued as unwanted meddling by a man to whom lethal violence came so easily.

For those who believe in 'an eye for an eye', capital punishment is probably the only penal measure that can be weighed against the despicable crimes inflicted on Aaron, and maybe even that would not go far enough for some. Rehabilitation and incarceration would be the more moderate view. Personally, I struggle to understand how a course in prison might help rehabilitate anyone capable of such things. Now, I believe passionately in the work that Graham and his team do both for and outside the show. I have actually seen the positive benefits of rehabilitation programmes and seen some lives which once seemed hopeless turned around by them. That said, there must be a limit. Graham or other members of his profession, even if they were using the best rehab programme ever devised by man, surely could not work a literal miracle in turning around anyone capable of the crimes I've discussed above, could they? I mean, how much work should society really be expected to invest in someone so far removed from and so sickeningly out of touch with all of the basic decencies that should bind us? To 'stand by and watch' without a care as your baby is tossed about a room and has the life battered out of him for no reason surely justifies the very harshest of penalties, right? It is the lowest of the low, the very rock bottom of the human spectrum and comes from a place so, well, evil, that no amount of counselling could ever wholly rectify, right? And all that aside, for the criminal acts alone, this couple who allowed a baby to be so hideously killed in their charge must surely have faced, AT THE VERY LEAST, a lifetime behind bars, no? Well, according to the courts of this country, a six-year sentence, of which she might serve only three and a half years, was sufficient for Becky. Andrew got twenty-four years, but I can't help thinking that there are millions out there who might view a firing squad as a much more efficient use of resources for him!

In 2005–2006 the average cost of housing a prisoner was £32,888. That's nearly £70,000 a year for this pair and nearly £800,000 for the cost of Andrew's full sentence alone.

Stories such as Sharon's haunt me sometimes. There is like a domino effect in my mind where one bad image triggers another and then one horrifying story crashes into the memory of another. At such times it is easy to despair and wonder just how far some people have moved on from the worst excesses of barbarism in the Middle Ages. I won't claim that sadist killings are in any way some sort of epidemic in the country, but the papers won't have to wait too long for another tragic tale to tell. I remember my shock at the story of Josef Fritzl and the reign of incestuous terror he wrought over his basement family in Austria. I thought such a thing could never be repeated in history and then, not too long later, it transpires that in Sheffield a man had been serially abusing two daughters in much the same way for the best part of twenty years! Is there really that much evil in the world and going on all around us? Just like the papers, my researchers don't have to wait too long to hear the phones ring with more stories of the most appalling abuse. Just working through this passage and Sharon's story has only reminded me of the evil abuse that rained down on another guest of mine.

She was a battered mother of two who used to cower in the corner whilst her husband thumped and kicked her repeatedly. She would take the beatings daily and sometimes provoke them, just to stop her assailant's attentions turning violently towards their children. After years of steady abuse that often left her face puffed up like an unrecognisable football, she got the call she had always dreaded. Her husband had driven off with the two young children and had decided to kill himself with them. He went through with it as he had always threatened he might in drunken rages. This sick, deranged and evil man had thrust a screwdriver into the ears of his own sons, despite the pained screams of their desperate mother on the other end of the phone. He wanted her to hear their last moments; he must have planned for it to be this way. She looked to me and everyone else for answers, but how can you explain such acts? Some people are just beyond my grasp of reality, of normality even. The people capable of the monstrosities lie completely outside my sphere of comprehension.

My anger when I recall these stories makes me feel we should rid ourselves of the vile filth who perpetrate such crimes. I can no longer see what purpose these killers might serve. Can anyone ever really be cured of the wiring in their brains that compels them to bludgeon a small baby to death, and just for fun? I can't see how they could ever reintegrate into society – or even if they were capable of functioning as part of a civilised community in the first place. I fear they have gone too far down one road for any therapist to bring them back. My first thought when I heard of those two kids killed by their own violent father was, 'Well, at least he killed himself too!' Anyone capable of such murderous cruelty towards anyone, let alone their own flesh and blood, to me just does not deserve to benefit from the spoils of civilisation. Too much futile effort is expended on criminals and never enough investment is made in the victims, comparatively speaking.

Of course, I can't blame governments, and in many cases I couldn't even point the finger at parents who have turned out evil individuals. Imploring anyone capable of any of the depraved acts I have described here to take greater responsibility for themselves will never likely work either. No. No matter how I look at it and however much I try to rationalise it, I just can't get away from the fact that SOME PEOPLE ARE JUST EVIL. Regardless of the personal investment a parent might make, regardless of any advantage society might provide, some people always have been – and I believe always will be – EVIL.

13

Let's Meet a Man in Turmoil

Imagine being given the chance to make your dreams come true. Imagine being asked to front a national television show. Imagine that show gradually building in popularity – from a start that saw your production team and a few strangers hastily dragged off the street and press-ganged into your studio audience – into a show with a six-month waiting list for tickets. Imagine the pride and camaraderie you and your team would feel when finally seeing the fruits of your labour rewarded. Imagine securing unprecedented recommissions on the back of unimaginably positive feedback from viewers and the network employer alike. Imagine the unrestrained joy that would course through your veins at repeatedly being told you have beaten the competition whilst securing record ratings for your broadcaster. Imagine then being nominated for a National Television Award at a live ceremony being broadcast from London's Royal Albert Hall. Imagine you, your wife and your show's producers all being invited to quaff free champagne, mix with your heroes, the glitterati, luminaries and leading lights – all the great and good of the TV world. Success acknowledged on a night where you get to meet all those people that still, to this day, leave you dumbstruck with awe and inspiration, invited to properly sample the full, five-star, red-carpet treatment for the very first time. You'd be pretty damned excited, right? Wrong! I wasn't. I was terrified . . .

Why? Well, it wasn't the ceremony that bothered me, and

I wasn't overly fussed that the award for 'Best Factual Programme' was inevitably going to go to the excellent team at *Top Gear*. No, the incomparable Clarkson, 'Hamster' *et al* were always going to win the award, and deservedly so, but for *The Jeremy Kyle Show* just being nominated was a serious and significant achievement. It validated the hard work of everyone on the show and gave us a legitimacy and credibility in the eyes of those industry insiders who so often sneered at us from the sidelines. Not seen as highbrow enough for some, jealously ignored by others, my producers have never really got the credit they deserve for what they pull together every day.

The snootier, sniffier media commentators focus their ire on me – or even the guests we try to help – but they forget the blood, sweat and tears that actually get invested behind the scenes by the people who work alongside me. As I have quickly learned in TV, it is only those who have worked with the unrelentingly pressurised environments and deadlines of talk-show television who really understand. Those who have served their time in the talk-show trenches never cast the same stones or aspersions as those who haughtily opine from afar in a manner that is every bit as ignorant and judgemental as they so often claim I am. No, the people who have been there on my show, on Trisha's, or wherever else, know the score. They've done the seventy-hour weeks, they've been up until five in the morning with contributors more intent on destroying their hotel rooms than resolving their differences in a TV studio four hours later! They've been there, done the hard yards, and not one of them *ever* disrespects the stamina, dedication and bloody hard work required to make a success of what we do. In fact, as one prominent executive producer recently told me, talk-show experience is something he always keeps an eye out for in prospective colleagues, precisely because he knows they will be prepared to give every last ounce of themselves for the show. But I have prattled off-piste again . . .

The reason I was so nervous was not down to any of the pomp and pageantry of my first big awards ceremony, nor the prospect of losing out to *Top Gear*. No, for the first time since I had taken to the nation's TV screens, I was genuinely fearful of facing the Great British Public. I saw the 29th October 2007 as my very own public day of reckoning. It was pretty much the first time I had stepped out of my house since an unfortunate incident on the show had precipitated a whole slew of media stories that threatened my future and the show's very existence.

Manchester district judge Alan Berg was the man who fired the pistol that started what felt like a race to 'get me', or at least take down the show. I had always been aware of that phrase 'media feeding frenzy'. In the past I had also unwittingly played my part in contributing to some of those feeding frenzies that engulfed people I now class as friends or colleagues, not by tipping off the press or selling anyone down the river, of course, but by paying money for whichever tabloid was that day promising the latest celebrity exposé. I had willingly lapped up every morsel on offer whenever the latest scandal broke. From royal love triangles to celebrity sex tangles, I have probably been as gripped as anyone by some of the sensations served up to us in the press. I certainly did not imagine for one moment that I might be caught up in a media maelstrom of my own.

Now, it wasn't Judge Alan Berg who brought me to my knees with his withering assessment of my show. However, his highly publicised judgement on a case involving a guest of the show started a run of stories that quickly went, as these things do, from a commentary on supposed professional failings to a pulling apart of my personal life, elements of which I had naively assumed might remain private or at least in the past. Judge Berg pulled no punches when he called *The Jeremy Kyle Show* 'a human form of bear-baiting'. He went further when commenting on a case that saw David Staniforth, a guest of my show, fined £300 for head-butting a love rival whilst on stage with me. Staniforth refused to deal maturely and sensibly with the fact that his wife had taken up with their one-time lodger, Larry. Staniforth refused to acknowledge any responsibility for his wanton act of unprovoked violence on stage. Such a refusal to admit responsibility, the wilful failure to acknowledge one's own culpability in anything that goes wrong, is something that a fair number of my guests are initially guilty of. Eventually many come to realise that they have at least played some part in their own downfall, break-up or addiction, and it is from there they can set about repairing the damage or rebuilding the bridges that have been destroyed. That Staniforth couldn't accept his wife had found love with someone else is perhaps understandable. That he perhaps held out some forlorn hope of reconciliation with the woman he claimed to love still is also perfectly plausible. I can even buy the possibility that his hopes for a happy reunion might have distracted him from a fair assessment of the fact that things had gone wrong and, moreover, gone wrong in part because of the way he had behaved in their relationship. However, I cannot abide the insinuation that Staniforth's decision to bury his forehead in the bridge of Larry's nose was anything other than a reprehensible act of unprovoked violence for which he alone is entirely responsible.

Staniforth's outbreak of violence was not the show's fault, nor my fault, any more than it was the effect of some external event or force. To claim 'they made me do it' really is the stuff of playgrounds, the most childish of cop-outs; it implies that violence 'sometimes just happens', like outbreaks of rain. If I went up to head-butt someone in the street, even if that person was my worst enemy and had run off with my wife, even if they called me every name under the sun, and even if I thought they were the reason it always seemed to rain when I film in Manchester, I – AND I ALONE – WOULD BE RESPONSIBLE FOR ANY DECISION TO ATTACK THEM. It would be wrong and I'd know it would be wrong. Frankly, I'd expect the police to throw the book at me, and I certainly wouldn't claim I'd been put up to it, or it was the result of anything other than my own temper or failings as a human being.

For the record, Staniforth was not wound up, provoked or anything of the sort. He was on stage with me for ten minutes before Larry even entered the fray, and I certainly didn't wind him up – I was only asking him how we'd come to be here in the first place. No matter, though, mud often sticks in the show-business world, and Judge Alan Berg heard enough from the Staniforth defence to set in motion the chain of events that so nearly finished my career before it had even really begun.

In his summing-up, Judge Berg said that my show was a 'human form of bear-baiting' that specialised in 'a morbid and depressing display of dysfunctional people whose lives are in turmoil'. He further went on to say that my show existed solely for the purposes of 'titillating bored members of the public who have nothing better to do in the morning than watch this trash on TV'. After also claiming the producers of the show should be in the dock with the defendant, the die was cast. The press had their headlines and a terrifying and lonely new chapter of my life had been opened for me.

I can't deny that my show does indeed feature some people in turmoil. Certainly we have filmed with some characters who might be termed dysfunctional. But we exist to help our guests achieve conflict resolution. Even cursory research into the show, its history or its obligations to the broadcaster and network would have told Judge Berg that. And with this in mind, it would surely also follow that most (but not all) of the guests featured would come to us with a problem that they have as yet been unable to resolve with the resources at their disposal. He is perfectly entitled to his opinion, of course, but rather than just denouncing the show as – at best – 'depressing', he and other like-minded detractors should perhaps consider the broken society that spawns it. Now, don't get me wrong. I am not saying that my show regularly features the Best of British, far from it. However, every guest on my show is home-grown, and the problems with which they daily come to me are seemingly endemic in our society. They are born of cultures and trends in Britain that increasingly I can't see as anything but broken or morally bankrupt. Some say my show holds a mirror up to the society we live in; others tell me we are just shining a very large light on a very small minority of the population. Well let me tell you: the problems people come to me with seem to be getting worse and more tragic, not any easier to fix. Now, I never condone any of the appalling behaviour I see or hear about in the studio – more regular viewers of the show than Judge Alan Berg would testify to that: my show and our efforts are geared towards stopping it. Meanwhile Judge Berg and critics like him seem to be of that breed that never offers an alternative solution. These people can only ever muster criticism of the idea you've come up with.

I used to hate such negative people at school and still get irritated by those kinds of people at work. You make a suggestion in good faith and it gets rubbished. The person trashing your idea without any thought for your feelings never comes up with an alternative of their own. They're just content to sit there in judgement on yours, protracted sighs and rolling eyes and all!

Anyway, as I have maintained throughout this book, I believe the show is a very real reflection of increasingly large pockets of Britain. People like Judge Berg would, I am sure, love not to see such people on their television sets in the morning, just as I am pretty sure they would choke on their cornflakes if they ever saw such 'ruffians' loitering about their leafy drive-ways. They would rather read about them in the press, conclude what a menace they are and feel relieved that they are someone else's problem on some estate far, far away.

The Jeremy Kyle Show is part factual entertainment, that is undeniable. People watch it for a great many reasons. The viewers I have spoken to say they get different things from it on different days. Some compare and contrast their own issues with those of the guests I have in studio. Some use the advice given on stage and apply it to their own lives. Some, I'm sure, watch for voyeuristic titillation, while others tell me they tune in to see certain people get told for the first time in their lives that they need to shape up, so fed up are the general public with seeing such people always being allowed to run riot without fear of rebuke. People are free to make their own choice over what they watch and when, no matter what Judge Berg thinks. I am sure a great many of my viewers would be offended that he classes them as 'bored' or with 'nothing better to do', but I'll waste no more time on him. What is more important is not why people *watch*, but why people feel the need to call in for my help. Surely even the most myopic of critics would be better advised to focus their attentions on fixing a country where so many cry out for help. Better that than decry the television show they feel forced to seek that help from.

Anyway, the damage was done with Alan Berg's judge-ment, and within twenty-four hours the show was headline news on most news networks. People once more queued up to slate us, many now basing their opinion on me and my show only from a few sound bites offered up by the usual commentators and talking heads. Many of the people that saw the news reports flashing up on screens – as the lead story (?!!) – every hour on the hour, would never before have seen my show and far less heard of me. Their first introduction therefore was to see me held up as some sort of circus ringmaster presiding over what some commentators then came to call a modern-day freak show. Many called in, again basing their views only on what was being reported and despite never having watched the show, saying that I should be taken off air. How could I allow such violence to happen on my show? How could I sleep at night now that Judge Berg had said my producers were also to blame?

I'd like to say here and now that NO VIOLENCE is allowed or condoned on the show. ALL guests are briefed about this and warned as to their conduct before appearing. Security are on hand and waiting in the wings throughout. At the first sign of heated emotion, raised voices, and certainly raised fists, they arrive on stage to deal with the situation. The fact that security immediately intervened as soon as was practicably possible in the Staniforth incident went pretty much totally unreported. That the whole production team then assisted Larry in dealing with the situation and its aftermath – medically and legally – was also largely ignored. No, with a story to sell and some undeniably shocking and compelling footage to show, the news channels went instead with repeatedly showing the head-butt before again reciting Alan Berg's judgement and then inviting viewer feedback.

I hate to bang on about it, but the repeated showing of the head-butt was a little unfair. Of course I understand any news editor's reasoning. I completely get why anyone would want to show that footage. It illustrates a point, gets people's attention and is very shocking indeed. However, the very reason it is so shocking is the very reason it is probably so unfair to show it. The simple truth is that *The Jeremy Kyle Show*, as well as never condoning violence, also NEVER BROADCASTS ANY VIOLENCE.

I would be lying if I said there had never been an altercation between guests on stage, or even that the Staniforth incident was the only example of a heated situation descending into violence on stage. It has happened before, it will likely happen again, but we always intervene and, more importantly, never show any of the violence that does take place. Some misguided souls have said to me in passing that they love to watch the show 'because sometimes there's fights'! Well, I don't know what show they've been watching, because we have never, will never, and are in any case legally required not ever to show fights on our television show. The TV regulators don't allow it and it is a road we just don't go down on a show that goes out at 9.25 on a weekday morning. Arguments are seen, but even they are edited down and tamed if our legal and compliance team deem them too vitriolic or aggressive to be suitable for broadcast.

As I said earlier, this was the opening paragraph of probably the darkest chapter of my life to date. What tends to happen when the media or the press have one story about you is that a whole run of other, vaguely associated stories will then appear. The common denominator that ties them all is invariably the celebrity name at the centre of them. So, while this episode started with my show being dragged through the mud, it soon went on to focusing on me and my past.

I was always warned that one day it would be my turn. Everyone knows that a media backlash is inevitable. I have never had a problem with the press or media. They have made my life unbearable at times, but equally they have helped me get where I am today. It is a double-edged sword, but anyone starting out in show business knows this and should recognise that one day the horse you have ridden to fame and fortune will throw you. As I found out, the challenge is to get back on, knowing full well that you will get thrown off again in the future, just as painfully, just as embarrassingly. It might be the next day, the next week, the next month or the next year, but it will happen. And if you don't like it or if you have found the experience too chastening, you always have the option to get off for good. Just as anyone who doesn't like my show can switch over when it comes on, so any celebrity who doesn't like so-called media intrusions or invasions of privacy can opt out. Cash in your chips, leave your microphone and six-figure salaries at the door and go join the nine-to-fivers.

From the head-butt came the criticism, and from that was spawned the interest that made it worth any journalist's while to find another story, angle or addition to the unfolding Jeremy Kyle canon. Within hours I learned that a disgruntled ex-producer had gone public with her assertion that everything Judge Berg had said was true. I can barely remember meeting her and think she contributed just three shows at the very beginning of my whirlwind introduction to TV, when all was new and equally confusing. I just felt so sorry for the former friends and colleagues whose livelihoods she endangered by going public.

With one storm weathered in the dailies, the next big wait was for what new revelation the big-hitting hacks at the Sundays might bring. The story itself didn't hit the pages of the *News of the World* for a good few weeks after Judge Berg's little diatribe. But the threat of it was ever-present. On a couple of Wednesdays, on my way to Manchester to film six shows, I would be informed that something was going to appear that Sunday. By Friday, midway through filming, I would be sent the transcript of the article they intended to print and be invited to comment. This seemed to go on and on, I was on a ceaseless treadmill of anxiety and I am not too proud to admit that the whole experience left me something near a gibbering wreck. Perhaps because it was my first experience of feeling hunted in this way, perhaps because I knew I stood on the verge of losing it all after such a short time on top. I had no other similar events or occurrences in my life on which I could call to compare what was being thrown at me now; no place from which to draw the reserves I needed to survive the onslaught. Looking back, I was glad I continued to film the six shows I did each week. My head was all over the place, but the work itself provided both a focus and a distraction from the 'off-the-field' events that were consuming me.

Once that article – *Vile Jeremy Kyle Preyed On Me When I Was Only 16* – went into the *News of the World*, my life was changed forever. But the time leading up to it was no easier to bear. Racked with guilt, worry, confusion and panic – most of it stemming from not knowing what might happen and not being in control of the events that were dictating my life, I descended into a pit of self-loathing and pity that few would recognise the on-screen incarnation they see each day as being capable of. I'm sorry to say I began to drink heavily. The occasional glass of red to wind down after work quickly became the obligatory two bottles to forget the troubles engulfing me. I slept only about an hour a night and could not find the right words to explain things to my wife. I didn't know what was going to be printed so I couldn't have an informed conversation with Carla about what was happening and how things might pan out. Hopefully you will understand, as Carla does now, that I just didn't want to have potentially marriage-wrecking conversations with my wife whilst I was at work and she was 250 miles away with our two young daughters.

I felt totally and utterly alone. Those who tried to comfort or assuage my fears did so without really knowing how it felt. They couldn't properly understand as they hadn't been there. Colleagues, of course, had one eye on the filming schedule, and their pep talks must surely have been as much about getting me ready for filming as making sure I really was OK. I did not know where to turn or what to think. I was about to be painted as some sort of sick pervert and I could do nothing about it; I could not even be assured of properly getting my side of the story across. Those who said to me 'there, there' were only being nice and supportive, but they could not possibly have reckoned on the difficulties I was to face at home with my wife and a daughter who was only one year older than the girl in question. They all tried to inject a bit of perspective into the situation, and I will forever be grateful to Dianne Nelmes and the McLennans, Tom and Lucy, for the support they gave me at the time. Dianne was the person who brought me through at ITV. She has been my mentor, guide and friend throughout every good and bad time since filming of *The Jeremy Kyle Show* began. I will forever be grateful to her for the way she supported the work our teams do each and every week. She put her head above the parapet when a lot of others at ITV went running for cover, scared off by the controversy unfolding in the press. Beyond that she was the one who helped me through internal difficulties at ITV when more than one twitchy executive held his finger hovering over some telly equivalent of the button James Bond baddies might use to send their victims to the shark tank.

My fate seemed sealed, my future doomed. The conversations taking place about me, but all too rarely with me, looked for some time to be hinged on how to get me a one-way ticket to the dole queue. On several occasions Dianne would stay up late with my agent and they would be in her office until way past midnight, waiting for the latest from the papers or the ITV bosses who doubted me. Her support was unwavering, she didn't flinch at all and I am sure she galvanised the support of ITV around me. I will never forget that.

Lucy and Tom McLennan, the husband and wife team at the helm of the TV show, and for a time my radio show, also took me in to spare me from myself in Manchester. They saw me at my very worst. Too much wine consumed and not enough coherent thought going on, at times I'm ashamed to say I was reduced to self-pitying tears. When I could no longer take the angst and voices of doom that continually circled in my mind I just capitulated, reverting back to something infantile, almost primal. My knees gave way and I found myself curled in a ball on Lucy's kitchen floor, tears flowing. It felt endless, and must certainly have seemed that way for poor Tom and Lucy, who stayed up with me each night past four a.m. before frogmarching me to my bed.

There seemed to be no let-up. My phone was constantly beeping at me, always bringing more bad news, and I just could not focus on anything else. I had something of a moment of clarity when one of my producers came through to brief me on an upcoming show. As I have already confessed in this tome, I am something of an obsessive-compulsive and my mind cannot be easily diverted from whatever issue is troubling it. A scratch on my car or a smudge on the screen of my phone can drive me to distraction, but this issue was something that threatened my very existence. I just couldn't stop thinking or panicking about anything else and, as is also typical of me, I would repeat my troubles to as many people as possible in order to see what advice came back. In truth, just talking about it was preferable to thinking about it and, whatever conversations I was having, even if they were the same ones repeated over and over, were a welcome if insufficient distraction. Everyone was as calming and understanding as they could be, but this one producer bucked the trend and actually quite shocked me with his response to my question of what he thought I should do to deal with the situation. 'Grow a pair of bollocks!' was all he said.

He later went on to explain that he was pretty sick of everyone rushing around to cajole me into a better state of mind. Always a bit of a bruiser, he contended that everyone's pity, sympathy and blind 'understanding' of my situation was merely keeping me locked into the same thought-processes. I could have done without a jibe hinting at any testicular inadequacy, but I did take the point, and to a large extent he was right. Whilst I told him that he would never understand the horror of what it feels like to be thrown to the wolves as I was, it is true: there is only one person in that situation who can pick themselves up, dust themselves down and deal with it. He helped me see that in this case that person was me.

He and others went on to explain that – ironically – being shot at in this way was quite a good indicator of success. The truth, as they explained, was that my life would be scrutinised and raked over precisely because the show had gone so well and my name had grown sufficiently big to become newsworthy. It is only now that such words of wisdom have sunk in and I truly realise that there will always be someone ready to sell or print an unflattering story about me. I can't control it, I can't stop it, and I know that these things will inevitably crop up from time to time – for as long as I am on television or classed as being anything close to a celebrity. As Graham Stanier, the show's director of aftercare, psychotherapist, genius and my closest friend, confidant and colleague, always says: 'That's it, we're done, move on!'

In hindsight I guess I should have seen some of this coming. There's no point in taking these people on, though, because you will never win. Max Mosley got to clear his name through the courts but at what cost? He didn't need the sixty grand the *News of the World* paid him, but he did want it on record that his predilection for kinky S&M spanking with a bunch of highly paid hookers did not have its roots in any affiliation to Nazism. Fair enough, everyone now knows that not to be the case, but he will be forever tainted by association. Like it or not, his decision to go so publicly through the courts only served to keep the 'Nazi Orgy' headlines on the tabloids' front pages – and therefore in all of our minds – for a great deal longer. Beyond that, he has clearly just made himself an even more appealing target to whomever he may have crossed when claiming the damages he sought.

As I have said, mud sticks in the celebrity world, and that is what can be so galling when you're at the centre of a storm that might only have a partial basis in truth. I admit I had a fumble, but this was some EIGHT YEARS AGO, when I was at a very low ebb and before I was even married to Carla.

I once watched the legend that is Max Clifford on TV and was intrigued by something he said about his job being more about protection of clients than promotion. That initially sounded odd to me. Naive as I was, I assumed that a 'PR guru' would necessarily spend his time promoting his clients to the public through the press or whatever medium was available. I now understand what he means when he states that for every story he helps into the papers, he has also been involved with keeping ten out. Now, I can't call on the services of the amazing Mr Clifford to help out whenever the press come calling. That said, I can see the truth of what he says because for every story you have read about me there have been quite a few that haven't made it to print. They range from the fantastical to the farcical. Again the process is the same. Early on in the week I'll get a call from one of the papers and they will explain their plans to print something that Sunday. I have until then to offer comment or come back on the veracity of their story. Again, I don't blame the press for this, they are only doing their jobs in line with market demands. If I were in their shoes I'd probably be doing the same, so I really don't bear any ill will to anyone in the press. I would prefer to stay on good terms with them all, defending my corner if necessary but certainly not picking a fight with them.

I'd like to say at this point I am not carping or begging for your sympathy. I don't want to run around like Kenneth Williams in *Carry On Cleo*, shouting, 'Infamy, Infamy, they've all got it in for me!' I have just tried to be honest about something of the flip side to the life I lead. My fame comes with a great many rewards that I know I am more than privileged to enjoy. However, it also comes with the willing – and although I say this honestly I do so with some trepidation – acceptance that you are 'fair game' for the press and associated media. If you court publicity, become a public figure, lead any form of public life, or if your success is in some way dependent on the support of the public, then you must also accept that you are subject to (at times scarily intense levels of) public scrutiny. The moral arbiters and ever-watchful scrutineers working on behalf of the Great British Public are the Great British Press. I submit to them with the full understanding that I am bound to have a whole load more of the sorts of run-ins that will leave me distraught, no doubt with career/future hanging in the balance once more.

There's no point in me taking personally what certain professionals in the press have to do to make their living, but I do take issue with the people who at times supply them with their material. I have had ex-guests trying to cash in on their appearance with me, as well as ex-friends and even an ex-employee trying to sell stories about me. Of course 'Jeremy Kyle Is a Nice Bloke Shocker' is never going to sell – we Brits demand something far more sinister or salacious than that – and so, for the right price, people you trusted, liked and sometimes even loved will betray you. For thirty pieces of silver (representing a fee that starts at about £300 for the stupidly desperate, rising to a maximum of about £5,000 for the more discerning Judas), I've had people I trust go to the press, giving sworn affidavits on everything from my hygiene (apparently too clean, and, horror of horrors, wanting to wear shirts that are ironed!) to an alleged refusal to shake hands with members of the public, even though anyone who's met me knows that not to be true – from the hordes who regularly besiege me and Graham when we are out filming on location to every guest I've met on the show (watch the show, you'll see I shake the hands of pretty much everyone I meet on stage), to the few late-night roadside stragglers who have caught me buying a burger at Knutsford Services on the way home from Friday-night filming. These stories never made it to print – I wonder why? – but it does show you the lengths some will go to to make some money from you.

As I've said, the effects of being caught in a media feeding frenzy can be terrifying. But you keep going and you gradually get used to it. What you don't get used to is how it affects those you love.

There were some moments at home I hope never to repeat. When that *News of the World* article came through, just before the National Television Awards, it caused mayhem. It arrived online, at ten to five in the morning and the minute Carla read it she exploded and hurled the computer across the room at me. I thought she was berating my weakness; my own stupid naivety at allowing my ego to be flattered by someone else and thereby threatening to bring down what we had both been working towards. I needn't have been so concerned. She was temporarily as bound up in the uncertainty as I was, but Carla's incandescence was rooted in the fact that someone could hold on to something for eight years before dropping the bombshell just days before what should have been the biggest night of our lives. Carla really is far stronger than me and her head soon cleared after the initial outburst. Personally, once I'd read the full article, I never wanted to leave the house again.

My daughter, Hattie, also struggled for a more philosophical grasp of the situation. We explained what was coming out in the press, and, as you might expect, she was disgusted. I often say to guests of the show that they should change their ways because one day they will have to answer to their kids. I faced the same judge, jury and executioner in Hattie, and it is an experience I hope never to face again. Eventually, she understood, and she like me has come to accept that press interest, with good or bad stories, are now part and parcel of the life we are embarked upon. We enjoy the spoils and positives, so we more than accept we have to endure some of the negatives. Nothing quite prepared either of us for the story that first tested our bond, though, and I am still occasionally haunted by the looks of disgust she shot me as I slowly explained all that she and her friends could expect to read about her dad in the Sunday papers.

The other principal casualty throughout was, I am sorry to say, Graham. He, like me, had a job to do during filming, but he also took time out to really go that extra mile as friend and counsellor when this was all at its worst. He would regularly sit with me until four a.m. and listen to my whining before urging me to adopt some of the techniques he uses with some of our guests to manage anxiety or face fears. He really was a trouper for me, and continues to be every bit the loving and loyal friend I so admire today. It is true what they say about discovering who your true friends are in times of adversity. One mate I know from radio has been approached with £5,000 (!!) to rake up some dirt on me, but he said no, and I'm proud to say that Graham too has marked himself out as a man of unsurpassed loyalty and commitment to the cause. This made it all the more upsetting when he was unwittingly sucked into my own spiralling media hell. He too became part of the feeding frenzy.

The breaking of this story clearly sounded a clarion call for other journalists. It is horrible to feel that everyone is out to get you, but the evidence of my own experience could only lead me to that conclusion at the time. Even the hotel I had regularly stayed at, two nights each week whilst filming in Manchester, seemed to be in on the act. Unbelievably, in a rented hotel room opposite where I'd always stayed (hmmm, interesting!) a watching journalist put two and two together, came up with ten and then notified his paymasters of the latest hot gossip from Jeremyland: JEREMY AND GRAHAM ARE HAVING A GAY AFFAIR!

At any other time I would have laughed, as indeed Graham and I often do today about that whole ludicrous story, but this little episode served only to heighten my enveloping sense of paranoia and persecution. It also dragged a friend into a place he just did not deserve to be. Both of us returned home after filming to find paparazzi outside our houses, our respective partners inside wondering what the hell was going on. Again, of course I accept that I have chosen a public life and know that at times I will pay a public price. However, my biggest fear throughout the whole time we were being spied upon was that my friend Graham's relationship would also be endangered by the lies being spread about us. Being accused of an affair is one thing but for him to be accused of having an affair with me really is quite another – especially when all he'd ever done through that time was support me as a friend. Thankfully he, like Carla, is made of sterner stuff, and he managed to laugh about it. And of course, like so many things it blows over after a while.

So all of my energies in the run-up to the National Television Awards had been focused on needless strategies of avoidance. I didn't want to leave the house but even before then had dreaded facing my team and even my own family. I was certain the British public would be baying for my blood, but again I was proved completely wrong. In the immediate aftermath of the exposé in the *News of the World*, the phone rang again. 'Oh no, what now? What next?' I thought. It was Matthew Kelly. He said nothing to me save, 'Pages Eight and Nine: don't they know who you are?!' Brilliant. The next time my mother-in-law walked through the front door, the only thing she said as she prepared to take my two youngest off up to bed – and it's something I will never forget – was: 'This'll make good bedtime reading!' With that she climbed the stairs, looked back over her shoulder and winked at me before mouthing 'You dirty bastard!'

Now, I'm not normally the best with criticism or piss-taking, but that was just what I needed. The team at work gave me relentless, merciless stick, all of them mocking my supposed preference for sixteen-year-old schoolgirls. There was a good deal of banter – all at my expense – as people went about their business as they always had. Kym Marsh spoke to me and said she never reads the papers, urging me to ignore them too, whilst Eamonn Holmes said something quite prophetic when he called me too: 'Don't worry too much about it now,' he said. 'If you ever get asked to write a book, this is precisely the sort of stuff you'll have to put in it.' He is good, that Eamonn.

Nothing seemed to have become too badly dislodged after the battering I had given myself over the whole experience. At work I was still ribbed as much as I ever was before, and home life quickly returned to normal after the initial shock. The last great unknown was the reaction of the public. And so it was that when I stepped out onto the red carpet at the Royal Albert Hall, I was still expecting to be pelted with eggs or carted off to the stocks for a public flogging. There were no boos, though, and no missiles launched my way. All around there was wild cheering for the casts of *Corrie* and *EastEnders*, while I walked past people unmoved by my appearance. They just didn't care and that, to me, was wonderful. I don't think I've ever been so happy to be ignored! The paparazzi, who I thought might be against me still, wanted pictures of me and Carla. A few fans not just there for Simon Cowell sought autographs, and I was swept inside to enjoy the event like everyone else.

I was a little puzzled as I looked around the Albert Hall and asked my agent, Grant, why there wasn't a more negative backlash. Not always known for the beauty of his language but never found wanting for his straightforwardness, Grant gestured around to all the celebrities being penned into their various holding areas: 'Look,' he said, 'half of these people here know exactly what you're going through because they've been fucked by the press, and the other half are sitting here terrified because they know it's only a matter of time before they get fucked too!' Not quite how I might have phrased things myself, but his is a theory that now seems sound to me.

As I mentioned, *The Jeremy Kyle Show* did get nominated, but one of our cameramen who was moonlighting at the awards explained to our party long before the ceremony started that we hadn't won. He didn't know the results, of course, but he did explain that we were seated too far back to be winners, who are apparently always placed near the front of the auditorium. Sure enough, the *Top Gear* team won and they made the short walk up to the stage from their exalted seats near the front (thanks for the tip, Alex, bruv, thanks very much indeed!). It really didn't matter to me, though: we had a whole lot of fun anyway, sitting at the back with the rest of the also-rans! I think I was glad not to be at the centre of anything, a feeling of having faded to relative anonymity was just what I needed. Of being involved and included without being scrutinised.

Some time after the ceremony, on the way back to the hotel, I asked some of my producers how the breaking of that story had played out with our viewers. They explained with typical sensitivity that I 'was a Marmite man, and ours was a Marmite show'! Apparently you either loved it or hated it, there was no middle ground in people's view of the show. This story had merely provided those who had always hated me with yet another reason to do so. Conversely, those who had always supported me seemed to be sending in messages of encouragement along the lines of 'keep up the good work' and 'don't let 'em get you down!' The ratings for the show had remained at the same level throughout and the papers had moved on to another story – after all, it wasn't as though they'd found me covered in bubble-wrap with cocaine shoved up my nose and a rent boy on my face! Nope, normality had returned for now. I was surrounded by my team, loved by my family, supported by my friends and was once more on my way back to a hotel before filming. Only this time I didn't feel the need to get drunk!

14

A Line in the Sand

Let me make one thing very clear: I am proud to be British. I love this little island of ours and would not have wanted to live anywhere else for the last forty-three years. It is the place that inspires me whenever I drive home; it is the place I long to return to whenever I venture abroad. There is so much that is so good about this country, and I have never lost sight of that. I marvel at our architecture, our history, our heroes. I love what this country has stood for, the beacon it has been during the greatest moments of our history. I am proud of our royal heritage. I am proud of our armed forces. I am so, so proud of the opportunities that exist for all who live in Great Britain even today. In fact, 'Great' is the only word I can think of to describe the way the freedoms that this country champions are upheld for the benefit of everyone who lives here. Despite our problems, I really do believe there is opportunity for all. No matter where you come from in this country, there exists, everywhere I believe, the chance for everyone to maximise their talents and better themselves in a way that can only be of benefit to the whole country. That is why I am so proud to be British.

I won't lie though. I can't pretend not to be a bit embarrassed by some of what this country has become. I can't pretend not to feel more than a little ashamed at the antics of so many of my compatriots up and down this land. I have come to feel regularly let down by a great many people I don't even know; people who have lost their way and make

wanton mistakes that the rest of us know we must continue
to pay for in so many ways. I can't pretend that there aren't
big problems to address in this country. Even the royal family,
which I once so revered, have disappointed in a way that my
father would barely have thought possible in his forty-one
years of work with them. From top to bottom I know this
country is facing many troubles. The problems we face are
inescapable, but I can't and I won't bring myself to give up
on my passionate belief that the people of Great Britain have
the necessary resolve within them to turn things around in
the long term. We have the tools and opportunities here
unlike anywhere else in the world. With so much available to
so many it is frankly criminal that so much opportunity is
so regularly wasted in this country. That such waste is also
allowed and then tolerated can surely no longer be acceptable. The time has come for us all to draw a line in the sand
and move this country on to new heights from which everyone
will benefit.

I am sure that my readers and viewers have had enough
of me harping on about all that is bad. I won't take that back
– I was only being honest! But if we are to set about improving
things, now is the time for the talking to stop. Now is the
time for us to begin the job of restoring our society to its
former glories. Now is the time to draw a line in the sand,
to fix 'Broken Britain' and once more make her Great again.

Some of this country's societal problems are undeniably
huge and they won't be fixed overnight. But I fervently
believe that just a little bit of tinkering from each of us individually could collectively effect a seismic change to the state
of the nation. It is all too easy to read the newspapers, believe
every headline and conclude that the problems we face are
too massive for us even to begin thinking about tackling
them. It is easy to become scared and then look only to
government to come up with big solutions to the big problems

that seem so impossible for us to crack individually. It is easy to think that one man can no longer make a difference. But to do so is to ignore totally the responsibility we all have to bear for improving and maintaining our country and our society.

I think we need to look upon these problems as those that will be remedied if we just commit to a personal policy of 'clean-as-you-go'. If we all just waited for the washing-up to be done, it would pile up day after day, and the task of clearing it would soon seem almost Herculean. Yet, if we just took two minutes to clean what we've used as soon as we've used it, the task would not be overwhelming at all.

I had a friend once who was about as good in the garden as I am in the kitchen. He had become known in part for an unkempt back lawn that he had effectively allowed to become a conservation area, untouched by any human. No one dared let their kids play out the back lest they be taken by the tigers we felt sure must live in the deepest darkest recesses of his own private jungle. I once asked him why he didn't just get out there and sort it out, but he replied that the job 'had got too big' for him to do alone. The grasses were neck high, weeds were everywhere; and I'm sure there was the odd Triffid stalking about out there too. He concluded that he now needed the help of professional landscapers, with industrial tools, or at least a large group of friends willing to muck in and give him a hand.

Nothing in this country is so rundown (or overgrown) that it can't be remedied. Some problems have become so endemic, some bad habits so ingrained that change will not happen overnight but, if enough of the right people behave in the right way enough of the time, change will happen. And, to quote President Barack Obama, it will be the change we need. My friend's unwanted forest was eventually tamed, but it need not have been the job it turned out to be. As with all things in life, if he had just kept on top of it, doing small jobs day by day, week by week, it would not have developed into such a seemingly insurmountable problem. In the end it took professional help, along with friends and family, to ensure that order was restored. That in itself is a metaphor for how so many of the larger problems this country faces could be tackled.

We all have it within ourselves to better our own lives, and our children's lives, if we just work hard to do the right things as often as we can. If we don't take the opportunities available to us, if we don't work hard to make the most of those opportunities when they do arrive, and, worse, if we can't see the opportunities out there at all, then our families will suffer. Beyond that, if we let the situations get too far out of hand, we will relinquish the power we have to determine our own destiny. Every one of us, every day, has at least some chance to go out there and work hard at something that could improve our lives and, by extension, the community we live in. Every one of us has the power to make a difference and has endless chances to do so. There really is opportunity for all: that is the beauty of Great Britain and that is why I still love this country.

I know that spirit of endeavour and entrepreneurialism still burns within a great many of our population. And I certainly know that there are few better countries than Britain for people to really make the most of their talents. I could name you any number of people from all manner of backgrounds who succeeded by maximising the opportunities available to everyone in this country. But no personal story shows the very best of what Britain has to offer quite like that of Surinder Arora.

I was absent-mindedly flicking through the TV channels recently when I caught a programme halfway through its transmission. I can't even remember what it was about, but

I will never forget the story it told. It featured Surinder Arora, the man behind what is now valued at nearly £1bn worth of business assets. Surinder Arora was given away to his aunt and raised in Punjab whilst his parents fled Pakistan to come to the UK. They wanted to build a better life for their children than ever would have been possible in the war-torn years following Partition. They did not see their son Surinder until he flew over to the UK to be reunited with them in 1972. Surinder was aged thirteen and did not know then that he was flying to meet his parents – he'd always assumed his aunt was his mother; but that's not even the half of this man's story.

Surinder Arora spoke not one word of English. At school in London he struggled to pick up the language, but nevertheless muddled through as best he could. When eventually he left school, he also left behind the Saturday job he'd had at Southall market for £1.50 per day, soon finding work with British Airways as an office junior paid £32 per week. Surinder had always wanted to be a pilot, so he worked from nine to five with BA before then working as a wine waiter at a local restaurant in the evenings until two a.m., all to get the money together to start flying planes. This diet of seventeen-hour days continued until eventually he got his pilot's licence. However, Surinder wanted to progress further, so supplemented his steady income at BA with extra work as a financial advisor for Abbey Life!

Surinder Arora worked from seven a.m. to two p.m. for BA before then working from three p.m. to ten p.m. as one of Abbey's best financial advisors before finally saving the money to invest in four rundown and derelict houses he bought at auction from Sheila Hancock! In between all of this he also found time to be a football referee, and a pilot, of course. From that first property purchase he developed his first hotel for airline staff on standby and from there he kept working and campaigning to build his empire. Surinder Arora is said to be personally worth about £225m now, and his business empire has gone from strength to successful strength.

I only chanced upon Surinder's story whilst watching television. The numbers are undoubtedly impressive, as is the hard work that underpinned them. Throw into the mix that he is said to know all of his staff by their first names and you also get the sense that he is probably a thoroughly decent bloke, too. I was looking for signs that Surinder might somewhere have been given a helping hand not available to the rest of us. But the truth is that everything he had, he had earned through his own hard work and determination. Surinder Arora is an example that should give hope to every British citizen who has ever wanted more.

Surinder Arora has himself said in most of his interviews that he owes so much to Great Britain. He has regularly spoken of his love for this country and the opportunities it gave him. He did not have the advantages of many of his contemporaries, but he made the best of what he had – and of the opportunities a country like this one provides to every citizen – to triumph. And, no matter what his other disadvantages, Surinder said he always enjoyed the unstinting love of his family. He had their support, just as he in turn now supports them in any way he can. Surinder's story represents in microcosm everything that I have ever tried to impart to any guest of mine who has not yet seen a way out for themselves. Surinder shows that Great Britain is the greatest place to be *if* someone wants to make the best of themselves. Surinder has reinforced the importance to me of family and how we all need to do our utmost to support our children at every step of the way. They by turn then have to support themselves and society as a whole by contributing positively as best they can.

Surinder Arora shows us all that life's riches and successes are there for the taking if you want them badly enough. But they have to be worked for. If you settle for second best, you might only ever achieve second best. If you want to be the best, you must be prepared to work hard, be determined and tenacious. More people in this country need to get thinking like that if Britain is truly to turn a corner and begin to leave behind the line in the sand I am imploring us to draw now.

Of course, I am not proposing that everyone in this country now trains their sights on becoming the next British billionaire hotelier. But his story does provide a simple template that anyone can use to achieve their own dreams in this life. It is the same template that has served me so well and the one that improves the lives of so many people I have tried to work with. All they ever need to do is commit to doing their best.

As I have already discussed, there has been a catastrophic bipartite failure of government and individual parents to get the right message through. Successive governments have allowed a culture of benefits dependency to grow. Where once there was pride, ambition and *a need* for every individual to work hard to support their family, now there exists an all too commonplace acceptance that it is OK for someone else to pick up the tab; that there is no shame in doing nothing, opting out. The parents who fail to guide and instil that work ethic in their children, or the need to choose right over wrong, are culpable on an individual level, but they too have been seduced by some of the easier options in life.

Now is the time for us to cut back on the easy options. If what I see most days is anything to go by, it really is time to stop being as soft as we have been. We have to tighten up across the board and make it an imperative, not just some high-minded ideal, for people to ally newfound aspiration with a renewed determination to work hard to achieve any goal. We have to learn not to give up. We have to rebuild within ourselves a resistance to giving up. People will fail from time to time, but that failure should not be one of the easiest options available in the first place.

Success stories in life are all well and good, but sometimes, I know, they can seem a touch unbelievable. The Aroras, or the Bransons or the Beckhams for that matter look like they inhabit fairy tales written for and not by them. Their successes can seem a bit inapplicable, inaccessible to those of us who content ourselves with more moderate ambitions. However, that would be to ignore the many success stories that walk quietly and without fanfare among us every day. Just as I see people who you wouldn't trust with your granny's purse on the show, so I meet a great many who stand up and show that we Britons do have it in us to bounce back from adversity.

This country carries a heavy burden. To dig ourselves out of the mess we have created will take the collective desire and combined efforts of ALL of us. But it can be done.

The reason I believe we can turn things around in this country is because I have seen that it can be done. I have watched the poorest and most disadvantaged turn their backs on crime and become properly engaged in society. I have seen the most hopeless addicts effect a turnaround in their own life with a little support and professional guidance. I have seen what can happen when a previously unmotivated stay-at-home finds it within themselves to get up, get out, get a job and provide for a family instead of claiming benefits they perhaps could have done without all along. Those people derided in the press, feared by the public, ranted at by Yours Truly on TV, any who have been doubted or chastised for good reason. All have made mistakes but some have turned it around, and it is from those we must take most heart. If the most hapless or the most determinedly indolent can turn their lives around, then anyone else can do the same. If just one person on society's fringes can choose to do the hard work to be better, then anyone in this world can, no matter what the problem. And as much as I see daily causes for much concern, I am also the proud recipient of countless calls from those who have risen to the challenge to improve their lot. Each week I will hear of someone from a previous show who has started to win their battle with themselves. More pleasing than any of the thank yous or the gestures of gratitude (I get quite a few home-baked cakes sent through to the office each month!) is the quiet understanding from those on the end of the phone that their life is a little bit better because they wanted and worked for it to be that way. It fills me with optimism, it restores my faith and it helps fuel the hope that future generations might continue to make progress too.

Take Charles for example. Charles was seventy-eight when he came to see us, hurried along to the studio by his wife of twenty-eight years, Anna. This lovely sweet couple's marriage was on the rocks because Charles was losing a battle with a foe I know only too well. Charles was a problem gambler. According to Anna, Charles had enjoyed the odd flutter from the moment they first met. However, now, nearly thirty years later, his harmless pastime had become a dread demon which threatened all Charles and Anna held dear. By his own admission, and he was almost comically honest in his confessions, he would ferret around the house playing some sort of cat-and-mouse game searching for the whereabouts of that week's housekeeping money which Anna had hidden. He would burrow into drawers or look in the airing cupboard until he found his bounty and then he would be off to the nearest bookies. A few bets, some more disappointment and a long, loser's walk home later and Charles would have to confess to Anna just why they would have to go without something else that week.

Charles's habit had become an addiction he could no longer control and he stood to lose all of his loved ones as a result. At seventy-eight you might be forgiven for thinking that this leopard could never change his spots. But do you know what? He took the talking-to I gave him and he resolved to work with Graham to conquer his problem. It surely wasn't easy to change the habit of a lifetime, but change he most certainly did. Step by step he put a halt to the problem gambling and as a result, his marriage started coming back to him. All of the spare pennies and pounds he used to squirrel away for a blowout on the nags was put instead towards romantic meals out with Anna. We revisited them some months later and still get letters from them to this day. Charles could not be more grateful, but on reflection I think it is I who wants to thank him: Thank you, Charles, for showing me and everyone else just what can be done if you apply yourself. At whatever age, no matter how ingrained the problem, it can be beaten. If you draw a line in the sand and resolve to move on, happier times can lie in wait for anyone.

In an average month of filming *The Jeremy Kyle Show*, there will be a great many referrals of guests, like Charles, to various agencies, counsellors or the registered professional most appropriate to deal with certain needs. In November 2008 we filmed twenty-six episodes and referred twelve people for anger management counselling, twenty-two couples for relationship counselling, twenty-three guests for individual counselling and fifteen people received programmes of Cognitive Behavioural Therapy. On top of that there were nine drug and alcohol referrals and fifteen DNA tests carried out at the show's expense. The cost of this runs into thousands every month and that outlay does not stop just there.

Counselling referrals start at three sessions but can go up to twelve or beyond, depending on an individual's need or progress. There are not always instantaneous results, but over time I have seen a steady flow of past guests coming back to us to say that our aftercare programme has worked for them.

I remember the first alcohol detox show we ever filmed. The star of this show was a guy who had been ravaged by years of excessive drinking. His skin was yellow and his eyes bulged and were glazed over. He seemed detached from the world when you spoke to him. No one who saw him arrive that day will doubt the enormity of the task he and we faced to turn his life around. As the producer of the show left me and strode across the car park to greet him, the man stepped gingerly out of his car and fell straight through the adjacent hedge! 'Game over' I thought, but then only seven days later this man, through a proper medicated detox in a residential unit, was sober for the first time in decades.

He endured the pangs, the convulsions, the sweats – hell, he even endured the cameras and the telly presenter trying manfully to give some encouragement on his long, lonely journey. But seven days later, just SEVEN DAYS LATER, I saw a fresh-faced, vital and vibrant young man. He seemed a little nervous at what life might hold in store for him now he saw the world through clear eyes, and a little embarrassed at all the fuss he had caused for so many years. But beyond all of that understandable angst was a palpable buzz of excitement. He had drawn his line in the sand and wrested back control of his life.

I swear, nothing gives me greater pride than hearing how someone I had doubted or maybe even shouted at has beaten the booze or got off the drugs. It is always a special occasion when someone who would be entitled to be angry with the world instead breaks their own cycle of deprivation and puts up their hand for help. There is often a collective outpouring of goodwill from the studio audience, applauding someone who has finally resolved to tackle their demons. Even a guest saying something as simple as 'sorry' can be the catalyst for wild whooping from the crowd. And it often marks the start of that person's new relationship with themselves and their loved ones.

I was raised in a monarchist family who themselves were founded on that Dunkirk spirit that saw this country rely not on just a few great leaders, but on whole legions of ordinary British men and women, who became heroes. The people who kept our island's backbone intact during the war, were not the political or military or industrial leaders, but the folk who would not be bombed into submission – those who rebuilt time and time again and who would not give up. These were the people who defended the freedoms we have to get back to today. They did not duck their duty and we must not now shirk our responsibilities.

It is tempting to be cynical in the celebrity age and assume that anyone who does well has somehow had it easy, that their fortune has been gifted to them. That is dangerous. Allowing that notion to permeate through society is what gives so many carte blanche not to do very much at all. As I write, this country is drowning in recession and it is undeniable that such a gloomy financial outlook will not augur well for jobs and prosperity in this country. People will suffer and, in the most deprived areas, the social problems I have detailed throughout this book will be brought into sharper relief once more. At such times of collective despair it might be easy to write off others' successes as 'lucky' or undeserved in some way, but that would be to fall prey to that attitude that makes it easier to accept defeat than press on in search of victory, even against the odds. Times are already tough for many and they will get tougher too for some, but let's at least draw some inspiration from what others in this country *can* do, and then resolve to test ourselves after first imbuing ourselves with that same can-do attitude. We've got to give it a go. It is at times like these that we should be more determined to overcome the social problems so often exacerbated by worsening economics. It is at times like these that we should all tighten our belts and try harder to set higher standards for ourselves. Work hard in the lean years and enjoy all the more those fat years to follow.

Thankfully we don't have to look very far to find contemporaries who can serve as an inspiration to us all. Look at our returning 2008 Olympics heroes. Chris Hoy, the monster-thighed, muscly king on two wheels. He won three Olympic gold medals. Look at the whole British cycling team, in fact, and at Rebecca Adlington, double gold medallist in swimming. They and most of the other Olympians who stood so tall and so proud for this country in Beijing are people we can really look up to. And why? It is because they could be any one of us. Of course they all had a special talent and were prepared to devote extraordinary amounts of time and hard work to hone that, but none is from a background that is so privileged that it would have excluded the rest of us. None is so genetically superior to us that they were predestined to beat everybody. No, these are ordinary people with a special talent, who worked and fought and scrapped and bled and sweated and cried and doubted and overcame until they could rightfully claim to be the best. That is why we respect them as much as we do.

Look at Chris Hoy, a virtual unknown not so long back. After the most glorious of triumphs in Beijing, he won the BBC Sports Personality of the Year award. A cyclist! That just shows you how real effort and real fighting spirit still resonates with so much of this country. It shows how we will always revere an honest champion over a pampered prima donna. That might help explain why on the flip side of that coin there is such ill feeling in this country towards those who don't make any effort to better themselves. One such man at whom many an aspersion was cast was Jordan Sabitini. Jordan who? JORDAN SABITINI! He may not have made headlines with any but the most loyal *Jeremy Kyle Show* viewer but he most certainly made an impact on me. His story summed up for me just what can be done with the right application and guidance.

Jordan came to the show as a man who had pretty much totally succumbed to his alcoholism. A divorced father of two, Jordan was a man who had never really come to terms with the fractured relationships that littered his upbringing. Alcoholism seemed to be woven into the fabric of his family and Jordan soon followed the well-trodden path his family had taken before him.

He started drinking at fifteen. The drinking was heavy from the off and Jordan gradually slid into destructive patterns of behaviour which saw him lose contact with most of those he loved. He ended up stealing thousands of pounds from his own mother to fund his drinking and by the time I met him, he confessed to drinking five bottles of wine per day, starting from the moment he awoke at eight a.m. Jordan felt worthless, had no sense of himself and felt he had nothing to live for. As a result, at the age of just twenty-nine, he had begun planning his own funeral, so convinced was he that he would not see thirty!

Jordan's liver was badly damaged and he probably did not have that long to live without our intervention. It fell to me to teach him about the harsh realities of his situation. And I did. I saw something in Jordan that day that gave me hope he could turn himself around. He was despatched to Graham and the aftercare team and we waited, as we do with all of our guests, for news on how he might progress. After an initial assessment, a fair amount of motivational counselling was prescribed to supplement the community detox programme on which Jordan was enrolled. We waited. And waited. And waited. And then a year later Jordan called our research team with the good news we all hoped for, but feared, we might never hear. He had drawn a line in the sand, and was rebuilding a life that just twelve months earlier he had all but given up on.

Jordan told me that it was me calling him 'a despicable young man' that gave him his first jolt. Beyond that, as our interview continued, he claimed that he started to become aware of all the misery his actions had brought on himself and those around him. He felt a great embarrassment at what he had become, and rather than letting that propel him further into the spiral, he used it as the springboard to completely rebuild his life. And more besides!

He did what I scream at so many to do – he made the full use of our resources. He milked every bit of help he could from us and fair play to him for doing so – that's what they're there for. He never lost sight of the fact that this was his battle to fight and his war to win. He dealt with past problems which for so long had been drowned in drink, built new friendships and rediscovered old ones. He once more seized control of his life and for the first time in fifteen years found myriad reasons to live, be happy and get excited. He set himself on the road to recovery and he deserves full praise for finding within himself the strength to carry on when the temptation to give up must at times have been overwhelming. What he did is remarkable, but it also shows everyone else how entirely possible such feats are – IF PEOPLE ARE PREPARED TO WORK HARD ENOUGH TO ACHIEVE THEM!

More than that though, and this is why I have singled Jordan out from most others who have similarly overcome the obstacles in their way, Jordan then resolved to help others

too. He came back to the show and was determined to
encourage, motivate and light a path for alcoholics on the
show who found themselves where he had been just twelve
months before. He wanted to show people what was possible
if only they applied themselves as he had done. Having
emerged from his own hell, Jordan proved himself anew as
a giant among men; it is that sort of spirit we should all
encourage ourselves to tap into to make a good fist of steering
this country back onto its proper course.

I believe that Britain might not be so much broken as just
badly bruised in certain areas. More needs to be done to
protect our country against the threat of crime and the breakdown of law and order. Education needs to improve, but
there also needs to be a reinvention of ambition for all.
Aspiration needs to be remarketed as a necessary tool in the
mindset of every British citizen. They all sound like big,
weighty governmental projects for which we should bear no
responsibility, right? WRONG!

We are all responsible for working in tandem with the
authorities. I don't want to be nannied by an overbearing
state, but my fear is that if things slip any further, then the
government will be forced to become more draconian. We
can only preach prevention so often before we have to lurch
towards more punitive measures. The real responsibility for
repairing the damage done in these areas starts with us as
individuals and then as parents. We all need to make a more
concerted, a more united effort to instil the right principles
into our children, to supply them with the appropriate moral
compass to guide them through life. We have to be there
through good and bad, through right and wrong, and not
give up on our duty to be the very best parents we can be.
I have often said on the show that it makes no difference if
you are the worst partner in the world; it makes no difference
if you have fallen on hard times and can't buy your child all

they might want each birthday. Being a good parent costs nothing but time, and all you invest in a child now will be paid back with considerable interest years later.

The tough times that are undoubtedly on the way bring with them a need to be tougher with ourselves. The 'prizes for all' culture has got to go, and with it that sense of entitlement that sees so many take before even seeing if they might have what it takes to earn. Government undoubtedly has a role to play, but the bottom line is that most of the responsibility for ourselves and our country is down to us and us alone. Again at the Olympics we saw what greater and more targeted government and lottery-backed funding can do for the sporting hopes of the nation. We should be proud at having turned out the world's best-prepared, best-trained and most successful cycling team. The money and the initiatives behind that team for all those years of hard training were undoubtedly important, but it wasn't the money nor any Whitehall penpusher who got on those bikes and pounded the miles to glory. It was Great British athletes who made the most of the opportunities available to them in this great country of ours.

In this book I have sought to be honest – about the good, about the bad and sometimes about the very ugly in this country. I can only call things as I see them and can only comment on what has been put before me. I am no great philanthropist with a plan to save humanity, nor am I any sort of anthropological expert, completely in tune with the latest societal trends in this country. I am an average, ordinary man. I have fought hard to make the most of what few talents I possess, and I recognise that I have been extremely lucky along the way. I have made mistakes but I have learned from them. I have hurt people but I have tried to atone. I have succumbed to temptation too many times but, thankfully, survived the worst excesses to emerge a better person in the end. I have epitomised much of what is good and bad in this country, but the fact I have been able to succeed in some small way only serves to show me how great this country truly can be.

I know it can be hard to recognise that there are problems in people's lives. I know it can be hard to acknowledge those problems when it would be far easier to ignore them. I also know it is harder still to put up a hand and seek help for problems we wished just didn't exist. But the harder something is to do, the more worthwhile it is too. There are problems in this country that can be fixed. As individuals and as a nation we have everything we need to fix them, and they won't cost us a penny in the long term if we invest what we can of ourselves from here on in. I am not trying to change the world and I am certainly not trying to distort the true picture of what I see each and every day. I am not trying to scare or sensationalise, pillory or patronise. I just want things to be better. I want to work hard at that and for others to share the burden too.

I want others to bask in that joy that comes from contributing to and being part of something bigger than just themselves. Start with being the best you can for yourself. Work hard and be the most productive you can be. Then strive to make your family the best it can be. Spend time on them, spend time with them, then watch as they blossom into assets for the community and the country.

Earlier in this book I talked of a 'Battle for Britain' and quoted the greatest ever of this country's wartime leaders, Sir Winston Churchill. Well, he's no longer around to deliver the sort of rallying cry we might need to rally the troops that constitute every single citizen of this country but his words do live on.

He once said 'the price of greatness is responsibility' and he was exactly right. If we all take responsibility for ourselves and our problems this country could truly be great again in no time. Personal responsibility, like the great man said, is all we really need to draw this country's line in the sand.

I can't close the final page on this book without first acknowledging one man who tragically is no longer with us . . . He gave me my first leg-up the ladder, he was the one who set me on the road to a life and career I could barely have imagined. I never accepted a job without first consulting him and not a day goes by where I do not think of him . . . my oracle, the Silver Fox, the much-missed and always loved Mr. Phil Easton. God bless you.

ACKNOWLEDGEMENTS

I simply could not let this book go to print without giving credit to those who made it happen – so thank you . . .

To Grant Michaels, my agent, and Paul March, my lawyer – it somehow wouldn't seem right to do something, even this acknowledgement, without giving you two a cut! Well, here's your usual percentage, this time paid in thanks for getting this deal done and securing a wonderful adventure for me – thank you.

To everyone at Hodder, my publishers, who made this whole process such fun. From Aslan and his fabulous sales team to the inimitable Mr. Ben Dunn – a happy Hammer and genuinely top bloke – and Jack Fogg, surely the greatest editor alive – thank you, and here's to the next one . . . and the next one – please!

To my wife, Carla, for printing thousands of pages for me to read when technology had got the better of me, and then shredding them afterwards when it had beaten me all over again. Thank you.

To Nadine, for allowing me to kidnap your husband each weekend and sharing him with me as we wrote this book. Thank you.

To Graham, for providing the oasis of calm and serenity

within which this book began to grow. For your unstinting support, friendship and loyalty and just for being a bloody genius – thank you.

To Kate Broadhurst, for the fastidiousness of your fact checking and for each day shining with typical uni-lunged brilliance – thank you.

And most of all to Kiernan, my right hand man and the best counsel I could possibly have wished for. Thank you for growing a pair yourself and making this so very simple for us both.